Mr Keynes
and the Post Keynesians

NEW DIRECTIONS IN MODERN ECONOMICS
Series Editor: Malcolm C. Sawyer, Professor of Economics, University of Leeds

New Directions in Modern Economics presents a challenge to orthodox economic thinking. It focuses on new ideas emanating from radical traditions including post-Keynesian, Kaleckian, neo-Ricardian and Marxian. The books in the series do not adhere rigidly to any single school of thought but share an attempt to present a positive alternative to the conventional wisdom.

Post Keynesian Monetary Economics
New Approaches to Financial Modelling
Edited by Philip Arestis

Keynes's Principle of Effective Demand
Edward J. Amadeo

New Directions in Post-Keynesian Economics
Edited by John Pheby

Theory and Policy in Political Economy
Essays in Pricing, Distribution and Growth
Edited by Philip Arestis and Yiannis Kitromilides

Keynes's Third Alternative?
The Neo-Ricardian Keynesians and the Post Keynesians
Amitava Krishna Dutt and Edward J. Amadeo

Wage and Profits in the Capitalist Economy
The Impact of Monopolistic Power on Macroeconomic Performance in the USA and UK
Andrew Henley

Prices, Profits and Financial Structures
A Post-Keynesian Approach to Competition
Gökhan Çapôglu

International Perspectives on Profitability and Accumulation
Edited by Fred Moseley and Edward N. Wolff

Mr Keynes and the Post Keynesians
Principles of Macroeconomics for a Monetary Production Economy
Fernando J. Cardim de Carvalho

The Economic Surplus in Advanced Economies
Edited by John B. Davis

Foundations of Post-Keynesian Economic Analysis
Marc Lavoie

The Post-Keynesian Approach to Economics
An Alternative Analysis of Economic Theory and Policy
Philip Arestis

MR KEYNES AND THE POST KEYNESIANS

Principles of Macroeconomics for a Monetary Production Economy

FERNANDO J.
CARDIM DE CARVALHO

Associate Professor
Department of Economics
Universidade Federal Fluminense
Brazil

Edward Elgar

Published by
Edward Elgar Publishing Limited
Gower House
Croft Road
Aldershot
Hants GU11 3HR
England

Edward Elgar Publishing Company
Old Post Road
Brookfield
Vermont 05036
USA

A CIP catalogue record for this book is available from the British Library

A CIP catalogue record for this book is available from the US Library of Congress

ISBN 1 85278 6531

Printed and bound in Great Britain by Billing and Sons Ltd, Worcester

Contents

Foreword

Joan Robinson has written that it was not until after *The General Theory* was published that Keynes fully recognized the vital distinction between the classical school and the analysis he was attempting to establish in his book. In the Foreword to Eichner's *A Guide to Post-Keynesian Economics*, Robinson wrote:

The main distinction was that he [Keynes] recognized, and they [the classical economists] ignored, the obvious fact that expectations of the future are necessarily uncertain. It is from this point that post-Keynesian theory takes off. The recognition of uncertainty undermines the traditional concept of equilibrium . . . When all the rubble of disintegrating [classical] equilibrium theories has been cleared away, post-Keynesian analysis can come into its own [as] an economic theory which is seriously intended to apply to reality [and] is neither an ideological doctrine, such as the presumption in favor of laissez-faire, nor a tautology true by definition.

In the initial chapters of this volume, Professor Carvalho firmly establishes the methodological connections between Keynes's uncertainty concept and the evolving Post Keynesian literature, while simultaneously demonstrating why the Hicksian IS/LM 'Keynesian' approach went off the careful analytical tracks laid down by Keynes.

In the remaining chapters, Professor Carvalho builds on the existing Post Keynesian literature to reset macroeconomic theory onto the path set out by Keynes. Professor Carvalho clears away the rubble of the classical equilibrium approach and therefore permits Post Keynesian economics to 'come into its own'.

Professor Carvalho has written a theoretical guide into the realities of the operation of a monetary economy. Both students and those teachers who wish to comprehend and work towards a pragmatic solution of the pressing economic problems of the real world in which we live, rather than spout out ideological platitudes or play tautological word games, will be indebted to the lucid exposition provided by Carvalho in this volume. He has provided us with a model textbook to bring students of economics into contact with the realities of the twenty-first century.

Paul Davidson

Acknowledgements

This book results from almost ten years of work in Post Keynesian economics. It concentrates the lessons, the influences and the help of many people over these years, even though the form some of its propositions ended up with may eventually be unrecognizable by some of those who inspired me. I cannot thank by name all those who had responsibility in shaping my ideas. In particular, I cannot list my students in the two universities where I have been teaching Post Keynesian economics since 1986; I have to thank them collectively for all the questions they raised, all the objections, the suggestions, or just the plain attention they have accorded me during these years. As a matter of fact, it was their constant prodding to put into book form the contents of my courses that gave me the stimulus to write this work.

Among the people I have to thank by name, I want to single out, firstly, my two mentors, Professors Paul Davidson and, in my younger years, Antonio Castro. It was under Professor Castro's influence that I began studying macrodynamics that eventually led me to Keynes. The opportunity of working with Professor Davidson, and of writing a PhD dissertation under his careful supervision, was decisive in my choosing to work with the Post Keynesian paradigm. More than as instructors of specific subjects, however, I must state their influence as examples of scientific honesty and caring professorship. I only hope I may be able to follow their steps in my academic life.

I also need to mention Professors Jan Kregel, Nina Shapiro, the late Alfred Eichner and the late Tom Asimakopulos for the numerous occasions on which they have generously helped me to develop most of the ideas that found their way into this book. Professor Kregel, in particular, was extremely helpful in sending me detailed comments on the drafts of this work. I have also to thank Professor

Malcolm Sawyer for his perceptive comments and useful suggestions.

I am also deeply indebted to many friends and colleagues for the help I was fortunate to obtain in my intellectual trajectory. A close friend of many years, and fellow Post Keynesian, Dr Carmem Feijo, has generously and patiently conceded me her time for an almost infinite number of discussions over more than a decade. It could be argued that some of the ideas contained in this book should carry joint authorship. My friends Johan Deprez, William Milberg and Andrea Terzi had more influence on my ideas than they can probably imagine. I must also mention how much I have learned from debating on a number of occasions with friends, some of whom work in traditions different from mine. I want to thank, in particular, Edward Amadeo, Mario Possas and Carlos Magno Lopes.

Ruggero Ruggeri and Carlos A. Afonso were extremely helpful during the preparation of the manuscript, knowledgeable as they are in the mysteries of word processing and computer printing.

Authors usually express gratitude for the patience their spouses show during the period they take to write their work. I have to thank my wife, Fernanda, however, for much more than patience. She has actively helped me since the project was conceived and if it is completed now it is due in no small measure to her own effort and determination to see it done. Whoever reads this book and finds it useful in any degree has her to thank more than anybody else.

Financial support from the National Research Council of Brazil (CNPq) made it possible for me to dedicate the time and effort necessary to complete this book.

F. C. Carvalho
Universidade Federal Fluminense, Niteroi
Universidade Federal do Rio de Janeiro, Rio de Janeiro

To my father, in loving remembrance

PART I
FOUNDATIONS

1. Introduction: Keynes, Keynesians and the Post Keynesians

In a famous letter sent to G. B. Shaw shortly before *The General Theory* was published, Keynes announced his new book as something that would revolutionize the way people thought about economic problems. According to Keynes, economic thought was dominated by Ricardian premisses, both in its orthodox version and in its Marxist branch, emphasizing allocative and distributive mechanisms but ignoring the question of the determination of the level of employment and aggregate income. *The General Theory* was to liberate economic thought from the Ricardian yoke and to set economic science on a new path (*CWJMK*, XXVIII, p. 42).

Reading Keynes's own assessment of his work in this period no one can doubt that he saw it as marking a new beginning in economics. In *The General Theory* he compared orthodox economics with Euclidian geometry trying to cope with a non-Euclidian world. The image reflects Keynes's view very accurately. Classical economics was believed to be a logically sound and coherent superstructure erected on inadequate foundations.[1] Some radical departure from orthodoxy was therefore needed to allow the development of a new economics. In Keynes's own words: 'Our criticism of the accepted classical theory of economics has consisted not so much in finding logical flaws in its analysis as in pointing out that its tacit assumptions are seldom or never satisfied, with the result that it cannot solve the economic problems of the actual world' (Keynes, 1964, p. 378).[2]

Keynes's hopes were surely disappointed. *The General Theory* faced some strong reaction from conservative circles, an enthusiastic reception by a small group of younger economists, but, generally, it seemed to have generated mainly perplexity among scholars who had great difficulty in establishing what exactly was the point of the book.[3] It is remarkable, for instance, that such an informed author as Harrod, who took part in the discussions surrounding the preparation of *The General Theory*, was rebuked by Keynes when writing a review of the book for not mentioning the propensity to consume, which Keynes saw as one of the main and newest concepts he was offering (*CWJMK*, XIV, pp. 84–6).

It has become a commonplace in economics to say that *The General Theory* does not do justice to Keynes's capabilities as a writer, that the book is obscure and sometimes contradictory, and so on. As with most commonplaces, such comments are only partially true. The image is perpetuated mainly by people who use it as an excuse not to spend the effort necessary to understand such an original and profound work as *The General Theory* is. One sees the same remark used again and again with respect to practically all epoch-making books.

Be it as it may, to recognize revolutionary ideas is always difficult and *The General Theory* really is not always helpful to this end. As is well documented in volumes 13 and 29 of Keynes's *Collected Writings*, the revolutionary message was somewhat disguised in the final published version, where Keynes substituted his criticism of Say's law in the second chapter for his originally intended discussion of economic paradigms, the cooperative economy versus the monetary or entrepreneurial economy, that was to constitute the opening chapter of the book. Keynes's frequent remarks that classical economics was right 'in its own terms', plus his not always consistent emphases on what was to constitute the real novelty of *The General Theory*,[4] misled many readers into playing down his departures from orthodoxy.

In this context, it should not come as a surprise that Hicks's 1937 paper, 'Mr Keynes and the Classics. A Suggested Interpretation', was so successful in moulding what the public was to understand as being the core of *The General Theory*. Arguing that arguments were not presented in the book in a fashion permitting the adequate comparison between Keynes's ideas and those of the Classics, Hicks set out to do what he modestly saw as no more than a systematization of both models in a way allowing one to confront them directly. Hicks's criticism was that Keynes attacked the classics for their labour market views and then tried to supersede them with a new monetary theory.

Endowed with a powerful logical mind, Hicks was able to show that the models could be represented as variants of the same basic structure that would confront Keynes directly with the classics. Of course the models are very well known. They led to the construction of the famous IS/LM curves that constituted (and to a large extent still do) the conventional wisdom in modern macroeconomics. According to Hicks, we could identify three models in this debate:[5]

I	II	III
$I = S(i, Y)$	$I = S(Y)$	$I = S(Y)$
$I = I(i)$	$I = I(i)$	$I = I(i)$
$M = kY$	$M = L(i)$	$M = L(i, Y)$

where I is investment, S savings, Y income, i 'the' interest rate, and M is (demand equals supply of) money.

Hicks calls model I the 'Classic' model, model II 'special Keynesian' and model III 'Keynesian'. The first two equations in the three models give us the IS curve. The third equation defines the LM curve. The models actually have two independent equations in two endogenous variables, i and Y, making it possible to find a simultaneous solution for the equilibrium in the goods markets and the money market.

In the way Hicks defines the models, the differences between models I and II are in the savings function and in the demand for money. Hicks plays down the first and emphasizes the second, which opposes the Cambridge Quantity Equation to Keynes's Liquidity Preference. But, Hicks argues, even this difference is not as important as it may seem at first sight because, even though Keynes emphasizes the role of interest rates in the determination of the demand for money (through the speculative motive to demand money), when one considers Keynes's transactions demand for money the model to be used is not model II but model III, which represents, according to Hicks, 'a big step back to Marshallian orthodoxy', making 'his theory ... hard to distinguish from the revised and qualified Marshallian theories ...' (Hicks, 1967, p. 134).[6]

If the different savings functions are not considered, and if, as Hicks correctly pointed out, the introduction of interest rates in the demand for money equation is not contradictory to the fundamental Quantity Theory (as demonstrated by papers such as Friedman,

1956, Tobin, 1956, or Baumol, 1952), the only opposition that may remain between Keynes and the classics refers to the parameters admitted as probable for the equations. On this it is pointed out that Keynes raised the possibility of the demand for money becoming infinitely elastic at some low level of interest rates, the so-called liquidity trap, an idea unknown to classical economists. But this situation is only likely to come about during a depression. Therefore, Keynes's revolution, in fact, amounts to no more than emphasizing the possibility that interest rates may become rigid downwards during depressions, which has the implication that policies that depend on the flexibility of interest rates would not work in these conditions, forcing policy-makers to appeal to other instruments, such as, for instance, fiscal policy. The identification of Keynesian economics with the economics of depression and with fiscalism, marks of what Samuelson later called 'neoclassical synthesis', begins with Hicks's 1937 paper.[7]

There has been much discussion as to how far the IS/LM model really represents the model of *The General Theory*. Hicks himself, in his later years, took part in it, warning against many of its misuses. He actually pointed out the atemporality of the scheme as well as its incapacity to identify causality relations, owing to its general equilibrium structure. On the other hand, one cannot ignore the fact that Keynes, having read Hicks's paper, commented that he had 'found it very interesting and really ha[d] next to nothing to say by way of criticism' (*CWJMK*, XIV, p. 79).[8] It is also arguable that it may be a not unfair rendition of the quasi-formal relations offered by Keynes in Chapter 18 of *The General Theory*. In this chapter Keynes encapsulates his theory of employment in three well-defined 'equations'. The first one is solved for 'the' interest rate, by equating the money supply, which is exogenously given, and the liquidity preference scale. The second equation gives us the value of investment read from the marginal efficiency of capital schedule when the interest rate is given. Finally, the third independent equation is solved for total income when the value of investment is known and combined with the propensity to consume. Although Keynes clearly emphasizes the causality relations that run from policy makers to consumers, we are given a system of three equations and three unknowns (the interest rate, the value of investment and total income) that can be solved simultaneously. In this sense, the IS/LM model can give us a description of an equilibrium state, understood as the set of values for the unknown variables that are consistent with each other given the value of the exogenous variables. But if the formal relations proposed in Chapter 18 are not wrongly depicted by Hicks, their substantive contents are much more problematic. As Kregel (1985, pp. 223–7) has shown, Keynes criticized Hicks's rendition of his opposition to the classics over the shape of the LM curve. A much more fundamental issue was actually at stake, the non-monetary nature of the interest rate in classical economics.

For our purposes, there are two main criticisms to be raised against Hicks's paper. Firstly, there is its inadequacy to obtain what it intended, a comparison between Keynes's and the classics' macroeconomic theories. It refers much more to the contrast in the specification of functions for econometric estimation procedures than for theoretical discussion. This becomes clear if we take the investment schedule in both models. Classical theory of investment makes it dependent on the proportion between labour and capital. As the interest rate is supposed to give the price of capital (and, thus, to measure its relative scarcity), investment becomes a function of interest rates because it reflects the intensity of the employment of capital. Keynes's theory of the marginal efficiency of capital has nothing to do with intensity of the use of capital, but with its amount, independently of the amount of labour being utilized. The interest rate is a discount factor, not a measure of relative scarcity. It is an opportunity cost with respect to financial placements, not with respect to labour. Finally, as Keynes pointed out, the marginal efficiency of capital would only coincide with its marginal productivity in stationary states. A theoretical study has to debate these issues. Hicks's examination, however, as, incidentally, may be suitable to an econometrics journal like the one which published the paper originally, is only interested in the variable that is made explicit in the functions, interest rates, ignoring what is held as constant in these relations, which is a matter of econometric convenience but not of theoretical relevance.

The main point, however, refers to the way Hicks approaches the very scope of *The General Theory*. In the drafts of *The General Theory*, Keynes insisted (and there are some remnants of this insistence in the published version) that he was not trying to provide a piecemeal alternative to classical theory but a full-fledged alternative. Of course, Hicks cannot be criticized for not considering what, after all, was not published. The result of treating Keynesian theory as Hicks did, in any case, was to favour the view that Keynes actually shared the same premisses as orthodox economics, differing from it only in terms of his expectations as to the value of the relevant parameters. Fundamental theoretical problems, however, are not touched in this kind of approach. It is implicit in presentations such as the one above that models I and II are comparable and if they are it is because they share a common structure.[9] They are, in other words, competing versions of the same fundamental theory. Research along Hicksian lines then took two forms, both of them characteristic of the neoclassical synthesis. On the one hand, empirically-inclined economists would try to estimate the relevant relations, trying to find out the value of debated parameters. On the other hand, theoretically-minded researchers tried to develop the concepts proposed in *The General Theory*, such as propensity to consume, liquidity preference and so on, within the framework of orthodox economics. Hicks himself, again, was one of the main contributors to this second line of work with his justly famous *Value and Capital*, where he developed models for consumption, investment and the demand for money, alternative versions to the building-blocks of *The General Theory*.[10] Keynesian economics became, in its neoclassical version, the development of that research programme.

Leijonhufvud (1968) has referred to a compromise that in a way defined the development of mainstream Keynesian macroeconomics. According to this compromise, empirically- and action-oriented economists would recognize Keynes's failure to develop a real theoretical alternative to classical economic theory, accepting that Keynes had done no more than examine the consequences of the existence of rigidities and other kinds of imperfections, something the orthodoxy had always accepted could take place. On the other hand, theoretically-minded economists would accept that the rigidities and imperfections Keynes had chosen to emphasize were very important in the real world and, thus, for the formulation of economic policies.

If Hicks had originally laid the foundation for accepting Keynes as a mildly deviant mainstream economist, the debate about the Pigou effect that occupied the 1940s and 1950s represented the closure of the discussion as to the possible theoretical originality of Keynesian ideas. The story came full circle when it could be demonstrated, to the satisfaction of most of the participants in the debate, that full flexibility of prices and wages would take any economy to a state of full employment. Even the liquidity trap could be escaped from if money wages and prices fell so low that wealth effects on consumption would cause the necessary recovery of aggregate demand. The Pigou-effect debate actually served also to consecrate the compromise denounced by Leijonhufvud, since the most important defenders of its theoretical importance, such as Patinkin, were also quick to recognize its complete irrelevance as a guide to policy making. The Keynesians' last stand was in the policy arena itself, in the late 1970s debate about the Phillips curve and the natural rate of unemployment, when monetarists of all colours seemed to eliminate any remnant of the notion of involuntary unemployment.

It seems that the vulnerability of such 'compromises' was not realized by many mainstream Keynesians. In the neoclassical synthesis, orthodoxy retained the scientific argument while Keynesians got the 'ad hoceries' of rigidities and imperfections, the reasons for which were never really understood. When, in the 1970s, the debate about the microfoundations of macroeconomics was proposed, to prepare the classical assault on mainstream Keynesians, the latter were found singularly lacking in arguments to sustain their views, having to retreat either into acceptance of such deeply unKeynesian or even anti-Keynesian concepts as the natural rate of employment or into the menu of irrationalities such as money illusions and the like.[11] One can assess the weakness of the Keynesian position when one sees the political compromise pointed out by Leijonhufvud translated into theoretical terms:

Clearly production and consumption are limited by supplies of labor, capital equipment and other productive resources, and by technical know-how. Almost all economists, Keynesian or classical or eclectic, agree that in the long run these supply factors call the tune and demand adapts. They used to agree also that short-run business cycles are principally fluctuations of demand; economy-wide capacity to produce changes slowly and smoothly. (Tobin, 1987, p. 127)[12]

We will discuss in the next chapter the significance of long-run concepts for the theoretical debate between Keynes and orthodoxy. At this point, however, all that needs to be stressed is that mainstream Keynesian economics was reduced to the collecting of rigidities and imperfections. Old Keynesians were accused by their classical critics of surrendering theory to the catalogue of ad hoc arguments. New Keynesians, such as those who gather round the debates at the Brookings Institution, keep the programme, trying, however, to reduce the arbitrariness of the assumed imperfections, searching for microeconomic foundations for rigidities, especially in models of imperfect competition.

One should not understand from what has been said that these latter studies are useless. They are not. Much to the contrary, they are very important, particularly as organized descriptions of empirical problems. What is being raised is their theoretical insufficiency. They try to identify problems starting from models where all problems are solved beforehand. In these kinds of models difficulties will always be generated only through the introduction of failures of markets to fulfil their function. Orthodox theory, however, does not have a theory as to how markets operate (Hahn, 1984). It has a theory as to what they achieve if they operate well. That is why malfunctioning of markets can only be considered in an ad hoc manner in these models. In reality, neoclassical theory gives no reason to know whether markets actually do or do not work well.

Post Keynesians take a different route. They revert to Keynes's own starting point, even though they may now arrive at different places. The world has changed since Keynes's time and economic thought has to follow these changes. The point, however, is that Keynes suggested an original angle from which we should look at modern economies. When preparing *The General Theory* Keynes felt the foundations of classical economics to be inadequate, not its superstructure. In searching for new foundations Keynes tried to define a new fundamental model of the economy and called it, on different occasions, monetary economies, monetary production economies, non-neutral economies or entrepreneurial economies. All these labels referred to economies of a different nature than those envisaged by classical economics, which Keynes referred to as cooperative economies.

Naturally, post Keynesians benefit from the publication in 1973 of Keynes's papers, notes, correspondence and drafts of *The General Theory*, in volumes 13 and 14 of his *Collected Writings*, and from additional material published in 1979, in volume 29, which confirmed all the hints offered in the two earlier volumes that Keynes spent a large part of the crucial years between 1930 and 1936 trying out the definitions needed to codify the new approach. Major contributions had been made before it, anyhow, by authors such as Kahn, Robinson, Shackle, Weintraub, Davidson, Minsky, Wells and others, even at the level of textbook production, as with Dillard (1948). After the publication of the drafts, those authors, along with scholars such as Barrere, Kregel, Chick and others, also made important contributions to the development of Post Keynesian thought.

What follows has little pretension to originality. This book is intended mainly as a codification of Post Keynesian thought organized around the notion of monetary or entrepreneurial economy. Robert Solow once observed that he felt Post Keynesianism to be mostly 'a state of mind'. This perception may be fed by the sometimes fragmented presentations of some Post Keynesian authors, dedicated to specific problems, the compatibility of which with other problems addressed by other Post Keynesian authors is not always clear. The notion of monetary economy can serve as the core (in the sense of Garegnani) of a Post Keynesian approach. To show this is the intention of this work.

SUMMING UP

Although Keynes claimed to offer a revolutionary approach to economic problems when *The General Theory* was published, most economists took it to represent a plea for giving special consideration to the implications of the existence of some rigidities and imperfections in the operation of some key markets, such as the labour market or the money market.

The work along Keynesian lines by mainstream economists was oriented by Hicks's codification of both Keynes's and classical macroeconomic models that discounted the former's claim to originality, suggesting instead that the main differences between them related to value of parameters rather than to essential matters of theory.

Keynesian theory therefore became the identification of rigidities and the examination of their implications, especially for aggregate employment and income. The neoclassical synthesis represented the compromise by which Keynes's views were absorbed by classical economics while having his concerns with short-run employment and income recognized by the new orthodoxy.

From the mid-1960s, Keynesian macroeconomics suffered attacks from classical economists, represented firstly by Friedmanian monetarists, to be followed by a new attack, this time from new classical monetarists. The vulnerability of Keynesian theory was shown to be rooted in the arbitrary nature of their assumptions as to the degree of imperfection of markets. This has led new Keynesians, heirs to the neoclassical synthesis, to search for less ad hoc assumptions derived from models of imperfect competition.

Post Keynesians, in contrast, break away from the mainstream by trying to resume Keynes's original path. The criticism of classical theory relates to its foundations, the 'vision' of a modern economy it entertains. It is a matter of opposing paradigms – to oppose the notion of an entrepreneurial or monetary economy to the classical notion of cooperative economy or, as suggested by Minsky (1986), to oppose Keynes's Wall Street paradigm to the neoclassical village fair paradigm. The notion of monetary economy can confer upon Post Keynesianism some unified core that, in the view of some critics, it has lacked.

NOTES

1. It is widely known that Keynes used the expression 'classical economics' in a somewhat misleading way, grouping together authors such as Ricardo, Mill, Marshall and Pigou, and taking the last two authors as representative of this approach. 'Neoclassical economics' was a term restricted to revisionist authors such as Wicksell and his followers. To avoid anachronisms and to preserve coherence with the quotations from Keynes's own works that are going to be made, we will follow Keynes's usage of the label 'classical economics' to refer to modern neoclassical analysis, restricting 'classical political economy' to the Smith–Ricardo–Marx approach.

2. In the short first chapter of *The General Theory*, Keynes did not deny that classical theory could be applied to some cases, but he warned:

   I shall argue that the postulates of the classical theory are applicable to a special case and not to the general case, the situation it assumes being a limiting point of the possible situations of equilibrium. However, the characteristics of the special case assumed by the classical theory happen not to be those of the economic society in which we actually live, with the result that its teaching is misleading and disastrous if we attempt to apply it to the facts of experience. (Keynes, 1964, p. 3)

3. Keynes actually seemed to be somewhat prepared for a lukewarm reception from those trained in the classical tradition, who would fluctuate between 'a belief that I am quite wrong and a belief that I am saying nothing new' (Keynes, 1964, p. v). Or, as Minsky put it later, between judging that what was new was not right and what was right was not new.

4. Compare, for instance, the preface for the French edition of *The General Theory*, where the propensity to consume and the multiplier are presented as the essential novelty of the book, and the famous paper 'The General Theory of Employment', where, although not denying the relevance of the propensity to

consume, the emphasis is clearly shifted to the concepts of uncertainty and its implications for the decisions to accumulate wealth. Although one can say (correctly, I believe) that both elements are essential in the creation of a new paradigm for economics, most readers of Keynes seemed to have felt the need to choose one of these emphases, leading to radically different interpretations of what Keynesian economics is about. Compare, for instance, Garegnani (1978/9) and Shackle (1967). We shall argue below that, to some extent, this is a false opposition rooted in the attempts by these schools to read Keynes into other schools or modes of thought, such as the Ricardian approach or the Austrian approach. In contrast, we suggest that, accepting Keynes's claim to have laid the foundations for an alternative paradigm (the 'monetary production economy' paradigm), we are led to state that we should not look for novel isolated arguments (although there are many of them) but for a new 'vision' (in the Schumpeterian sense) where these new concepts are articulated. The point will be better developed in the next chapter.

5. I am not using the original notation, appealing, instead, to the more familiar symbols used nowadays.

6. The relation between Keynes's ideas and Marshall's is actually very complex. Some aspects of it are explored in the next chapter.

7. This relates both to the 'pessimism of elasticities', criticized by Leijonhufvud (1968), and to models such as Klein's that assumed that investment and saving would be coordinated by the interest rate but that this rate could be negative, making equilibrium impossible. See Klein (1952).

8. Actually, Keynes did criticize Hicks's presentation of the investment function because of its reliance on current income instead of expectations. See *CWJMK*, XIV, pp. 80–1.

9. This was the case, for instance, with the debate between Friedman and Tobin in the early 1970s, in which both participants appealed to the IS/LM model. See Friedman (1970) and Tobin (1972).

10. Clower's remark that most of what one knows of modern macroeconomics is due to Hicks rather than to Keynes is fully justified. See Clower's introduction to Hicks (1974).

11. As an example of conversion to anti-Keynesian notions one could mention R. J. Gordon. The appeal to irrationalities is made by Modigliani (1983).

12. See also Tobin (1980, p. 27). Tobin, however, seemed to be very hesitant as to the compatibility between Keynes's theory and general equilibrium models. See, for instance, his contradictory statements in 1987, pp. 17 and 41. One would think Keynes himself dissented from that unanimity mentioned by Tobin. In fact, he wrote in 1934:

I have said [economists] fall into two main groups. What is it that makes the cleavage which divides us? On the one side are those who believe that the existing economic system is, in the long run, a self-adjusting system, though with creaks and groans and jerks, and interrupted by time lags, outside interference and mistakes . . . On the other side of the gulf are those who reject the idea that the existing system is, in any significant sense, self-adjusting. They believe that the failure of effective demand to reach the full potentialities of supply in spite of human psychological demand being immensely far from satisfied for the vast majority of individuals, is due to much more fundamental causes. (*CWJMK*, XIII, pp. 486–7)

Keynes called the latter group 'heretics' and added: 'Now I range myself with the heretics' (ibid. p. 489).

2. Towards the Keynesian Revolution: Some Methodological Considerations

Orthodox economics has been the object of constant criticism since its birth in the 1870s. Internal or immanent criticisms, such as, for instance, the attack on the concept of capital by Joan Robinson in the late 1950s, were aimed at the internal logic of the theory. In this kind of criticism one searches for mistakes made in the construction of basic models, be they faulty fundamental concepts or defective developments of arguments. This kind of criticism may be powerful in the negative sense of demonstrating intrinsic weaknesses or limitations of the theory that is the object of examination. On the other hand, the internal critique frequently fails to prevail because to develop it one has to remain within the limits set by the criticized theory itself. Searching for logical insufficiencies, one cannot show them to exist by appealing to new concepts or assumptions that are not recognized by the theory itself. As a consequence, one may often see the critique, even when accepted, being diluted or even downright ignored by the supporters of the theory under attack.[1]

An external critique, in contrast, is not concerned with the power of a theory in its own terms but with an examination of the terms on which it is valid. In other words, an external critique generally comes from a different paradigm, from an alternative way of seeing the fundamentals of the subject. This kind of criticism does not raise questions as to the internal coherence of the theory but as to its starting points. The difficulty involved in this attitude is that one can demonstrate that some developments are simply mistaken (as in the case of the internal critique) but one can only suggest that some starting points, some foundations are more powerful in their theoretical potentiality than others. On the other hand, the advantage of this mode of debate is that the critique itself is in general the starting point of an alternative. In other words, an external critique does not perform just the purely negative role but also a positive one of criticizing one theory from the point of view of another theory in the making. If one can convince a theory's proponents of the superior power of the proposed new foundations one can at the same time develop these new proposals.

Keynes's attitude with respect to classical theory clearly indicates that he took this second line: 'For if orthodox economics is at fault, the error is to be found not in the superstructure, which has been erected with great care for logical consistency, but in a lack of clearness and of generality in the premises (Keynes, 1964, p. v).[2]

Keynes was convinced, in the early 1930s, that a new 'vision' of a modern capitalist was necessary, to be opposed 'in totum [*sic*]' to the fundamental vision of classical economists.[3] In a sense, his 'long struggle of escape' established modes of thought can be seen as the process of recognizing the fundamental insufficiency of the classical vision of capitalism that resulted from the attempt at analysing its problems using not only classical instruments but also, and more importantly, the classical hierarchy of concepts. As we will see, Keynes's main point of attrition with classical thought was the position it conferred upon money.

The seeds of Keynes's revolt against classical theory may have been planted by his forays into philosophy before becoming an economist and from which resulted his *Treatise on Probability*, which will be discussed in Chapter 4. The ideas he then developed found in his later Marshallian training in economics a fertile but conflictive ground that eventually led him to adopt an increasingly critical attitude towards classical postulates and ultimately to their abandonment.

MARSHALL AND KEYNES

Keynes's Marshallian background was very important in shaping both his attitude as to the object and nature of economic science and the creation of his most important analytical instruments, notably the aggregate demand and supply functions.

In one important sense, one may perhaps argue that Keynes took Marshall's approach to economics to its limits. The Keynesian revolution should be seen as simultaneously the culmination and the superation of the Marshallian programme. Keynes observed in his obituary of Marshall (*CWJMK*, X) that the latter's influence on English economic thought went far beyond his published works. Nevertheless, Marshall's *Principles of Economics*, even though not dealing with matters the author judged to be inadequate for a volume on fundamentals, such as money, international trade and so on, contains some key elements of his method that were part of the heritage Keynes criticized and developed.

Marshall seemed to have assessed his own work rather modestly. He saw the *Principles* as a work of synthesis of the propositions of the first authors in economic theory, like Smith and Ricardo, and the participants of the marginalist revolution of the late nineteenth century. Marshall's view of the divide between classical and neoclassical authors (using anachronic terms for clarity's sake) was that the opposition was illusory, being a matter of emphasis rather than of substance. For this reason, writing with a proper perspective given by the interval of time between the marginalist revolution in the 1870s and the publication of his *Principles* (whose first edition appeared in 1890), Marshall believed that the time was ripe for a codification of economic theory that would show its fundamental unity, as against the appearance of conflict and dissension.

One aspect of the Marshallian synthesis is very well known and will not be treated in detail here. This is the famous scissors image, used to show that the conflict between Ricardians and marginalists over the theory of value was the result of the partial nature of both theories. Ricardians emphasized cost conditions and marginalists emphasized demand conditions, but just as the two blades of a pair of scissors are necessary to cut a piece of paper, value would be determined by both cost and demand conditions. The apparent opposition between the schools was rooted in their misunderstanding of the influence of time in the determination of value. Cost or supply conditions changed more slowly than demand. So, for short intervals of time, all changes in value one would observe would be explained by demand shifts. Given time, however, supply could also be changed to adapt to demand, so it was the interaction between the two that should be studied instead of the narrow concentration on one of them, as proposed by each of the contending schools.

One sees that the explicit consideration of time exercises a crucial role in this argument. Marshall changed the framework within which value theory was discussed to consider an explicit analytical role of time (Bharadwaj, 1978). This was to have an important influence not only on Keynes's ideas but on all economics practised by heirs to Marshall.

It is to another aspect of Marshall's attempts to build a synthesis that we wish to call attention. Marshall also inherited the classical concern with the identification of 'laws of motion' of society or the economy.[4] It was suggested that these 'laws' gave 'sense' or 'meaning' to the evolution of modern economies over time. Classical political economists (including Marx), however, determined these laws from an approach to economic dynamics that privileged the action of collectives, social classes, defined by their assumed function in the productive process. The notion of law was then used to postulate the distinctive behaviours of these collectives and their interactions. Workers were those who produced income and, particularly, surplus income. Manufacturers or capitalists transformed surplus product into new capital, and so on. These were necessary, almost definitional, roles and it was from them that laws were derived.

The notion of law was of central importance also for Marshall, who wrote that a 'science progresses by increasing the number and exactness of its laws' (Marshall, 1924, p. 25). Writing, however, after the marginalist revolution he could not ignore its arguments as to the importance of individual decisions in opposition to the classical stress on collectives. Marshall himself stated that one characteristic of modern times was:

a certain independence and habit of choosing one's own course for oneself, a self-reliance; a deliberation and yet a promptness of choice and judgment, and a habit of forecasting the future and of shaping one's course with reference to distant aims . . . It is deliberateness, not selfishness, that is the characteristic of the modern age. Ibid., pp. 4, 5)

Marshall was to have great difficulties in reconciling the idea of law with the freedom he recognized modern people to be endowed with. On the one hand, he was led to play down somewhat the meaning of laws in economic science (ibid., p. 27). In addition, Marshall developed the notion of 'normality' to substitute for the behavioural iron laws of the classical political economy. As we will see below, the notion of normality was to have a very important role in Keynes's own theory that had to face the same dilemma between the notions of 'order' (which supposed some form of social coherence and, therefore, of 'laws') and individual freedom to choose. To transcend the individual Marshall offered the idea of 'normal behaviour':

... normal action is taken to be that which may be expected, under certain conditions, from the members of an industrial group. (Ibid., p. 6)

If men have similar motives and face similar conditions one may expect they will have similar behaviours, the 'normal' behaviours that could be observed and understood by science, the economic science. Idiosyncratic behaviours, on the other hand, cannot be the subject of a social science like economics.

As Marshall put it: 'the economist has little concern with particular incidents in the lives of individuals' (ibid., p. 83); 'economists study the actions of individuals but study them in relation to social rather than individual life; and therefore concern themselves but little with personal peculiarities of temper and character' (ibid., p. 21); 'For our present purposes the pliability of the race is more important than the pliability of the individual' (ibid., p. 638).

Marshall postulated that economic motives are similar in the average (pp. 15, 83) even when considering that some demands are so widespread as to be conventionally assumed as basic needs (p. 58). The notion of convention was to have an important role in Keynes's own theory. Finally, some appeals to 'human nature' were made when Marshall lacked better arguments (as in the relation between savings and interest rates in book 6, chapter 6).

If we know what individuals, in the average, want, what they actually do will depend on what it is possible for them to do. In other words, it will depend on the restrictions on the freedom of choice that the environment imposes on agents. If we suppose agents to be capable of correctly assessing these restrictions, we may be able to identify normal strategies or behaviours for each set of restrictions.

Marshall in fact not only postulated that this is possible but also took a much bolder step and proposed the fairly intuitive idea that the number of restrictions on individual decisions we should consider depends on how much time we allow the whole process to take. In the short period the agent would face many more restrictions on his choice than in the long period. If he knows these restrictions he will adopt the 'normal' procedures to achieve his goals, and his actions (and those of everybody else who is like him) will be intelligible, allowing the identification of a 'law' of behaviour. The period, however, is not a real duration of time. Its time dimension is entirely due to our intuition that the more time we consider, the fewer 'permanent' factors we will have to consider as restraining an agent's choice. Rigorously, however, short and long periods differ only to the extent that we consider different sets of restrictions in each of them. This is actually how Marshall defined them: 'For short periods people take the stock of appliances for production as practically fixed . . . In long periods they set themselves to adjust the flow of appliances to their expectations of demand . . .' (ibid., p. 310).

Two conditions are required for the 'normal' action to become actual behaviour. The first is that the environment has to remain stable while the action develops; the second is that the agent has to be able adequately to assess the environment when making his choices. The second condition was to occupy Keynes. The first condition is recognized as an important difficulty by Marshall himself:

It is true however that the condition that time must be allowed for causes to produce their effects is a source of great difficulty in economics. For meanwhile the material on which they work, and perhaps even the causes themselves, may have changed; and the tendencies which are being described will not have a sufficiently 'long run' in which to work themselves. (Ibid., p. 30)

A run is a duration of time: it is the amount of time it takes for a process to achieve its end. If the environment keeps changing the process will never reach its end. A long-period normal position may be a purely notional state if it is not given enough time for it to be achieved. In other words, a long period exists in the present, here and now, as Joan Robinson used to say. It is, in fact, an expectational concept (Marshall, 1924, p. 278) that can only be an actual state, a kind of terminal point of actual economic processes, if conditions remain the same for the process of adaptation to be completed, in the long 'run'. Marshall's 'solution' was to recognize that 'under certain conditions' long-period normal values will be achieved in the long run. For the processes where 'conditions' allow it, then, laws of motion can be derived.

KEYNES AND MARSHALL

The somewhat long digression on Marshall above helps us to understand a fundamental aspect of Keynes's and Post Keynesian theory
that will face pretty much the same dilemma as did Marshall: how to
reconcile the notion of order with the acknowledgement of individual freedom?[5]

Keynes wrote in Marshall's obituary that the distinction between
the short and the long period was 'path-breaking'. But he added that
'this is the quarter in which, in my opinion, the Marshall analysis is
least complete and satisfactory, and where there remains most to do'
(*CWJMK*, X, p. 207). We may venture the hypothesis that Keynes's
objection may have had to do with the identification of long period
with long run and thus with the gravitation process that unifies both
notions.

The long period was thus important to Marshall because it was
the way to reconcile the search for long-run 'constants' with the
behavioural analysis of actual markets that concerned him. The
notion of normality was fundamental to justify the possibility of
stable equilibria, whenever conditions were sufficiently permanent to
allow agents to find their most desired positions. Long-period
results, in this sense, could always be defined; whether they could be
actually reached depended on the degree of permanence of their
determining conditions.

Keynes, like Marshall, also saw the long period as the realm of full
equilibrium. When discussing a paper submitted by Kalecki for
publication in the *Economic Journal*, in 1941, Keynes asked Robinson whether it was 'not rather odd when dealing with "long run"
problems to start with the assumption that all firms are always
working below capacity' (*CWJMK*, XII, p. 829). When she replied
that Kalecki was working with a different view of the long period,
Keynes retorted:

If he is extending the General Theory beyond the short period but not the
long period in the old sense, he really must tell us what the sense is. For I am
still innocent enough to be bewildered by the idea that the assumption of all
firms always working below capacity is consistent with a 'long-run
problem'. (*CWJMK*, XII, p. 830–3)

When developing the concept of a monetary economy, on which
The General Theory was to be founded, Keynes observed that Mar-

shall had not 'explicitly settled' the meaning of long-period equilibrium. He saw three possible ways to define it:

The first suggestion conveyed by the term 'long-period' is that it relates to a position toward which forces spring up to influence the short-period position whenever the latter has diverged from it. The second suggestion conveyed is that the long-period position differs from the short-period positions in being a stable position capable cet. par. of being sustained, whilst short-period positions are cet. par. unstable and cannot be sustained. The third suggestion is that the long-period position is, in some sense, an optimum or ideal position from the point of view of production, i.e. a position in which the forces of production are disposed and utilized to their best possible advantage. (*CWJMK*, XXIX, p. 54)

The sense of long period which Keynes actually used in *The General Theory* was the second, with one relevant exception: the concept of long-period employment, presented in Chapter 5 of *The General Theory* (see below). This sense of the term is weaker than the other two. In it one recognizes only that there may be some stimuli to change implicit in a given situation even if it represents a short-period equilibrium. This is, for instance, the case of the short-period equilibrium between supply and demand being coexistent with a desire to change the stocks of capital equipment in use. The concept does not refer to a terminal but to an initial position and reactions to it that are implicitly contained in its construction.

In the discussion of meanings presented above, Keynes did not try to resolve the ambiguity of the concept, choosing instead to focus his criticism on the 'uniqueness' of the equilibrium position:

For the root of the objection which I find to the theory under discussion, if it is propounded as a long-period theory, lies in the fact that, on the one hand, it cannot be held that the position towards which the economic system is tending or the position at which it would be at rest or the optimum position is independent of the policy of the monetary authority; whilst, on the other hand, it cannot be maintained that there is a unique policy which, in the long run, the monetary authority is bound to pursue . . . On my view, there is no unique long-period position of equilibrium equally valid regardless of the character of the policy of the monetary authority. (*CWJMK*, XXIX, pp. 54–5)

Some points in the statement above should be highlighted: first, it has nothing to do with the second meaning of long period, which does not specify the nature of the final equilibrium position; secondly, it touches directly on the orthodox way of equating long-period normality with long-run equilibrium; finally, it is the existence of money and its institutional apparatus that is at the root of the problems with orthodoxy.

At this point, one should have in mind why monetary policy can have the kind of long-period influence Keynes expected; that is, affecting the 'course of events'. It does so by exercising a lasting impact on the accumulation of capital. We will argue later that Keynes's most original insights referred to the possibility of money becoming a substitute for other types of assets in the portfolios of agents, including real capital assets. Other theoreticians, following Wicksell, considered that monetary policies could affect real investment through their effects on credit conditions. Keynes, in contrast, approaches this process by emphasizing the role of money as an asset, absorbing demand that otherwise could be directed to productive assets. Under certain conditions it could be more attractive to retain liquid assets rather than income-generating, but riskier, capital assets. If confidence on the expectations of returns from the latter is weak, agents may prefer the safety that liquid assets confer on their holders.[6]

This quality of money of being an asset, according to Keynes, derives from the uncertainty that surrounds private economic decisions under capitalism. The liquidity of money lies in its unique capacity to liquidate debts (*CWJMK*, v, p. 1; Keynes, 1964, pp. 236–7). It is because other assets are subject to income or capital risks that money, the legal tender and its closest substitutes, have a 'return'.

Uncertainty is particularly strong in relation to investment in long-lived capital assets, where current conditions cannot give the decision maker the relevant information about the future to guide his acts. This does not mean that agents cannot perceive current inadequacies of their capital stock or differences in current profit rates. It only means that there is no mechanism to coordinate their perceptions and decisions towards a consistent, stable, long-run equilibrium position.

Keynes, like Marshall, approached the long period to sustain the notion of 'normality'.[7] But 'normality' is a behavioural concept. It refers to the reactions that consistently accompany a given stimulus. The latter has to be sufficiently permanent or repetitive to allow agents to develop 'normal' behaviour. Investment of capital would fail on this criterion. In this case, the outstanding fact is the extreme precariousness of the basis of knowledge on which our estimates of prospective yield have to be made. Our knowledge of the factors which will govern the yield of an investment some years hence is usually very slight and often negligible' (Keynes, 1964, p. 149).[8]

The present is not then sufficient to 'determine' investment decisions: 'regarding the marginal efficiency of capital primarily in terms of the current yield of capital equipment . . . would be correct only in the static state where there is no changing future to influence the present' (ibid., p. 145).

If investments were 'primarily' decided in terms of current conditions one could postulate conditions under which long-period values would be obtained in the long run induced by those conditions. Keynes, however, interposed the predominance of personal interpretation, states of confidence and animal spirits between current conditions and investment decisions.

In this picture, long-period equilibrium values might exist behind, or as a shadow to, any short-period configuration, because they would represent that situation which would constitute a full equilibrium consistent with economic 'data'. We also may consider, as Keynes did, that, if short-period and long-period values diverge, the economy will move towards another short-period position and will keep moving as long as the divergence remains; precisely because of not being in a state of full equilibrium agents will continue to try to change their position. This would indeed be the main role assigned to the notion of long-period equilibrium. Nevertheless, one should emphasize that there is no longer any necessary connection between the long-period equilibrium values an external observer can identify at any given moment and the specific strategies that will be adopted by actual agents at the same moment. What matters to Keynes in explaining the actual path of the economy is the 'state of long-term expectations' rather than 'objective' long-period conditions.[9] These long-period values cannot then be called 'normal' because they do not correspond to the information that will be actually available to agents. Therefore, even if long-period values can be calculated, nothing can guarantee that they will ever become, in the long run, 'normal' values.

The difference stated above between the concepts of run and period was very clear to Keynes. In a debate with Hubert Henderson about the influence of money supply, Keynes noted that 'the above deals with what happens in the long run, i.e. after the lapse of a considerable period of time rather than in the long period in the technical sense (*CWJMK*, XXIX, p. 221). Keynes then proceeded to state that a long-run equilibrium situation might not exist (which was not the case of long-period values 'in the technical sense'): I should, I think, be prepared to argue that, in a world ruled by uncertainty with an uncertain future linked to an actual present, a final position of equilibrium such as one deals with in static economics, does not properly exist' (ibid., p. 221).

That the question revolves around volition in an environment of uncertainty is not open to doubt. In a letter to Harrod, Keynes wrote, in 1938:

I also want to emphasise strongly the point about economics being a moral science. I mentioned before that it deals with introspection and with values. I might have added that it deals with motives, expectations, psychological uncertainties. One has to be constantly on guard against treating the material as constant and homogeneous. It is as though the fall of the apple to the ground depended on the apple's motives, on whether it is worth while falling to the ground, on whether the ground wanted the apple to fall, and on mistaken calculations on the part of the apple as to how far it was from the centre of the earth. (*CWJMK*, XIV, p. 287)

But what can one say about short-period equilibrium? Would it not share the atemporal nature of the long period? For Keynes, some crucial differences between the two notions could be pointed out. Firstly, Keynes saw the short-period framework as being closely related to the virtual stage in which agents make their decisions. It was not just an idealized scenario but a fair rendering of the restrictions under which flesh-and-bones agents would act. The data for which the short-period theory of employment is solved coincide with the actual conditions under which short-run decisions are made, thus allowing one to define not only a short-period equilibrium but a short-run equilibrium as well. This is very clearly the meaning of the following quotation:

Thus we are supposing, in accordance with the facts, that at any given time the productive processes set on foot, whether to produce consumption goods or investment goods, are decided in relation to the then existing capital equipment. But we are not assuming that the capital equipment remains in any sense constant from one accounting period to another.

If we look at the productive process in this way, we are, it seems to me, in the closest possible contact with the facts and methods of the business world as they actually exist; and at the same time we have transcended the awkward distinction between the long and the short period. (*CWJMK*, XXIX, pp. 64–5)[10]

One should notice that the difference that is being brought to the fore is precisely that the short-period framework includes the data of the actual environment where agents act, while the long-period situation has no such 'reality'. They do not relate in the same way to actual processes that are to take place in definite 'runs' of time.

For this reason the idea of short-period equilibrium is more than just an analytical abstraction to Keynes. As he stated in *The General Theory*, short-run decisions, like the decision to produce, are made in an essentially repetitive fashion (Keynes, 1964, pp. 50–1).

As long as the environment does not significantly change, learning can originate a kind of gravitation process towards equilibrium:

Entrepreneurs have to endeavour to forecast demand. They do not, as a rule, make wildly wrong forecasts of the equilibrium position. But, as the matter is very complex, they do not get it just right; and they endeavour to approximate to the true position by a method of trial and error ... It corresponds precisely to the higgling [*sic*] of the market by means of which buyers and sellers endeavour to discover the true equilibrium position of supply and demand. (*CWJMK*, XIV, p. 182)

One could ask, then, whether it is really useful to extend *The General Theory* to the long period. Keynes's own use of long-period notions in that work strengthens that feeling of doubt. The long period is briefly introduced in the chapter on expectations, after a discussion of the notion of 'long-term expectations', in which the word 'term' refers to a definite time-horizon for which the agent is forming his expectations to state that, 'if we suppose a state of expectation to continue for a sufficient length of time', the economy will reach the level of employment that is entirely due to that state. This will 'be called the long-period employment corresponding to that state of expectation' (Keynes, 1964, p. 48). This is a notional state, as happens with other long-period configurations that may or may not be achievable in the long run. It should be noticed that Keynes does not use the term 'normal', as Marshall used to do when referring to long-period values. This is probably due to the fact that Keynes proceeded from that definition to state that 'expectation may change so frequently' that the precise level of employment may never be attained in reality. In any case, as Asimakopulos (1984–5; 1985) has already pointed out, Keynes's discussion of this concept has the nature of an aside, without any consequence for the model presented in the book. What really matters for Keynes is the 'state of long-term expectations', because this is the driving force acting on agents. Long-period employment is just a notional configuration that does not have to coincide with the employment that is expected to occur actually in the long term. It is a reference for the outside observer, not a guide for the decisions and behaviours of agents.

NORMALITY

Marshall built his long-period analysis when trying to obtain behavioural foundations for the notion of normality. Keynes proposed that, in an economy that operates under uncertainty, to be able to determine long-period values was not sufficient to establish a long-run tendency to reach those values.

For both Keynes and Marshall, the point of the idea of normality was to explain the existence of rules, the continuity that economic life exhibits, despite the fluctuations and interruptions of activity that are also typical of capitalism. As observed by Keynes:

It is an outstanding characteristic of the economic system in which we live that, whilst it is subject to severe fluctuations in respect of output and employment, it is not violently unstable ... Fluctuations may start briskly but seem to wear themselves out before they have proceeded to great extremes, and an intermediate situation which is neither desperate nor satisfactory is our normal lot. (Keynes, 1964, pp. 249–50)[11]

Furthermore, in a letter to Joan Robinson in 1936, Keynes had warned that one 'must not confuse instability with uncertainty' (*CWJMK*, XIV, p. 137). The capitalist economy shows a remarkable degree of stability for a system with the characteristics Keynes described. In a sense, it is not the explanation of fluctuations that should be the problem for economists but of how a system like this simply does not collapse under its own contradictions.

As we have seen, for Keynes order and continuity were not a result of the 'attraction' forces contained in a long-run set of equilibrium values. The divergence between short-period and long-period values was sufficient to move the system but not to direct it towards any definite position. This was so because investment decisions were only partly informed by current signals and long-run equilibrium values could not be translated into 'motives and behaviours' of entrepreneurs determining their state of long-term expectations. Mostly investment was determined by extremely uncertain expectations that in no way could be coordinated among different individual agents. Continuity (and normality) should thus be explained in another way. According to Keynes, continuity was actually guaranteed by 'exogenous' factors: 'Now, since these facts of experience [those mentioned in the 1964 quotation] do not follow of logical necessity, one must suppose that the environment and the psychological propensities of the modern world must be of such a character as to produce these results' (Keynes, 1964, p. 250).

Keynes went on to list four of these characteristics, namely, that the multiplier is not very large; the investment schedule is not very elastic with respect to a change in expectations or in the interest rate; the money-wage rate is not very sensitive to changes in the level of employment; and that changes in investment tend to react on the marginal efficiency of capital in such a way as to counteract the initial impulse (ibid. pp. 250–1).

These features refer basically to the 'psychological propensities of the modern world'. To those we should add a very important concept developed elsewhere in *The General Theory*, the notion of convention. This is

our usual practice . . . to take the existing situation and to project it into the future, modified only to the extent that we have more or less definite reasons for expecting a change . . . The above conventional method of calculation will be compatible with a considerable measure of continuity and stability in our affairs, so long as we can rely on the maintenance of the convention. (Ibid., pp. 148, 152)

The notion of convention is the closest substitute Keynes offered for the concept of 'normal' values. It isolates a very important characteristic of behaviour under uncertainty: its stickiness. This behaviour will be examined in more detail.

As important as the 'right' psychology are the features of the environment that strengthen continuity. Foremost among these features are institutions created to reduce or socialize uncertainty, coordinating plans and activities. The most important of them is the emergence of forward contracts denominated in money connecting the present to the future (see Davidson, 1978a; 1978b; pp. 57, 60). To sustain a system of forward contracts one also needs to define a monetary standard endowed with rules of management that may be seen by agents as limiting the future behaviour of the monetary unit to a manageable range, allowing them to form predictions with greater confidence. In addition, there are also material elements of continuity, such as long-lived capital goods, which limit, at any given moment, the range of alternatives that are open to agents. Finally, in modern capitalist economies, one cannot forget the action of the state in informing and coordinating economic agents and assuring them that 'normal' business conditions will be maintained.

All these 'environmental and psychological' factors are sufficient to create a stable framework within which agents can form a picture of 'normality' without reference to long-period equilibrium values that cannot be operational at the behavioural level. As suggested below, in chapter IV, Keynesian normality is a feature of the short period rather than the long.

SUMMING UP

Garegnani (1983) has correctly stressed the methodological continuity between classical and neoclassical economics as regards the use of the long-period method. Both schools took long-period equilibrium values as being long-run gravitation centres for the economy. In the short run the economy would be subject to erratic influences and unsustainable plans would emerge. In the long run, however, only the fundamentals would prevail, since it would be sensible to suppose that erratic influences would be cancelled out, given time. In addition, both classical and neoclassical schools tended to identify only 'real' long-term forces. Monetary influences work like 'veils', obscuring real motives and restrictions in operation.

As we have seen, Marshall tried not only to remain in the orthodoxy as regards method but also to synthesize what he thought were the essential propositions of each school. Keynes broke with orthodoxy firstly on methodological grounds, and this is the meaning of the shift towards the short period as against the traditional emphasis on long periods. Moreover, Keynes saw clearly that his break had to do with volition and the freedom that the existence of money in a modern capitalist economy confers on individual agents. However, if this meant that one had to take into consideration 'motives and behaviours' of individuals, it was not conducive to an extreme methodological individualism along Austrian lines. Order and social organization are essential elements of Keynes's vision, as much as uncertainty and individual freedom. To a large extent one can see Keynes's economics as the attempt to reconcile these two elements, order and freedom, without surrendering to either one of them, as did the classical determinists who only saw order, or the Austrian irrationalists, who could only see the individual.

Keynes understood that the key to developing his project was the role of money in modern economies. Most of the debates mentioned in this chapter began with the consideration of the power of monetary policy to affect the path of an economy. The increasing clarity of this point in Keynes's own mind is the story of the preparation of the Keynesian revolution, that Keynes himself identified as the codification of a theory adequate to analyse the workings of a monetary economy. This is the subject of our next chapter.

NOTES

1. More than 30 years after the emergence of the so-called Cambridge critique of neoclassical capital theory a quick examination of the main economics journals shows that, despite Samuelson's famous acceptance of defeat in the matter, aggregate capital and production functions still abound in the mainstream literature. This can be partly explained by plain ignorance fomented by the poor quality of textbooks that avoid questions about fundamental concepts in favour of a 'technical school' approach that emphasizes mathematical skills rather than theoretical reasoning. An often used argument states that, whether theoretically correct or not, aggregate capital and production functions concepts are useful empirical instruments. These are very fragile practices. The failure of the Cambridge critique to change the ways economics is practised can be attributed, however, mostly to its incapacity to present an alternative. An internal critique is naturally developed in the interior of a theory and can only be developed in that environment. When one tries to proceed from the negation of a theory to the construction of an alternative, one realizes that the critique per se does not set clear bases for a positive proposition. In other words, to deny content to the concept of aggregate capital is not sufficient to establish new foundations. An internal critique, per se, in sum, is not sufficient to define a new alternative paradigm around which the economics practitioners can be regrouped. As Kuhn showed, a paradigm is replaced only when there are competitive paradigms to be adopted. It does not disappear just because it faces difficulties.
2. One should note that an important implication of this discussion is that an

external critique, when rejecting a paradigm rather than trying to work in its interior, is in fact rejecting not only particular concepts but also, and more importantly, the hierarchy of concepts presented by the vision under attack. This means that a new paradigm not only poses new problems but also rejects as irrelevant some of those that the superseded tradition entertained. A new paradigm poses its own questions. Its task is not to answer the old questions except when they happen also to exist in the new paradigm. In this sense, the neo-Ricardian criticism of Post Keynesians that the latter do not offer an alternative construction to neoclassical models of long-run equilibrium may be out of place. As Garegnani (1983) makes clear, neo-Ricardians accept the same fundamental questions as classical and neoclassical economists. As will be argued later, this is not the case with Post Keynesians. On the need to consider Keynes's vision as a whole instead of taking the Keynesian revolution as just the development of new instruments, see Barrere (1985).

3. Keynes had a lifelong concern with persuasion, initially through his political and economic pamphlets and later with *The General Theory* itself.

4. Marshall possibly inherited this concern not only from classical political economists but also from philosophers who admittedly influenced his views, such as Hegel, referred to in the preface to the first edition of the *Principles*. The present author has explored these points in Carvalho, 1990.

5. The attempt at reconciling these two notions is a specifically Post Keynesian goal that distinguishes it both from the neo-Ricardian models, where there is no individual decision and order is the only problem, and from extreme Shacklean views that, in common with the new Austrian school, can only study the individual but is powerless to understand orderly 'social' systems.

6. The substitutability between capital and liquid (monetary) assets is emphasized at many points in *The General Theory*, and formally modelled in Chapter 17. See Keynes (1964, pp. 160–1; 212–3; 226–7; 357–8). The substitutability between money and goods had already been raised in a 1933 draft of *The General Theory* (*CWJMK*, xxix, pp. 84–6) although not yet in a portfolio choice framework. We will return to this point in Chapter 5.

7. Keynes had written: 'By means of the distinction between the long and the short period, the meaning of "normal" value was made precise' (*CWJMK*, vii, p. 207).

8. Keynes's inclination to develop concepts that could reflect what takes place 'in the real world' was already clear in the way he chose sides in the Malthus/Ricardo debate. See, for example, *CWJMK*, x, p. 87: 'Malthus was already disposed to a certain line of approach in handling practical economic problems which he was to develop later on in his correspondence with Ricardo – a method which to me is most sympathetic, and, as I think, more likely to lead to right conclusions than the alternative approach of Ricardo.'

9. When forming expectations an agent builds a scenario of the future within which he locates his own expected position. The divergence between short- and long-period values could show itself by falsifying his forecasts of scenarios, even if the particular results he achieves coincide with what was expected, leading him to seek additional changes of strategy.

10. As Keynes wrote in 1937: 'I have said in another context that it is a disadvantage of "the long run" that in the long run we are all dead. But I could have said equally well that it is a great advantage of "the short run" that in the short run we are still alive. Life and history are made up of short runs' (*CWJMK*, xxviii, p. 62). Conditions are seldom permanent enough to guarantee any long-run gravitation process to work. Prediction may be a fool's work: 'The inevitable never happens. It is the unexpected always' (ibid., p. 117).

11. The correspondence between the notions of normality and equilibrium, the

latter being understood as absence of stimuli to change, is established by Keynes as follows: 'I define "equilibrium" real wages as those which are paid when all the factors of production are employed and entrepreneurs are securing normal returns, meaning by "normal" returns those which leave them under no incentive either to increase or to decrease the money offers which they make to factors of production' (*CWJMK*, XIII, p. 178).

3. Foundations of Post Keynesian Economics: The Concept of a Monetary Economy

As we saw in the preceding chapter, Keynes's departure from orthodoxy happened because of his dissatisfaction with the classical treatment of money. What he called in *The General Theory* his 'long struggle of escape' from established modes of thought took the form of an increasing discomfort with the way the classics conceived the insertion of money in the economy.

Classical and neoclassical theories basically postulate the neutrality of money with respect to the determination of long-period equilibrium values. All the fundamental theorems of these theories are established in real terms, by the direct consideration of goods, preferences and technical constraints. Thus in classical political economy the laws of motion are all proposed as a result of the interaction between elements such as the surplus rate, the organic composition of capital, real wages and so on. The central propositions of neoclassical theory refer to the reconciliation between the limited availability of resources and the consumers' preferences obtained by the system of relative (real) prices. Money cannot influence the basic choices to be made, except to the extent that it can obscure the informational content of market prices. In the long run, when all erratic influences are cancelled out and agents learn to separate information from noise (created by monetary disturbances), all that matters is real variables.

Keynes was trained in this tradition and one possible way of reconstructing his trajectory towards breaking with orthodoxy is to identify his attitude with respect to money in his main works. Although this is not the place for an exhaustive historical reconstruction of Keynes's monetary thought it may be useful, in order to evaluate adequately its relevance for the understanding of the content of the Keynesian revolution, to follow, in broad lines, the way money was approached in his three main works in monetary theory: the *Tract on Monetary Reform* (1923) (*CWJMK*, IV), *A Treatise on Money* (1930) (*CWJMK*, V) and *The General Theory* (1936) (*CWJMK*, VI).

When writing the papers that were gathered in the *Tract*, Keynes was a convinced Marshallian quantity theorist. As Kahn, perhaps his closest collaborator, wrote: 'Keynes showed himself in his *Tract on Monetary Reform* as a fanatical believer in the Quantity Theory, in the full causal sense of the determination of the price-level by the quantity of money (Kahn, 1984, o. 53). Keynes did actually state about the Quantity Theory during this period: 'This theory is fundamental. Its correspondence with fact is not open to question' (*CWJMK*, IV, p. 61).

In the *Tract*, Keynes presents a discussion of the Marshallian quantity theory of money. In this version the quantity equation is used to define a money demand function connected to the level of nominal income. The connection is given by a velocity coefficient that measures the convenience of holding money to bridge the interval between receipts and expenditures.

The Marshallian approach to the Quantity Theory was essentially behavioural, in contrast to the Fisherian approach of a heavily mechanistic nature (Fisher, 1926).[1] In a sense, with the Marshallian (or Cambridge) version of the Quantity Theory one was led to concentrate mainly on adjustment mechanisms rather than on the properties of an equilibrium state. One of the main subjects of the *Tract* is precisely the behaviour of economies suffering deep inflationary disequilibria, like the German or the Russian hyperinflations of the early 1920s. In this situation, one cannot expect elements like velocity to remain constant, as is assumed in equilibrium exercises. To understand the variations suffered by these assumed 'parameters' was crucial to explaining the dynamics of hyperinflations.

In the *Tract*, Keynes was also interested in exchange rate theory, particularly in the qualifications one had to introduce into the purchasing power parity theory of exchange rates when considering the existence of forward exchange markets. As shown by Kregel (see below, Chapter 5), this discussion has a strategic place in the development of Keynes's thought that eventually took him to *The General Theory*.

Despite the intrinsic interest aroused by Keynes's study of hyper-inflations,[2] the analysis may be seen as strictly orthodox, or at least strictly Marshallian. Money is not neutral but the non-neutrality happens in the short run, something perfectly acceptable to the orthodoxy. Keynes's comments on the idea that in the long run everything would return to normality are mildly derisive: he does not question its validity in theory but its practical relevance. Here, one of his most famous statements, makes its appearance: 'In the long run we are all dead. Economists set themselves too easy, too useless a task if in tempestuous seasons they can only tell us that when the storm is long past the ocean is flat again,' (*CWJMK*, IV, p. 65).

Money is still a means of circulation of commodities. Hyperinflations are circulatory disturbances of some gravity but there are no long-term consequences following from circulation problems. Money, existing only as a circulation device, as a means to facilitate the turnover of the flow of goods, does not leave its mark on the economy beyond the limits of the short run.[3]

A crucial change takes place between the appearance of the *Tract* and the *Treatise on Money*. As realized by many authors, despite Keynes's continuing reverence for the Quantity Theory in the *Treatise*, a fundamental change of vision had taken place that implied the abandonment of the traditional approach to money,[4] even though some of the most dramatic implications of the new approach were only to be perceived in the preparation of *The General Theory*.

To put it in one phrase, the fundamental change that occurred was the change in the way money was perceived: from a means of circulation that is eventually held as a convenience to bridge definite intervals between transactions, to a representation of wealth, an asset that can be held as purchasing power in pure form, to be spent at some indefinite future date.[5]

The first departure from orthodoxy takes place with the identification of a financial circulation that breaks the linkage between money and the circulation of goods, that Keynes called industrial circulation. In the latter, money is merely a means to facilitate the circulation of goods. The financial circulation, on the other hand, includes the operations with assets, stocks of wealth, that have no necessary relation to the turnover of goods. In fact, even within financial circulation, money could be seen as merely a means of circulation of assets but not necessarily as an asset itself. It would break the relation between demand and money supply but would not represent any substantial rupture with orthodoxy. However, asking about forms of wealth, dealt with in financial circulation, Keynes advanced to the examination of notions such as waiting and speculation, and particularly to money as a form of waiting and speculating about asset values. The retention of positions in money affected the prices of debts and assets and actually affected the allocation of wealth among its various forms, making money non-neutral.

Of course, Keynes was not postulating money illusion. Ultimately, money is a means not an end, even in financial circulation. Nevertheless, in contrast to industrial circulation, money held as an asset is not associated with any definite plan of expenditure. It is held to be spent eventually, but it allows its possessor to postpone the decision as to when to do so. It is thus more than a bridging convenience and its behaviour cannot be adequately described by the Quantity Theory in any form, except if one takes the latter as just a truism or an accounting identity.

The seeds of dissent had been with Keynes for a long time. His earliest ideas on liquidity preference were presented in his 1913 examination of bank behaviour during the cycle (*CWJMK*, XIII, pp. 2–14) and the more complex interaction between banks and other financial institutions at the outbreak of the First World War (*CWJMK*, XII, ch. 4). These very suggestive works, however, still suffered from an excessively empirical tone and from a still confused use of terms such as capital, savings and so on. Together with the second volume of the *Treatise on Money*, they are very important for an extension of liquidity preference theory to bank behaviour and to the determination of the money supply. In a more definite sense, however, we may say that Keynes's new approach starts from a feature of money that he had been emphasizing since at least 1925 (*CWJMK*, XXVIII, pp. 252, 255) which was the importance of the existence of contracts denominated in money for the organization of modern economies. In the *Treatise* this point occupies the very first pages, it being stated that to serve as unit for contracts (money of account) is the primary function of money and one from which the other properties of money are derived (see below, Chapter 6).

The object that liquidates contractual commitments denominated in the money of account is money and for this very reason it is 'liquid'. Being liquid it can be held to assure debtors that an agent's obligations will be liquidated as they come due. Money then becomes what Davidson has called a 'liquidity time machine', to transport purchasing power over time. The importance of this change of attitude cannot be exaggerated.[6] Now the effects of money do not vanish at the end of a period but persist from one period to another. Money affects the choices that are made as to the means of conserving wealth, being a substitute for other assets. In this way it was bound to affect not only the short-run operation of the economy, but also its long-period positions and its long-term trajectories.

The elements for the identification of long-period non-neutrality of money were indicated in the *Treatise*. Nevertheless, Keynes did not seem to have realized the contradiction between his new approach and the desire to keep the pragmatic attitude of the *Tract*, avoiding the conflict with orthodoxy. In the *Treatise*, as in the *Tract*, Keynes still wrote that his new ideas were 'formally compatible with the traditional quantity theory – indeed it must be, since the latter is an identity, a truism' (*CWJMK*, VI, p. 5).

The pragmatic posture could be adopted in the *Tract*, however, because Keynes was still sticking to a theory in which money did not have long-run impacts. This was not so in the *Treatise*. To accept the orthodox view required the acceptance that money could not be seen as a durable form of wealth. To say the opposite was precisely the outcome of the new treatment.[7]

The theory offered in the *Treatise* connected money and other assets and suggested a theory of capital goods prices in which they were determined by mechanisms operating in the money and financial assets markets (*CWJMK*, V, chap. 10). The criticisms Keynes received even from sympathetic readers, such as the participants of the Cambridge Circus, led to further developments and to the perception that a new work was needed to sort out the issues. The new work was to be *The General Theory*.[8]

As one can follow in volumes XIII and XXIX of Keynes's *Collected Writings*, the way to *The General Theory* was difficult. The central point, however, was that Keynes soon realized the impossibility of keeping the theoretical innovations of the *Treatise* and the overall orthodox framework he still accepted. The perception grew in Keynes that perhaps some more radical change was needed to establish those propositions, instead of just amendments or qualifications to the dominant approach.

This is not a speculation but precisely what one gathers from the material collected especially in volumes XIII and XXIX of Keynes's works. In fact, in a somewhat cryptic paper published in 1933,

Keynes stated that he was looking for a new set of fundamental concepts, a new 'vision', to allow him to understand the operation of a 'monetary economy':

The distinction which is normally made between a barter economy and a monetary economy depends upon the employment of money as a convenient means of effecting exchanges – as an instrument of great convenience, but transitory and neutral in its effect . . . It is not supposed to affect the essential nature of the transaction from being, in the minds of those making it, one between real things, or to modify the motives and decisions of the parties to it. Money, that is to say, is employed, but it is treated as being in some sense neutral.

The theory which I desiderate would deal, in contradistinction to this, with an economy in which money plays a part of its own and affects motives and decisions and is, in short, one of the operative factors in the situation, so that the course of events cannot be predicted, either in the long period or in the short, without a knowledge of the behaviour of money between the first state and the last. And it is this which we ought to mean when we speak of a monetary economy. (*CWJMK*, XIII, pp. 408–9)

The need for a thorough reconstruction of economic theory from its foundations is made unmistakably clear by Keynes in the same paper: 'The idea that it is comparatively easy to adapt the hypothetical conclusions of a real wage [classical] economics to the real world of monetary economics is a mistake' (ibid., p. 410).

The first tables of contents Keynes prepared for his new work had as their first chapter precisely the exposition of the principles of operation of a monetary economy; that is, one in which money is not neutral either in the short or in the long period. *The General Theory* was to become the codification of the new vision, the formal statement of the rules of operation of this new conceptualization of what a modern economy is. For many reasons, including, apparently, the attempt to reduce attrition with the economics profession, Keynes minimized in the final version of *The General Theory* the innovative or radically new aspects of his approach, avoiding in particular more extended discussions of the concept of monetary economy. This choice seems to have failed in its objectives and Keynes, in the most important contribution to the post-*General Theory* debate, the paper 'The General Theory of Employment', tried to reestablish the radical character of his propositions.

In the view of the present author, Post Keynesians have as their programme precisely to develop the new vision, that of a monetary economy. This is the unifying concept that organizes the Post Keynesian paradigm and that makes it possible to overcome the very common impression (even among Post Keynesians themselves) that this school is united more by the arguments they refute than by positive tenets of theory reconstruction.

In the next section, the fundamental features of a monetary economy are presented to allow the precise identification of the rules and limits of work within this paradigm. Afterwards an overview of the analytical construction of the *General Theory* model, as an analytical representation of this paradigm, is offered. The theoretical model synthesized in this overview is then discussed in detail in part II.

A MONETARY ECONOMY

The crucial years in the development of Keynes's thought towards *The General Theory* seem to have been 1932 to 1934. In this period Keynes clearly realized that some kind of radical rupture with classical theory was really necessary, that economic theory required the definition of new foundations if it was to have any relevance to the analysis of modern economies. The key idea, as we saw above, was the non-neutrality of money in the long period; that is, there was a need to find a characterization of the economy that implied a substantive role for money, in contrast to the more superficial means-of-circulation function that was recognized by classical theory.

In the period between the publication of the *Treatise on Money* and *The General Theory*, Keynes, in his drafts of the new book and in his university lectures, was groping his way towards an outline of the new economics. In particular, Keynes was concerned with defining the principles or postulates that would characterize his fundamental 'model' of a monetary economy as something distinct from the real-wage or neutral economy that informed classical theory.

Keynes's first attempts at conceiving a monetary economy seemed to have been essentially negative. He knew what he did not want to keep from the classical view. The discussion of the features of the new model was more fluid. According to Keynes, in the kind of economy conceived by the classics the factors of production were either paid directly with goods or in some means of payment but, in the latter case, 'there is a mechanism of some kind to ensure that the exchange value of the money incomes of the factors is always equal in the aggregate to the proportion of current output which would have been the factor's share in a cooperative economy [the first case, where payments are made in kind]' (*CWJMK*, XXIX, p. 78).

Economies of the cooperative type admit sectoral disequilibria, local imbalances between supply and demand, but aggregate imbalances are ruled out. There are no disequilibrium-amplifying income effects, such as multipliers and the like. All income generated in the production process returns to the market as demand for produced goods, even if it is not for the precise basket of goods that is available. This kind of imbalance is removed by the operation of the price system in which relative scarcities and excess supplies are signalled by disparities between market and natural (or long-period equilibrium normal) prices. Gravitational processes are conceivable in these economies since the information on excess supplies are coexistent with information on excess demands (being market prices below natural prices in the former and the converse in the latter).

This conception of an economy, that Minsky nicknamed the 'village fair paradigm', sees it as constituted by independent consumers–producers that trade on the surpluses of their production above their needs. As Ricardo wrote, productions are exchanged for productions, and productive effort is made only because agents need or want the additional product.[9] These consumers–producers have their targets set in real terms, the goods that satisfy their needs; money is a convenience that can only be non-neutral in the short run, when it is possible for agents to confuse it for real wealth. In the long run, people learn to see through money and therefore to realize that it is only a means to an end, not an end in itself.

The mechanism that sustains global equilibrium is in fact the assumption that economic agents are primarily consumers facing scarcity of goods.[10] Productive decisions are made with a view to increasing the availability of goods to satisfy the insatiable demands of consumers. To remove this 'mechanism' one has to examine whether this characterization of a modern economy as an agglomerate of Robinson Crusoe fits well the fundamental structure of modern capitalist production.

Keynes's answer was that it did not fit. He offers instead the concept of a 'money-wage or entrepreneur economy' (alternative labels to monetary or monetary production economies) in which 'the entrepreneurs hire the factors for money but without such a mechanism as the above' (*CWJMK*, XXIX, p. 78) and wraps up this discussion by stating: 'It is obvious on these definitions that it is in an entrepreneur economy that we actually live to-day' (ibid.).

The task, then, was to elaborate the concept of monetary or entrepreneurial economy so as to give it the necessary theoretical rigour to allow the development of formal analysis on the basis of it. Actually, the examination of the defining features of the entrepreneurial economy was performed in a rather unsystematic way by Keynes and it is confined almost entirely to the drafts of *The General Theory*, being left out of its final form. However, there are enough clues in these works and in later discussions of some of his followers to allow some reconstruction of the concept.[11]

Modern neoclassical theory presents its foundations in the form of axioms upon which, by deriving its implications and corollaries, one constructs formal analytical propositions. Using Keynes's language with regard to these modern endeavours, we would say that these neoclassical axioms define rigorously the foundations or the defining principles of operation of a cooperative economy, embodying the fundamental vision of a consumer–producer economy.

Keynes's concept of monetary economy, however, cannot be adequately portrayed in the form of the specification of axioms. The application of the axiomatic method requires that the proposed axioms have two properties, firstly, they are starting points, statements that are irreducible to other principles. As Hahn put it, axioms 'mark the stage beyond which one does not seek to explain' (Hahn, 1984, p. 6). Their adequacy cannot be proved: one has to be convinced of their worth to use them. Again, as Hahn put it, 'The axioms have summed up what one regards as pretty secure empirical knowledge' (ibid., p. 7). There is a second property of axioms, however, that is not unrelated to the first; that is the need for axioms to be independent of one another. The application of the axiomatic method of construction building requires phenomena to be reducible to 'fundamental particles', upon combinations of which the rest of the theoretical construction is sustained. These fundamental particles cannot be themselves a combination of other elements because this would only mean that the necessary analysis had not been taken to its completion when the axioms were proposed.

For the second property to be valid it is then necessary that the object under study be approached in an 'atomist' perspective, that phenomena are thus reducible to a combination of fundamental elements. Fitzgibbons has correctly observed that in his early studies on probability Keynes was an atomist (Fitzgibbons, 1988). He is not convincing, however, when he argues that this aspect of the young Keynes's ideas remained a characteristic of his later work in economics.[12] In his biographical essay on Edgeworth, Keynes observed:

Mathematical Psychics has not, as a science or study, fulfilled its early promise ... The atomic hypothesis which has worked so splendidly in physics breaks down in psychics. We are faced at every turn with the problem of organic unity, of discreteness, of discontinuity – the whole is not equal to the sum of the parts, comparisons of quantity fails us, small changes produce large effects, the assumptions of a uniform and homogeneous continuum are not satisfied. (*CWJMK*, X, p. 262)

An object characterized by 'organic unity' cannot be conceived as a mathematical combination of independent elements and this is what happens with the economy. While neoclassical thought reduces the economy to the mechanical interaction of individual particles (the independently defined consumer–producer) taking place in a vacuum, Keynes's approach is based, even in its most abstract form in an institutional (and therefore organic) concept; that is, money. Money is a form of interaction that is supposed by Keynes to go far beyond the merely 'frictional' status visualized by neoclassical theory. It affects 'motives and decisions', and therefore the very definition of the economic agent. Because of (or, at this point of the argument, related to) money we will have market uncertainties plaguing the economic activity. Uncertainty is partly an axiom, but also partly a consequence of the nature of modern monetary arrangements and so on.

These characteristics of Keynes's thought prevent us from being able rigorously to formulate axiomatic systems as neoclassical theory does. On the other hand, to engage in the debate with orthodoxy it is certainly useful to try to identify, if not the axioms, at least the fundamental principles orienting the conception of a monetary economy.

As has already been said Keynes never presented these foundations in this form. The drafts of *The General Theory*, however, show that this was not a concern foreign to him since they contain a large amount of material of this nature. Since there is no systematic presentation of these principles by Keynes himself, one can organize his remarks made during the period of preparation of *The General Theory* as well as its defence against critics after publication in the most adequate way to allow contrast with neoclassical axioms.

Davidson (1984) has summarized the foundations of Keynes's and Post Keynesian economics in the refusal of three neoclassical axioms, to be replaced by alternative principles. The three axioms to be abandoned were those of gross substitution, of reals and of ergodicity. The axiom of gross substitution, which roughly states that everything is, in some degree, a substitute for everything else, was incompatible with Keynes's postulate that money was unique in the roles it could perform and therefore one of its fundamental properties was that of having low elasticity of substitution. The axiom of reals consists in assuming that only goods and services generate utility and therefore agents set real targets for their strategies unless they suffer from some kind of irrationality, such as money illusion, a possibility denied by another axiom (not necessarily incompatible with Keynesian ideas), that of rationality. This was the foundation of the neutrality of money that, as we saw, was precisely the object of Keynes's most important criticisms. Finally, the axiom of ergodicity assumes that economic processes are basically stationary, so in the long run agents can learn how they operate and, by adapting their behaviour to the environment, long-period equilibrium positions can be attained. The axiom of ergodicity is, as will be discussed in more detail in the next chapter, incompatible with the notion of uncertainty as presented by Keynes.

According to Davidson, the Keynesian revolution would consist in the substitution of three alternative principles for these rejected axioms. The first principle would be the non-neutrality of money; that is, the idea that it affects 'motives and decisions'. Secondly, the irreversibility of time generates non-ergodic environments in which the tendency to gravitation towards a long-period equilibrium does not operate and in which the kinds of behaviour described by neoclassical models are themselves irrational. Inergodic processes exhibit statistical averages different from temporal averages, making learning through trial and error impossible (Davidson, 1984, p. 185). Finally, the third principle would be that in a non-ergodic world, where production takes time, societies develop means to deal with uncertainty, the most common and widespread of which is the creation of a system of forward money contracts.

These three principles certainly summarize the core of Keynes's proposed revolution. They have one limitation, however, if one thinks of a system of axioms – that of not being intuitive enough and therefore perhaps not 'originative' enough. In the rest of this chapter we will present what could be perhaps a more intuitive alternative, especially as regards the first and the third of Davidson's proposed principles. Before outlining these principles, however, it is important to set down some preliminary points related to the conception of economic activity and to the identification of economic agents.

Keynes's notion of economic activity is essentially Marshallian, which is close to the notion entertained by classical political economy and very different from the Walrasian approach. Firstly, it recognizes production as the essential economic activity, in contrast with the Walrasian emphasis on exchange. This means that, while the study of characteristic features of the productive process, being time-consuming, cooperative, involving long-lived equipment and so on are an essential part of Keynes's economics, the Walrasian approach to production is confined, as Walras himself put it, to the formation of factor prices (Walras, 1954, p. 40). The second difference is the conception of market. Again, for Keynes, markets are institutions, a set of practices, rules and procedures. For the Walrasian approach, markets are in fact an illusion. They do not have any reality and the more perfect they are the less visible their operation is.

To sum up, the concept of entrepreneurial economy is applied to an economy where agents are organized to produce and where goods are distributed through market relations between independent units. In the basic model of an entrepreneurial economy there are three kinds of inhabitants (in a more extended model one could add at least two more types of agents, the state and foreign agents): firms, families and banks. Firms organize production and its related activities. Families have a double role: that of supplying factor services and of consuming goods. Banks create money. It is important to note at the outset that these three types are not reducible to one another as in neoclassical theory, where firms are either indefinable ghosts or are special forms that families assume to reach particular ends.[13] They will be fully recognizable individuals to the extent that one can recognize goals and objectives for each that are not reducible to the goals and objectives of others; in particular, that are not reducible to the search for satisfaction maximization on the part of families.

At this stage we can formulate six fundamental principles of operation of a monetary or entrepreneurial economy. The first we call the 'principle of production', according to which we recognize

the particular individuality of the firm as an agent in these economies to the extent that it is possible to define both an exclusive
activity for it but also that it has its own motives and goals that are
not mere modifications of goals set by other agents, such as families.
The principle of production states that production is performed by
firms with a view to obtaining profits.[14] The goal of the firm is set in
quantitative terms: to produce profits to be able to produce more
profits, and so on. A firm does not exist to generate utility to its
owners. In Keynes's view, 'An entrepreneur is interested not in the
amount of product, but in the amount of money which will fall to his
share' (*CWJMK*, XXIX, p. 82).

The abandonment of the anthropomorphic figure of the 'entrepreneur' in another draft is even more telling: 'The firm is dealing
throughout in terms of sums of money. It has no object in the world
except to end up with more money than it started with. This is the
essential characteristic of an entrepreneur economy' (ibid., p. 89).

Finally, it is also meaningful that it is in the context of conceiving
this independence of goals of firms in this form of production that
Keynes made the only friendly reference to Marx's view that one can
discover in the whole of his *Collected Writings* (ibid., p. 81). Here
Keynes acknowledges the 'pregnant observation' by Marx that the
attitude of business is 'of parting with money for commodity (or
effort) in order to obtain more money'. The firm exists, in other
words, to accumulate wealth and its 'satisfaction' is reached when it
is able to increase the command it has over wealth. This implies that
it is wealth in general, not specific forms of wealth, that is sought by
the firm. It is thus wealth in the form of money that is the goal of the
firm.

The existence of such entities as the Keynesian firm, for which
money is the goal, the end instead of merely a means, is enough to
establish a non-neutral role for money as much as the demand of
consumers for a given good is enough to establish the 'non-neutrality' of this good. One should notice, in any case, that Keynes is not
appealing to any kind of money illusion in his argument. On the
contrary, the monetary form is precisely what defines the general
nature of wealth in contrast to the particular forms represented by
specific goods that are wealth only with respect to some uses. Money
is wealth because it is a potentiality of all uses, since it is purchasing
power in its universal form.

On the other hand, firms have an index of this purchasing power of money that is not given by any particular commodity or basket of commodities but, in Keynes's theory, by the money wage. The money wage measures the extent of the command on real wealth or on the power to generate real wealth represented by an amount of money. Specific goods may be meaningful indices in specific sectors, but only labour is of interest to all firms and that is why the money wage is the most strategic price for the decisions of firms as a whole (see Kregel, 1989; Kahn, 1972, p. 105 and 1984, p. 126).

The second principle of a monetary economy refers to its hierarchy and will be called the 'principle of dominant strategy'. Keynes's notion of an entrepreneurial economy clearly recognizes differentiated powers of agents to determine the dynamics of that economy.[15] This notion is made very clear in *The General Theory* and accompanying papers. In the former, the examination of the markets where families and firms meet, such as the labour markets or the savings market, shows that the dominance of firms is clear: both the amount of employment and of savings depend on the decisions of firms to produce and to invest. Labourers and savers adapt themselves to the firms' decisions even if they do not realize it and part of the innovative content of *The General Theory* is to show how this takes place. On the other hand, in his post-*General Theory* debate with Ohlin, Keynes made clear his view that banks hold the key to the investment process, in another hierarchical relation central to the notion of an entrepreneurial economy.

This principle is based on the idea that the distribution of productive resources is unequal among agents. As Keynes stated in *The General Theory*, in an entrepreneurial economy capital is 'scarce' relative to labour (Keynes, 1964, p. 213). Although the capacity to work is possessed by practically everyone, the control of means of production is not equally accessible. Of course, this scarcity is not natural in any sense: it is organized by the system itself, the operation of which restores it every time it is threatened as happens, for instance, during boom periods when the labour force also becomes scarce. Minsky (1975) suggests that the business cycle can be seen as the way through which the scarcity of capital is preserved (and with it the hierarchical basis of the system, an insight that is very important to anybody proposing the possibility of sustaining full employment).[16]

In addition, one should consider that financial and material wealth is usually storable and can therefore be withheld from use for as long as its possessor desires if the conditions in which it would be utilized are not satisfactory. Labour force, in contrast, if not spent, is just lost.

The most fundamental argument explaining this principle, however, may refer to the fact that to produce it is necessary to have finance available, allowing the producer to buy appliances, materials and the labour force needed. Naturally, firms, much more than families, have access to discretionary funds, created by banks. Firms (or, if one wishes in this context for a more anthropomorphic concept, capitalists) have preference in the access to credit, given the nature of the assets they possess. Firms have assets that can be absorbed by banks in case of non-compliance with contractual obligations. Families, generally, possess wealth mainly in the form of 'human' capital, that cannot be taken by banks, or durable consumption goods, that are very illiquid.

The third principle in the portrayal of a monetary economy is the principle of temporality of economic activity. Production takes time. This implies that firms have to decide on scales of production based on expectations of demand. They have to commit themselves to the purchase of labour and other inputs in advance of the actual sale of finished goods in the markets. Besides, different industries employ different methods of production. The duration of productive processes is not, then, uniform. Keynes and Post Keynesians consider explicitly the delays and asynchronies that characterize economic activity and that impose the necessity to consider how plans are conceived and implemented and what is the nature of the interaction between individual agents that is established.

During the productive process, factors are remunerated by money. They do not commit themselves to spending this money in any specific form or at any specific date. Firms operate on their expectations of demand, not on commitments assumed by the 'market'. Producing is inevitably speculative in a capitalist economy: 'Whether it likes or not, the technique of production under a regime of money-contract forces the business world always to carry a big speculative position' (*CWJMK*, XIX, p. 114).[17]

If the principle of temporality makes us consider the necessity of taking expectations into account it is not yet sufficient to imply the consideration of uncertainty in the sense used by Keynes. For that we need a fourth principle, borrowing from Davidson the principle of inergodicity.[18] At this point we do not have to add anything to the summary of Davidson's argument presented above, except to emphasize that it is inergodicity that is responsible for the fundamental (non-distributional) uncertainty that surrounds some of the decisions agents must make in entrepreneurial economies.[19] For this reason, it is inergodicity, not the mere temporality, that will imply the notion of irreversibility of time and the opposition to other theories of expectations, particularly those built in neoclassical models. This point will be developed in more detail in Chapter 4.

The fifth principle is the principle of coordination. It is a characteristic of modern economies that the social division of labour refers not only to final products (as, for instance, in backward agricultural communities) but that productive processes are themselves fragmented into a large number of independent producers that extract the raw materials, process them in various stages and, finally, obtain the finished good. The process from the extraction of iron and coal to the production of an automobile is actually performed by a very large number of independent productive units that are not only autonomous but are actually involved in many other productive sequences (the producer of steel, for instance, is involved in the production process of a great number of other final goods).

As we saw when discussing the principle of temporality, entrepreneurial economies do not have command mechanisms by which the coordination of productive plans is pre-established, whether in terms of amounts to be produced or in terms of timing according to which intermediate goods have to be available for the next step in the productive sequence or, again, in terms of the final matching of the availability of goods and the structure of needs perceived by society. It is often said that in these economies coordination is obtained ex post facto, by the revelation by the 'market' of which decisions were right and which were not. Such mechanisms would obviously be costly, because wrong decisions would be pointed up by the imposition of losses on producers. But one should not say that these economies lack any pre-coordinating mechanism whatsoever. As Keynes pointed out, under uncertainty (that is, under the possibility of suffering future losses resulting from taking the 'wrong' decisions) agents develop some 'techniques' of behaviour (*CWJMK*, XIV, p. 114). Important among the ways to deal with the uncertainty caused by market coordination is the development of institutions to socialize losses and reduce risks to each individual agent.

The most characteristic and widespread of these institutions is the forward money contract. A contract reduces uncertainty by establishing flows of resources, real and financial, their timing and their terms, assuring producers of the availability of inputs, on the one hand, and of the existence of outlets for their products, on the other. It serves as a cost-controlling device for entrepreneurs and as the basis for the calculation of relative rewards that are the field of application of entrepreneurial rationality. Not all flows of goods can be defined in forward contracts (in particular, consumption goods are not produced 'to order'), so uncertainty cannot disappear completely. But time-consuming productive processes that would be too risky otherwise can be organized on the basis of a system of contracts that ensure its continuity, at least in the face of predictable contingencies.[20]

The strategic importance of the existence of forward money contracts takes us to the last defining principle of a monetary economy. We will call it the 'principle of the properties of money'. This principle is closely related to the preceding one in the sense that Keynes states that, for a complex system of forward money contracts to be feasible, it is necessary that money have some properties that guarantee its survival. According to Keynes:

Money of account, namely that in which debts and prices and general purchasing power are expressed, is the primary concept of a theory of money . . . Money itself, namely that by delivery of which debt contracts are discharged, and in the shape of which a store of general purchasing power is held, derives its character from its relationship to the money of account, since the debts and prices must first have been expressed in terms of the latter . . . Perhaps we may elucidate the distinction between money and money of account by saying that the money of account is the description or title and the money is the thing which answers to the description. (*CWJMK*, V, p. 3)

Money of account is the measurement standard for forward commitments. As a measurement standard its content must be stable (*CWJMK*, XIX, p. 117; XXVIII, p. 257).[21] It would not serve as an uncertainty-reducing device if agents could not trust, when they entered into contractual obligations, their assessment of what those obligations implied for them. But money of account is a 'description'. This means that the stability property that is a feature of the 'description' must be true also for the 'thing which answers to the description'. In other words, there must be some degree of stability in the value of money as recognized by agents for them to accept contractual commitments. Therefore, for money to fulfil its role, some restrictions have to be imposed on its creation to guarantee that it wil not violate the 'description' to which it must correspond.

These restrictions are represented by Keynes's statement that money in an entrepreneurial economy is characterized by zero or negligible elasticities of production and substitution (Keynes, 1964, p. 230). These properties sustain the 'liquidity' of money, its capacity for liquidating debts and for constituting purchasing power in its general form. If the liquidity of money is not doubted, agents will accept obligations denominated and dischargeable in money and a contractual system will be erected. But, Keynes argued,

it is unlikely that an asset, of which the supply can be easily increased or the desire for which can be easily diverted by a change in relative price, will possess the attribute of 'liquidity' in the minds of owners of wealth. Money itself rapidly loses the attribute of 'liquidity' if its future supply is expected to undergo sharp changes. (Keynes, 1964, p. 241n)

A model of an economy built on the above six principles will present the results Keynes expected: the long-period non-neutrality of money, the full realization of the meaning of the concept of financial circulation, created in the *Treatise on Money*, and the principle of effective demand. *The General Theory* can be seen as the analytical development of the concept of monetary economy, where those principles are translated into analytical propositions that allow a rigorous description of its dynamics.

In the perspective of the above discussion, one can think of the core propositions of *The General Theory* as follows. In a monetary economy, money is not only a means of circulation but it is also an asset, a means of conserving wealth, the main attribute of which is the capacity to liquidate debts and to represent purchasing power in its purest form. The existence of a demand for money as an asset affects the demand (and prices) for other types of assets, alternative forms of conserving wealth with different attributes.

For a given state of expectations, wealth owners will then have to demand the available stocks of assets, including money. Prices will move in order to obtain the compatibility between demand and supplies for the various items. For those assets that are reproducible, the prices that are obtained in the market are important to indicate their relative 'scarcity'. This will happen if reproducible assets are being transacted at prices that are greater than their cost of produc-

tion (their flow-supply price). If current prices are higher than the
flow-supply price, new items will be produced, increasing the availability of that asset (and, thus, the accumulation of capital in this
economy).

The production of additional quantities of the reproducible assets
requires the employment of production factors, particularly labour.
The newly employed labourers will then be able to demand consumption goods, leading to an expansion of employment also in this
industry. On the other hand, if an additional expansion of employment has to take place to face the demands of those employed in the
production of reproducible assets, a further impulse will be given to
the consumption goods industry that has to supply goods for their
own newly employed workers, and so on. In Keynesian terms, the
expansion in investment gave rise, through multiplier effects, to a
secondary expansion in the consumption goods industry. The total
amount of income and employment that are thus created will
depend on the amount of the secondary demand for consumption
goods that is created. Of course, the whole mechanism would operate in a contractionary direction if we had supposed that current
prices of reproducible assets fell below their flow-supply prices. This,
in a nutshell, is the principle of effective demand that Keynes supposed to be characteristic of (and exclusive to) a monetary economy.[22]

SUMMING UP

In this chapter we have proposed that Keynes's revolutionary endeavour was the formulation of a new concept of economy that would
better depict the workings of the real world. Keynes's key to developing this new concept was the long-period non-neutrality of
money; that is, the possibility of showing the conditions under which
money can become an asset, a form of wealth to be retained by
individual agents in place of other assets, affecting thereby the
rhythm of capital accumulation of the whole economy.

Keynes called this new paradigm a monetary production economy, which was to be seen as an original form of social organization
and not as a derivation of cooperative economies, as it was by
classical economics. The main features of this monetary production
economy were presented in the form of six postulates: of production;

of dominant strategy; of temporality; of uncertainty; of coordination; and of the properties of money.

It was proposed that such a monetary production economy would show the characteristics Keynes identified in real-world market economies, such as the non-neutrality of money and the possibility of unemployment resulting from a deficient effective demand. Agents, feeling the uncertainty of the future, could choose liquid but irreproducible forms of wealth accumulation which could depress prices of reproducible assets below their production costs. This would lead to a reduction in production and of employment that would exert a secondary impact on consumption goods industries as well. Involuntary unemployment would then result from these shifts of the demand for assets towards non-reproducible assets.

In most of what follows, we will explore this mechanism. Before we do so, however, there is one last preliminary question to be attacked; that is, the notion of uncertainty adopted by Keynes and Post Keynesians. As we saw, it is an essential aspect of Keynes's vision that the role money performs in a modern economy has to do with the peculiar form of uncertainty which reigns in these economies. It is to this that we turn in the next chapter.

NOTES

1. As Davidson (1978b) has noted, Keynes's approach to the quantity theory of money was much more flexible and behavioural than Fisher's heavily mechanistic models. This was not, however, unusual among Marshall's students, being a feature of Marshall's own approach to monetary theory. For an excellent, succinct presentation of Marshallian quantity theory and Keynes's views on it, see Kahn (1984).

2. One can argue that the lessons Keynes derived during this period about the behaviour of money under hyperinflation were never really abandoned. The direct relation between availability of money and aggregate demand in highly inflationary conditions discussed in the 1920s was never denied in *The General Theory*. The change in Keynes's thought was that under normal conditions the relation was more complex, since money could be hoarded, but when 'flights from money' occur, the validity of his early 1923 propositions was reaffirmed.

3. The long run was, and still is, the refuge of the orthodoxy that seems to feel under no obligation to explain how one can get from a short-run situation that can be very disequilibrated to a long-run equilibrium. Even some otherwise non-orthodox schools share this 'faith' in long-run equilibria, sharing also the limitation of being unable to show how they would be attained. For a more detailed discussion see Carvalho (1983/4 and 1984/5).

4. Cf. Leijonhufvud (1968). Also Kahn has noted that 'the great innovation of the *Treatise* was the abandonment of the Quantity Theory of Money – apart from some few parting gestures . . .' (Kahn, 1984, pp. 64–5).

5. Only under fundamental uncertainty can money really play this role. As Davidson and Davidson (1984) observed: 'Only in a non-ergodic world can the precautionary demand for liquidity be comprehended as a shield against forces that may threaten the very existence of individuals and organizations' (p. 60).

6. It is a central proposition of Post Keynesian monetary theory that money, in a monetary production economy, is an asset for the holder and a debt for its issuer. Cf. *CWJMK*, XIV, pp. 109–23; see also, for instance, Minsky (1982, p. 131), among many other works in Post Keynesian theory that stress the same point.

7. In the *Tract*, Keynes took the Quantity Theory of Money as a theory, while in the *Treatise* he took it as truism. In the latter, Keynes pointed out the limitations of the Quantity Theory as being its inability to show any causality relation (*CWJMK*, V, p. 120), for not capturing relevant forces in operation (ibid.), for being unable adequately to identify the functions of money (p. 135) and for being applicable only to income deposits (p. 207).

8. The evolution of Keynes's thought between the *Treatise* and *The General Theory* as regards the determination of the prices of debts and of assets is brilliantly described in Kregel (1988).

9. Classical authors as well as Walras considered the producers' demand for their own goods as part of demand functions, confirming their fundamental view of a market economy as one of independent consumers–producers. See, for instance, Ricardo: 'No man produces, but with a view to consume or sell . . . By producing, then, he necessarily becomes either the consumer of his own goods, or the purchaser and consumer of the goods of some other person' (Ricardo, 1971, p. 291). This view is radically opposed to Marx's and Keynes's.

10. Insatiability of consumer demands was assumed by Ricardo. See Ricardo (1971, p. 292n), where Smith is criticized for assuming otherwise.

11. Other attempts have been made to systematize the concept of monetary economy. Among them we should mention Davidson (1978a, 1982 and 1984); Kregel (1980); Minsky (1975 and 1986); Barrere (1985). A recent work with views that are close to those presented here is Feijo (1991).

12. This does not mean that there is any fundamental discontinuity between the *Treatise on Probability* or other works prepared in the same period and Keynes's later works. In fact, in the next chapter, we will argue that there is a line linking the *Treatise* and *The General Theory*. It is, however, a line of development, where some ideas are kept and others are changed, not of static, immutable views.

13. On the difficulties of neoclassical theorists to deal with firms, their very existence, their role, and so on, see Hahn (1984).

14. The firm is a strategic concept in the construction of Post Keynesian models. In contrast to the neoclassical black box, the machine that transforms inputs into outputs, the Post Keynesian firm is primarily a policy decision centre (Shackle, 1970, p. 20). Its primary goal is not to produce goods but to make money (Davidson, 1984). Some Post Keynesians propose that a modern firm should be studied as if it were a bank (Minsky, 1982, pp. 19, 145, 206). For a full discussion of the Post Keynesian concept of firm, see Feijo (1991, chap. 2) and Shapiro (1981, 1984).

15. The same point is made by Barrere (1985).

16. A very sharp analysis of the political problems involved in the maintenance of full employment in capitalist economies is presented in Kalecki (1943).

17. Minsky has paid particular attention to the speculative nature of production and investment decisions by firms. See Minsky (1975, chap. 4 and 1986, p. 177).

18. In an ergodic process, learning from experience is possible, allowing agents, in the long run, to decide with certainty and to eliminate the need for speculation.
19. Uncertainty results from two main sources. On the one hand, money, in its role of a 'liquidity time-machine' (Davidson, 1978), allows agents to save without investing or without placing orders for future consumption (Chick, 1983a, p. 5; Kregel, 1980, p. 38). On the other hand, if innovations are possible any long-term commitment to specific production techniques is uncertain (Shackle, 1970, p. 21).
20. Keynes was explicit as to the essential nature of a monetary economy as a 'contractual' economy in the sense discussed above. See, for instance, *CWJMK*, xxviii, p. 255. In modern Post Keynesian theory this line is closely followed by Davidson. See Davidson (1978a, 1978b).
21. As Vicarelli (1984) has pointed out, inflationary processes had to be seen as critical for economies organized on the basis of forward money contracts (p. 35).
22. Davidson and Kregel (1980, p. 137) emphasize that the principle of effective demand is characteristic of monetary economies, since it is the existence of a non-producible resting place for wealth that causes unemployment. Only money allows a complete severance between financial and physical provision for the future that may create unemployment:

In so far as our social and business organization separates financial provision for the future from physical provision for the future so that efforts to secure the former do not necessarily carry the latter with them, financial prudence will be liable to destroy effective demand and thus impair well-being, as there are many examples to testify. (*CWJMK*, xiii, p. 439)

In this sense, one cannot accept contentions such as Kaldor's proposition that liquidity preference has nothing to do with unemployment in Post Keynesian macroeconomics. See Kaldor (1982, p. 26).

4. Probability, Uncertainty and Expectations

Of all the theoretical innovations offered in the concept of monetary economy discussed in the last chapter, two of the principles may be the most revolutionary, taken in themselves: those of the properties of money and of uncertainty. The properties of money will be examined in further detail in Chapter 6. In this chapter, Keynes's and Post Keynesian views on uncertainty will be explored.

We begin with an examination of Keynes's views on probability and uncertainty, before proceeding to a discussion of the implications of these views for the way expectations are formed. The contrasts between the Keynesian treatment of expectations and the neoclassical approach are briefly presented. Finally, some implications of the consideration of uncertainty for the development of analytical models are listed.

PROBABILITY

Keynes was a student of probability before he became an economist. He was concerned, however, with probability as the foundation for decision making rather than with descriptive statistics or with probability as a feature of the world as such. To follow Keynes's views on probability and uncertainty it is important to keep this interest in mind. The changes we observe in his views seem to be due to his deeper understanding, as time went by, of actual decision-making processes rather than to the study of the logic of probability itself. Keynes first approached probability when searching for criteria to support practical decisions. Under some conditions one could devise rational methods of decision whereby a choice would be made of a sequel that could be shown to be a 'logical consequence' of a given proposition or premisses. In many cases, however, neither certainty nor impossibility could be obtained by logic alone. In these cases, the relation between premisses and sequel was said to be probable. Partial belief then had to be substituted for certain belief and probability became the basis for a decision. For equally desirable outcomes, then, 'we might put it . . . that the probable is the hypothesis on which it is rational for us to act' (*CWJMK*, VIII, p. 339). According to Braithwaite, 'Keynes's main motive in writing the *Treatise [on Probability]* was to explain how a degree of belief could be rational, and thus not merely a matter of the believer's psychological make-up but one which all rational men under similar circumstances would share' (ibid., p. xxi).

It was a distinctive British tradition (Kregel, 1977) to approach economics as being 'specially concerned with the making of decisions, and with the consequences that follow from the decisions' (Hicks, 1979, p. 5). If decision making is to be seen as one of the fundamental objects of economic science rather than just a side-issue, it has to fulfil two conditions. It has to be creative (or 'uncaused' in Shackle's terminology). This means that to make decisions is not just to react in an automatic fashion to ongoing stimuli. To decide cannot be reducible to mere adaptation, which means that one cannot link directly environmental conditions to behavioural results. One is not denying the existence of systemic requirements, of natural and social laws or of any other outside influence on the decision maker. These are seen, however, as pieces of information for, not of command over, the process of decision.[1]

A second requirement is that the process itself through which decisions are reached may be analysed into consistent and logically connected steps. There must be a criterion of decision and a method of constructing the sequels of a set of premisses to inform the decision. Decisions are made with reference to the sequels each choice is believed to generate. Rational choice is the one which maximizes the possibility of obtaining the most desired sequel. Application of reason means then the search for the alternative in which the desired sequel can be shown to result most directly, given the perceived or expected constraints, from the choice to be made. The judgement of rationality can only be made if the decision maker can show how each step follows its antecedent and shapes the next in the chain connecting the decision to the expected outcome. If the construction of sequels obeys the rules of logic it will be independent of the 'believer's psychological make-up' and it will be possible to study it scientifically.

When a decision is made thus a given sequel is chosen through which the premisses, the description of the starting point of the decision maker, are connected to the aimed outcome. A process of choice could then be seen as being constituted by two elements: the initial data and the reasoning process leading to the outcomes. The second of those elements, the construction of the relation between starting propositions and final outcomes, was the central subject of Keynes's *Treatise on Probability*.[2] The ultimate goal is to find the laws of rational decision making to serve as the foundations of behavioural sciences, including economics. As Keynes put it, 'Between two sets of propositions . . . there exists a relation, in virtue of which, if we know the first, we can attach to the latter some degree of rational belief. This relation is the subject-matter of the logic of probability' (*CWJMK*, VIII, pp. 6–7).

The theory of probability is thus part of epistemology. It does not deal with events or material processes as such but with propositions. Keynes is concerned with determining the extent to which it is rational to accept as true a proposition that is obtained by argument from another: 'Probability is the study of the grounds which lead us to entertain a 'rational' preference for one belief over another' (ibid., p. 106).

'Rational belief' referred to the logical plausibility of the derived proposition with respect to a given starting proposition. The extent to which the resulting idea is true knowledge depends on the truth and completeness of the starting point and on the adequate construction of the probability relation. The initial proposition, or premisses, may be an assumption or a datum of observation. In the *Treatise on Probability* Keynes simplifies the point by assuming that all premisses are, in fact, results of observation, which he calls direct knowledge. In an even bolder assumption, Keynes then proposes considering direct knowledge true knowledge (ibid., chap. 2).[3]

Assuming that the starting proposition is true allows Keynes to concentrate on deriving knowledge by argument. The space of probability is defined then as the application of logic to propositions to obtain other propositions: 'Given the body of direct knowledge which constitutes our ultimate premisses, this theory tells us what further rational beliefs, certain or probable, can be derived by valid argument from our direct knowledge' (*CWJMK*, VIII, p. 4). Which arguments are valid can be logically ascertained. Belief in the conclusion is then rational because it does not depend on individual peculiarities but on criteria of consistency with formal logic. The outcome, being a logical derivation of the premisses, shares the truthfulness of the latter. The choice of the premisses is in any case the domain of the individual. Probability, however, is not concerned with the choice of premisses but with their logical unfolding into a conclusion.[4]

At this point it may be interesting to contrast Keynes's views of probability with the dominant, frequency-theory, view. The most important contrast between Keynes's approach to probability and the frequency theory is the very definition of the object of study. For the frequency theory, probability is a relation between events, a characteristic of the world itself. The accumulation of knowledge does not change probabilities because randomness is a feature of the object of knowledge, not of knowledge itself. The theory of probability thus consists of the accurate description of the forms this randomness may assume, and their properties. If the stochastic processes are stable enough, repeated observation leads to the knowledge of their underlying structures.

While for Keynes each probable relation is an individual one by itself, with frequency theory probability can only be ascribed to a particular relation as part of a larger family of individual observations. It distributes certainty among events. It is the whole distribution function that matters. An isolated statement of a probability relation is basically meaningless: 'the probabilistic laws governing the answers to the original question are known in their entirety. There is no uncertainty or ambiguity of meaning in the statement that event A has probability $p(A)$' (Katzner, 1986, p. 60).[5]

But if the premisses are true and the arguments are logically derived,[6] why are the conclusions merely probable instead of certain? Probability is approached by Keynes as part of the process of learning. The larger the body of knowledge gathered as premisses, the more complete and certain the conclusions obtained by argument can be. At the limit, we can imagine a set of premisses that is sufficient to imply logically a certain result. In this case, probable belief becomes certain belief. But, under certain circumstances, direct knowledge may not be capable of generating a sufficient set of true premisses to sustain an outcome with certainty. Processes may be too complex to be reconstructed in imagination. In some other cases direct acquaintance may be downright impossible (for example, in sequential processes some premises may refer to events that can be contemplated only in the future). In this case, the logic or reasoning cannot substitute for the insufficiency of knowledge to obtain certain outcomes.

This new discussion, however, could not be taken further in the *Treatise on Probability*, where Keynes seemed to be unsure of (or uninterested in) the epistemological status of the premises themselves. As a matter of fact, the development of Keynes's ideas on decision making gradually changed from the focus on probability to a focus on uncertainty. This change, however, did not require any important change in his basic framework. It followed from his increasing attention to the premises for decision, shifting from the assumption of true knowledge gained by direct observation to expectations and the fragility of the information on which they are anchored.

UNCERTAINTY

The above point was first raised by Ramsey, when he pointed out that belief was not only a problem of formal logic. Belief, even if rational belief, was also a question of human logic, those 'mental habits' that are 'also a sort of logic' (Keynes, 1951, p. 243). Keynes conceded the point, although still unsure of its implications.[7] Human logic, however, cannot annul formal logic. They have to have different domains. Human logic can only be a process of appraisal of the premises themselves rather than of its manipulations.

Keynes had met this question for the first time in the *Treatise* when he introduced a discussion of the 'weight' of arguments. The weight of an argument is not determined by a comparison 'between the favourable and unfavourable evidence, but between the absolute amounts of relevant knowledge and of relevant ignorance respectively' (*CWJMK*, VIII, p. 77). The kind of evidence does not reveal any new logical link between the propositions, nor does it deny any other. It merely corroborates or repeats some already known argument (in a positive or a negative sense). In these conditions, this new evidence may not change a probability but it alters its 'degree of belief'.[8] The degree of confidence in a proposition obtained by probability depends on the strength of the signs that not only is the proposition certain with respect to its premisses but that it is actually true, which means that the premisses upon which it is built are true. This is the field of 'human logic'. This 'logic' did not find a place, however, in the *Treatise on Probability* because, if the premisses are true knowledge and their manipulation is logical, the weight of an argument is irrelevant.

Concerned with logical connections alone, Keynes evaded the point by keeping it isolated from the rest of the *Treatise*. The weight of arguments was to be revived only much later, when Keynes's approach to uncertainty was much better developed, in the discussion of states of confidence in *The General Theory*.

How could confidence (or belief) be introduced into Keynes's theory of probability? Certainly not in the method of construction of sequels. If one wants to preserve the rationality of methods of decision, reasoning has to develop along logical paths. If this is accomplished through the use of formal logic the sequel has to be contained somehow in the premisses themselves. Formal logic does not 'create' sequels; it can only reveal whatever is already implicit in the premisses. If the set of premisses is not 'complete', logic cannot be applied to this effect. Even if we accept that all direct knowledge is true knowledge, this does not imply that all direct knowledge is complete knowledge.

But what if direct knowledge is not complete? Then the decision maker has to fill in the voids, has to 'create' the additional premisses which may be needed in order to apply logical methods to them. Now direct knowledge, the observed premisses, can sustain different outcomes depending on how the set of necessary data is completed by imagined premisses. In situations of this nature, some of the premisses may represent true knowledge but the remaining ones will be just hypotheses. These hypotheses may themselves be probable relations, but they may also be 'figments of imagination', to use again Shackle's imagery.

Therefore, as Lawson (1988) correctly concludes, the weight of arguments, the uncertainty of a relation, is defined by the degree of 'completeness' of the available information at the moment of decision. The incompleteness of the set of observable premisses may be an insoluble problem in sequential processes. In these processes, the final outcome, about which one has to reach some degree of belief to induce action, may depend on premisses that are nonseparable (Hicks, 1979, chap. 2), but are not contemporaneous. In addition, some of the variables that work as premises may be influenced (but not necessarily determined) by the very decision the agent has to make in the present. This typically happens with an investment decision. One of the premises of such a decision is the expected size of future markets. These, however, are influenced (although not determined, for there are other forces shaping demand curves) by the variations in income that may result from the investment decision itself plus the reactions they may induce in competitors. The longer the duration of the process under consideration, the more the possibilities that may have to be taken into account, and the smaller the set of direct knowledge elements that, even being assumed to be true knowledge, will be relevant to sustain a decision.

The point, thus, is that the set of observable premises is not sufficient to establish certainty and the agent has to 'create' the additional premises needed to build a sequel. In this sense we can say, following Shackle, that the agent does not choose from a given list of possibilities; he actually has to create the list, by creating the premises from which each alternative is generated.

In Keynes's concept of uncertainty not only may some premises be unknown at the moment of decision but they may actually be unknowable. This is easily perceived when we think of decisions such as those of production or investment. The entrepreneur has to form expectations about other entrepreneurs' conduct as well as about his customers'. His competitors are naturally compelled to do the same. In this way it is logically impossible to include these conducts as observed premises alongside the premises he does know, such as the amount and technical efficiency of his equipment, the contractual obligations of workers and suppliers, and so on. The missing premises just do not exist. They have to be created by the decision maker in order to build a sequel but they are not 'knowledge'. Rather, as Shackle put it, they are 'unknowledge'.

When we think in terms of real-world economies evolving in historical time, the number of unknowables of this kind is much increased. Now at each step the decision maker has to fill in new voids and create new premises in increasingly complex algorithms and a growing number of possible sequels. Uncertainty means the acknowledgement of the impossibility of dealing logically with this complexity.[9] In cases of this nature no meaningful numerical probabilities can be obtained. It is not possible to limit the universe of possible outcomes to distribute probabilities among them. A numerical probability would then be meaningless.

A different situation is one in which the premisses may be known but the way in which they are combined is too complex and 'the weakness of our reasoning power prevents our knowing what [the] degree [of probability] is' (*CWJMK*, VIII, p. 34). For practical purposes, however, the two cases may be taken as equivalent in the sense that they are likely to induce the same kind of behaviour by economic agents. Social processes developing in historical time may be, perhaps, the most important example of situations where the power of reasoning is too weak to derive the global picture necessary to the identification of numerical probabilities. In both cases, the agent has to limit somehow the set of conceivable premisses to a workable group of alternatives and to build sequels, in the knowledge, however, of its unavoidable incompleteness. The awareness by the agent of being at least partially ignorant of the influencing elements in a given process will be a crucial feature distinguishing behaviour in Post Keynesian and neoclassical models.

Uncertainty thus surrounds the process of decision making because of the consciousness of the extent to which ignorance leads to imagination substituting for knowledge as the basis to establish premisses. Formal logic can sustain robust expectations only if we trust the premisses to be correct. When we know some (perhaps most) of the premisses to be no more than figments of imagination, human logic comes to the fore, the weight of arguments becomes relevant and uncertainty finds its place alongside probability in Keynes's sense.

This is precisely the way Keynes introduced the uncertainty that surrounds investment decisions in *The General Theory*: 'The outstanding fact is the extreme precariousness of the basis of knowledge on which our estimates of prospective yield have to be made. Our knowledge of the factors which will govern the yield of an investment some years hence is usually very slight and often negligible' (Keynes, 1964, p. 149). As we have pointed out, this is typically a case where the premisses on which to build a probability relation cannot be based on knowledge, especially on direct acquaintance. Nevertheless a decision has to be made. However 'flimsy' may be the foundations for this decision, the entrepreneur has to gather whatever knowledge he can accumulate (for example, in terms of current technologies, current financial conditions, demand elasticities and so on) and to create premises in terms of the way his customers as well as his competitors will behave, future technological changes, changes in relative prices, and so on. Given these premises, a probable relation can be built. Uncertainty pertains to the premises and from them it spreads to the outcomes.

Human logic and the role of weight of arguments reappear in this context as the degree of confidence, or the state of confidence. The equivalence of concepts is pointed out by Keynes himself when he observes: 'It would be foolish, in forming our expectations, to attach great weight to matters which are very uncertain.' At this point Keynes introduces a footnote, saying: 'By "very uncertain" I do not mean the same thing as "very improbable". Cf. my *Treatise on Probability*, chapter 6, on "The Weight of Arguments" ' (1964, p. 148).

Rational belief, when the decision process can no longer be established in terms of true premises, cannot attach to expected outcomes only on the basis of a logical development of those premises. Rational belief will also have to depend on the confidence in the premises themselves. As Keynes proposed, the confidence will depend 'on how highly we rate the likelihood of our best forecast turning out quite wrong' (1964, p. 148). If we assume that the agent will handle adequately formal logic methods, that likelihood can only depend on the accuracy and realism of the premises.[10]

UNCERTAINTY AND ERGODICITY

We could, of course, conceive of conditions where the creation of the missing premises was rather an objective process of 'discovery'. If social processes were ergodic, as discussed in the preceding chapter, trial and error could lead agents to identify gradually all the necessary data to orient their decisions. Ergodicity, however, demands replicability, which means that processes should be time-independent. It cannot survive a world where 'crucial decisions' are possible, because the latter destroy the environment in which they were made. Replicability, even notional replicability, does not make sense for 'crucial experiments'. In a Keynesian world, a non-ergodic world, there are no inevitable, pre-defined paths to the economy. Agents have to create by themselves their own images of sequels and act on them. As a result, history will result from the fusion of men's actions, in a way that is not really predictable to anyone of them nor even to an external observer. If innovations are a theoretical possibility, ergodicity cannot be sustained.

Uncertainty, therefore, is not simply a result of defective methods of reasoning. The insufficiency of premisses is rooted in objective features of actual social processes. The lack of knowledge about, for instance, future demands of goods to serve as premisses to an investment decision in a monetary economy cannot be overcome by observation or by developing better means of information. As Kregel put it, there is a 'crucial feature [in] a monetary economy that allow[s] consumers not to spend all their income, not to know what they would consume in the future, and to forestall decision over the expenditure of their income: a store of value that preserves the purchasing power of current income' (1980, p. 39). Under these conditions, 'no future market signal is given because there is nothing more to signal' (ibid., p. 36). Uncertainty is the result on the decision process of considering these characteristics. The social world is, then, non-deterministic.

Social reality has an existence external to the mind of the observer but not independent of agents' views and behaviours. After the emergence of quantum mechanics even physical phenomena are no longer assumed to be independent of the observer, at least in the field of subatomic particles. As for social processes, their orientation and evolution, they are certainly not independent of the way agents perceive and conceive them. It is the acknowledgement that action oriented by perceptions and mental elaborations is not impotent that makes uncertainty a feature of reality rather than just of knowledge.

In this sense, Keynes's views as to the reality of probability have to be studied considering not only the *Treatise on Probability*, where his position is more ambiguous, but also his mature work, where uncertainty becomes a feeling rooted in the reality of social processes.[11]

BEHAVIOURAL IMPLICATIONS

Starting from Keynes's concepts of probability and uncertainty, Post Keynesians will postulate that the behavioural relations that are affected by them will tend to be strikingly different from those accepted by neoclassical theory.

Even though one can identify some diversity among neoclassical authors on probability,[12] it is possible to state with some tranquillity that modern neoclassical theory accepts a realist view of probability (that is, the idea that randomness is a feature of reality itself) and that, in addition, social processes are ergodic, meaning by this that they are replicable and obey stable statistical laws of distribution. This is the basis for their use of the notion of risk, as represented by the dispersion of results around their expected average values (see Lucas, 1981, pp. 223–4).

Neoclassical economists are seldom clear as to how agents are supposed to learn about the distribution functions that describe these social processes.[13] One may think of repeated observations (trial and error) or of Bayesian inference, if conditions are propitious for this kind of method.[14] In any case, if the process under study is ergodic we can assume that it will be known, in the long run.

The importance of approaching probability along these lines is that it makes it possible to consider random processes in economic theory without having to change the fundamental postulates that were developed for a deterministic world. Modern neoclassical theory actually just proceeds to a redefinition of the notion of goods rather than of behaviours (Debreu, 1959).

In this modified approach, developed by von Neumann and Morgenstern (1953), agents choose not only goods but actually probabilities of goods. In their words, 'If v is preferable to u, then even a chance $1 - a$ of v – alternatively to u – is preferable' (p. 27). This treatment allows the building of a continuous preference scale among probabilities of goods that may be used in consumers' satisfaction maximization problems just as well as before. Now the utility of a good is given by a combination of its useful features and the chances of actually getting it. If I prefer one apple to an orange, I also prefer some chance of getting one apple to an orange.

Given the widespread existence of lotteries, it was particularly attractive to consider these schemes in terms of values rather than in terms of specific goods. Naturally, as in standard consumer theory problems, money is just a proxy for the goods that actually give satisfaction. Translated into monetary terms, one could say that if I prefer $1 to $0, I also prefer some chance of getting $1 to getting nothing. Of course, a chance of getting $1 is worth less than having

$1 for sure. In the former case I have to subtract the 'risk' of not getting $1. If one could find a formula to do it, we would have defined three 'goods': $1, $0, and the given chance of having $1, in terms of which the consumer could make his choice using precisely the same instruments as when choosing between any three goods x, y and z.

The way to define the new 'good', 'chance of getting $1', was to take the value of the prize and multiply it by its probability. If we were considering the two prizes above as resulting from a tossing of a fair coin, with each value associated to the turning up of one of its faces, the probability of getting $1 would be 50 per cent. The value of the lottery was then 1 times 0.5 plus 0 times 0.5, or 50 cents. The consumer would then face three goods $1, $0 or 50 cents. All that was needed to obtain the value of the lottery was to know its probability distribution.

But what does it mean to say that the value of a lottery with those prizes and odds is 50 cents? It means that, if the game could be repeated an indefinitely great number of times, the results of each tossing would be a sequence of 1s and 0s averaging, in the long run, between gains and losses, 50 cents. Whoever could bet for an indefinitely long period of time would be 'indifferent' (if there was no pleasure derivable from the very act of gambling itself) between having 50 cents and accepting this lottery. If the knowledge about the probability distribution is true, in the long run there is no uncertainty about what one can get with the game, so the agent can consider it as a good like any other and make his maximizing choices in the usual way.

For Post Keynesians, this procedure is not acceptable, at least as a general theory of behaviour under uncertainty, because it is based on the replicability of the experiment which requires its stability over time, that is, that it be ergodic. The coin-tossing mechanism does not suffer any change from the first to last tossing, as a result of the betting activity. The initial conditions are restored after each toss independently of the face which turned up in the preceding toss. This view excludes what was called 'crucial experiments', those that are essentially unique in the sense that the conditions for which they are a stage are destroyed by the experiment itself. In these cases, the context is not external to the agent, as happens with the coin-tossing mechanism. The conditions change depending on the decisions that are made. The agent cannot always count on stable environments that wait for him to know them through repeated experiments. The agent knows that he is shaping the context, even though he may not (and most probably does not) know how much and in which direction.

A frequent criticism is raised that, even if the experiment was notionally repeatable, the agent could not have the chance to repeat it. If he could toss the coin only once, what is the value of the lottery to him? This objection is only superficially valid and is the basis on which a neoclassical model of insurance can be developed. If the experiment can be performed in the aggregate it does not really matter who performs it to make it possible to reach the above solution. Let us suppose that each individual agent has limited resources, so they are unable to try for long-run results. If agents are risk-neutral, they may trade their lottery tickets for each toss for an insurance policy worth 50 cents to obtain the long-run prize in the 'short run'. If all gamblers do the same, the insurer does not lose because, if he has all the lottery tickets, his average gain is precisely the 50 cents. So the experiment may seem 'crucial' for each agent, because he cannot repeat it, but it is not really so, for another agent can make it repeatable. One can make the scheme a little more sophisticated by considering agents risk-averse. In this case, they would accept less than 50 cents for their lottery tickets, and the insurer would have a profit given by the difference between the 50 cents he gets on the average for each toss and the lower amount he paid to each individual for the lottery ticket.

One can thus see that the von Neumann–Morgenstern scheme allows us, with just some superficial changes in the basic model, to deal with uncertainty, if by uncertain we are referring to the dispersion observed in given and known probability distribution functions. The crucial hypothesis is therefore the ergodic principle that sustains the assumption that agents may know the distribution. In this case, all one has to do is to redefine good, allowing for its 'risk', keeping all the rules of behaviour developed for strictly deterministic kinds of choice.

Keynes's notion of probability and uncertainty, as we have seen, differs from the orthodox concepts and rejects the idea that the same methods can be applied to deterministic and uncertain decision processes. If the distribution function cannot be known and the agents are conscious that experiments may be 'crucial', it is their behaviour that will change as they will try to build defences against disappointments. The consideration of non-distributive uncertainty makes it impossible to appeal to the well-behaved methods of decision as those described by neoclassical theory.

Keynes's and Post Keynesian economics are frequently accused of being nihilistic because of the importance uncertainty came to assume. This is certainly the result of misapprehending the role of uncertainty in their models. In a nutshell, uncertainty is important because recognizing it changes behaviour. Economic theory is not replaced by an 'all is possible' game. Keynes's point is that behaviour or conduct is different in an uncertain world; that is, one where the possibility of crucial experiments is recognized. The criticism that is levelled against the neoclassical treatment, in this particular, is precisely that it ignores the complexities of decision making under uncertainty, echoing a similar point made by Keynes in 1937: 'I accuse the classical economic theory of being itself one of those pretty, polite techniques which tries to deal with the present by abstracting from the fact that we know very little about the future' (*CWJMK*, XIV, p. 115). The techniques have changed but the essential character has been kept intact: to assume ergodic processes is the same as assuming the future to be equal to the present (or the past).

The alternative, however, is not to suppose that anything is possible, because this is also false. The need to create practically the premises on which to base decisions gives the agent the degree of freedom he lacks in deterministic worlds. But if the world admits the novelty it also displays continuities. Although in the strictest sense the world changes continually, for practical purposes there is enough continuity in social processes to allow some space for induction and the identification of rules of behaviour.

Learning by experience requires enough repetitiveness to allow agents to observe and recognize patterns to understand phenomena. It also requires that the degree of complexity of the experience itself be not excessive, lest agents fail to understand the nature of the experiment and draw its lessons. These requirements are obviously not fulfilled in the case of investment decisions. These decisions are crucial and non-repetitive. their sequels too complex to be apprehended beforehand. Past experiences in the case of investment do not safely indicate the direction of the future. Production decisions, in contrast, are seldom crucial. They do not imply irreversible commitments of resources and can be checked after very short intervals. Markets tend to be continuous for short periods, so similar experiments can be realized and generalizations drawn. The missing premisses in the case of production decisions are not, under normal conditions, impossible to visualize with some assurance. For investment decisions, human logic dominates formal logic and induction is impossible. For production decisions, the premisses are safer, formal logic can dominate expectations formation, and the possibility of induction is preserved.

One of the most important innovations of *The General Theory* was the distinction proposed between short-term and long-term expectations: 'The process of revision of short-term expectations is a gradual and continuous one, carried on largely in the light of realized results' (Keynes, 1964, p. 50). Experience guides these expectations because 'it would be too complicated to work out the expectations de novo whenever a productive process was being started; and it would, moreover, be a waste of time since a large part of the circumstances usually continue substantially unchanged from one to the next' (ibid., p. 51). It is in the formation of short-term expectations that agents can learn from experience and to derive logical conclusions from mostly known premisses.[15] Here one recognizes the environment and adapts to it. Predictable behaviour and formal logic reign:

Entrepreneurs have to endeavour to forecast demand. They do not as a rule make wildly wrong forecasts of the equilibrium position. But, as the matter is very complex, they do not get it just right; and they endeavour to approximate to the true position by a method of trial and error. Contracting where they find they are overshooting their market, expanding where the opposite occurs. It corresponds precisely to the higgling [*sic*] of the market by means of which buyers and sellers endeavour to discover the true equilibrium position of supply and demand. (*CWJMK*, XIV, p. 182)

Investments, in contrast, are crucial decisions. They are based on long-term expectations 'that cannot be checked at short intervals in the light of realized results . . . Thus the factor of current long-term expectations cannot be even approximately eliminated or replaced by realized results' (Keynes, 1964, p. 51).

Keynes's economics recognizes that long-term expectations are, thus, exogenous, because they cannot be definitely related to any current economic variable. They are based on 'flimsy foundations' and are 'liable to sudden and violent change'. This does not deny continuities or the possibility of theory but it explicitly acknowledges the theoretical intractability of long-term expectations, where the human logic of belief predominates over the formal logic of probability.[16]

SUMMING UP

In this chapter we have discussed the notions of probability and uncertainty offered by Keynes that play a crucial role in the development of Post Keynesian theory. We argued that Keynes's notion of uncertainty is connected to the unknowability of the relevant distribution functions that preside over social processes. The impossibility of appealing to treatments such as the neoclassical that reduces uncertainty to the dispersion of a known probability distribution forces Post Keynesians to consider other answers to the problem of uncertainty.

For Post Keynesians, as for Keynes, what matters is to discuss why and how economic processes are surrounded by uncertainty in order to identify the defensive strategies agents adopt to cope with it and to avoid paralysis. Neoclassical theory, in contrast, uses probability theory to evaluate events themselves in order to keep unaltered its choice-theoretic models built originally for deterministic conditions.

The clues for an alternative are offered in *The General Theory*, where one differentiates processes that can be predicted with some margin of safety from the observation of current events and those that cannot. For the former, agents will act on expectations that may be taken as endogenous to the operation of the economy. But for those processes where the future cannot be predicted from current values of variables, such as long-maturity investments, the only possible treatment is to take the expectations that orient their decisions as exogenously given and to derive their implications.

NOTES

1. As Penrose aptly put it in her discussion of entrepreneurial strategies. 'It is not the environment "as such", but rather the environment as the entrepreneur sees it, that is relevant for his actions' (1980, p. 215). Of course, 'whether experience confirms expectations is another story' (ibid., p. 5).

2. Professor Tony Lawson has called my attention to the distinction between rational belief and rational choice, the latter being directly connected to action while Keynes focused on the former. The distinction is very important and I believe that it had a central role in the development of Keynes's ideas on the subject. However, in the *Treatise on Probability*, Keynes did not seem to be fully aware of it or of its importance. Between belief and decision making (or action) we will find the 'human' logic (of confidence, for instance) to which Ramsey and Keynes himself will refer later (Keynes, 1951, pp. 240–4). In the *Treatise*, Keynes still directly related belief to action, as the quotation taken from p. 339 (above) shows. The point is further explored below.

3. Lawson (1987, p. 959) points out that not only observation but also intuition is considered by Keynes to be a form of direct knowledge. Keynes makes a rapid incursion in the field of the theory of knowledge in Chapter 2. His intention seems to be to define his epistemological assumptions rather than discussing epistemology per se. In this chapter, Keynes proposed that direct acquaintance with things is the source of knowledge about them, 'experience, understanding and perception being three forms of direct acquaintance' (*Treatise on Probability*, p. 12). The objects of knowledge, comprehending sensations, meanings and perceptions, are then called 'propositions' (ibid., p. 12). 'About what kinds of things we are capable of knowing propositions directly, it is not easy to say' (ibid., p. 14). Keynes argues that 'we cannot know a proposition unless it is in fact true' (ibid., p. 11). This sense of the term 'knowledge' is, however, too strong and Keynes later opted for something weaker but closer to common sense: 'To employ a common use of terms (though one inconsistent with the use adopted above), I have assumed that all direct knowledge is certain' (ibid., p. 17); 'I assume then that only true propositions can be known' (ibid., p. 18). As will be proposed below, uncertainty emerges when we focus on the starting propositions rather than on the method of argument.

   In any case, Lawson's view that Keynes was not an 'extreme' empiricist is supported by Keynes's quick but meaningful remarks on memory and the difficulty in distinguishing the remembrance of knowledge from the remembrances generated by 'irrational associations of ideas which cannot fairly be called knowledge' (*CWJMK*, VIII, p. 15). Keynes concluded: 'We cannot always tell, therefore, what is remembered knowledge and what is not knowledge at all' (ibid., p. 15). Of course, we can ask if there is any knowledge that is not 'remembered' knowledge.

4. In the sense important to logic, probability is not subjective. It is not, that is to say, subject to human caprice. A proposition is not probable because we think it so. When once the facts are given which determine our knowledge, what is probable or improbable in these circumstances has been fixed objectively, and is independent of our opinion ... What particular propositions we select as the premisses of our argument naturally depends on subjective factors peculiar to ourselves; but the relations, in which other propositions stand to these, and which entitle us to probable beliefs, are objective and logical' (*CWJMK*, VIII, p. 4).

5. Frequency theory and the construction of distributive probability functions are usually supposed to be descriptions of actual states of the world. Lawson (1988) raises the point that subjectivist authors, such as Friedman and Savage, also consider probability to be a feature of knowledge gathering instead of being characteristic of reality. Two points, however, deserve to be explored. First, how are the probability distribution functions generated? As Keynes has shown in the *Treatise*, the use of prior probabilities, based on some version of the Princi-

ple of Insufficient Reason involves great difficulties in defining the alternatives. In addition, the decision maker may have reasons to suppose, although with an indefinite degree of exactitude, some events to be more likely than others. How can one distribute intuitions? Second, are agents supposed to behave 'as if' they could trust these probability functions as true (and insurable) descriptions of reality? The most characteristic forms of behaviour discussed by Keynes, such as liquidity preference, conventional behaviour and so on, result precisely from the negative which answers this question. After all, as Shackle has pointed out, 'subjective probability ... has no claims to be knowledge' (quoted in Lawson, 1987, p. 18).

6. I am using the term 'logic' in the same sense of formal logic as accepted by Keynes: 'Formal logic is concerned with nothing but the rules of consistent thought' (Keynes, 1951, p. 243). Given sufficient premisses, one can rigorously combine them into relations that lead to conclusions that are not contradictory to the premisses themselves, are consistent with each other, and are no more general in meaning than the premisses themselves. It is undeniable that Keynes sometimes used a more elastic idea of logic, not easily reducible to formal rules like the above. O'Donnel (1989) mentions Keynes's reliance on the idea of similarity as one of the keys to his notion of logic. On the other hand, claims such as Carabelli's (1988) that Keynes was actually opposed to formal logic do not seem sustainable in the light of Keynes's own writings. An especially informative clue to Keynes's use of logic is found in the contrast between practical certainty and logical certainty (*CWJMK*, VIII, p. 177), a distinction that gives some support to O'Donnel's view but none to Carabelli's.

7. 'So far I yield to Ramsey – I think he is right. But in attempting to distinguish "rational" degrees of belief from belief in general he was not yet, I think, quite successful ... Yet in attempting to distinguish a "human" logic from formal logic on the one hand and the descriptive psychology on the other, Ramsey may have been pointing the way to the next field of study when formal logic has been put into good order and its highly limited scope properly defined' (Keynes, 1951, p. 244).

8. 'Weight cannot, then, be explained in terms of probability. An argument of high weight is not "more likely to be right" than one of low weight; for the probabilities of these arguments only state relations between premiss and conclusion, and these relations are stated with equal accuracy in either case' (*CWJMK*, VIII, pp. 82–3).

    An example may help. Let us suppose an entrepreneur is deciding the volume of output to be produced during the next 'day'. The observation of his market operating for a day is, in principle, sufficient to serve as a base for his calculations. Can he trust his data? New observations may repeat the same data, maintaining his original calculations unaltered. They will, nevertheless, increase the weight of his evidence, the degree of confidence in the premisses that were adopted, strengthening the urge to action based on those expectations. If, on the other hand, we had assumed that the original observation was true knowledge, nothing could be gained by the mere corroboration of the evidence.

9. Keynes's famous passage in his 1937 article, 'The General Theory of Employment', fits very well in this interpretation. Lotteries and roulettes do not demand the creation of new premisses. However, the prospects of a war in Europe, the market for copper or the behaviour of the rate of interest, 'twenty years hence', demand the creation of premisses *ex nihilo*. It is not a question of formal logic or probability as he discussed in the *Treatise*. In this case, 'we simply do not know' (*CWJMK*, XIV, pp. 113–14). A similar posture, now related to international

political affairs, is offered by Keynes when he writes: 'I believe in living from hand to mouth in international affairs because the successive links in the causal nexus are so completely unpredictable' (*CWJMK*, XXVIII, p. 120).

10. That is why two individuals sharing the same premises have to share the same expectations (formal logic) but may be led to choose different courses of action (human logic). We must, however, be careful with this statement. To the extent that part of the premises is in fact created by each agent, the sets of premises adopted by different agents do not have to coincide, even if all of them start with the same set of observational data. In other words, 'animal spirits', for example, can influence not only the urge to action in the face of given premises but also the way the set of premises is completed.

11. In the *Treatise*, Keynes seemed still hesitant to consider reality itself in a non-deterministic way. The remarks about experiments like the tossing of a coin point to the imperfect technique of experimentation rather than to a random nature of the world itself. Physical reality seems to be considered deterministically. As to social reality, however, Keynes's views were not so clear in the *Treatise*. In any case, in *The General Theory* there is a clear understanding that it is social reality itself that is uncertain.

12. Lawson (1988) offers a very comprehensive guide to the epistemological and ontological differences in the treatment of probabilities by the most important schools of economic thought.

13. Rational expectationists, for instance, simply propose that the agents' views coincide with the objective probabilities distribution functions (cf. Muth, 1961; Lucas, 1981). For a criticism of this rather cavalier 'solution' to the problem of learning see Arrow (1983, p. 278).

14. Two important conditions are that one has to conceive a set of possible events that is complete (so as to make possible the distribution of the certainty one has that one of those events will occur among the alternative events being considered) and well-defined (a consistent set of events that make them comparable, so as to exclude events such as an object being green or not green, which are clearly non-comparable characteristics). An adequate definition of alternatives is necessary for the application of the principle of insufficient reason. By this principle, if there is no reason to assume that any event of a given set is more probable than any other we can just assign equal probability to each of them. In this sense, if alternatives are not well-defined (as is the case with green and not green above) or if there are reasons to suppose that they are not equally probable, the inference cannot be made.

15. The world is always changing and, rigorously, every process is non-ergodic in an organic universe in which at least one process is non-ergodic. The argument, however, is not whether there are stochastic processes that are really stationary or not but whether agents should behave as if every process is non-ergodic or not. Keynes's point in Chapter 5 of *The General Theory* is clearly that it is not worthwhile, when forming short-term expectations, to take the world as radically different from one 'day' to the next. Post Keynesians are concerned with the way agents behave and this depends on whether they think it worthwhile to reexamine thoroughly the context in which they operate every time they make a decision. Keynes's hypothesis is that they do not. They save the effort of reexamining something that, although never remaining the same, is nevertheless similar enough to justify assuming things to be the same.

16. Before *The General Theory*, Keynes did not adequately distinguish short- from long-term expectations. As a result, he tended to overemphasize the influence of current facts on the formation of expectations, including those orienting the

decision to invest. For a sample of Keynes's pre-*General Theory* treatment of expectations, see *CWJMK*, v, pp. 143, 178: xiii, pp. 358–9, 363–4, 457; xx, p. 366.

PART II
THE OPERATION OF A
MONETARY ECONOMY

5. Asset Choice and Accumulation of Wealth

The General Theory is the analytical codification of the forms of operation of a monetary production economy. It translates into formally defined functional relations, patterns of interaction and causality flows the intuitions that sustain Keynes's new paradigm, the foundations of which were described in Part I.

The essential model of a monetary economy has to account for some crucial characteristics:

1. It has to recognize that production activity is organized and directed by firms according to their profit expectations. These expectations are intrinsically speculative, since they refer to the uncertain future behaviour of markets. Once expectations are formed and decisions to produce are made, firms enter into money forward contracts that allow them to reserve factors of production in advance of their actual utilization so as to guarantee not only their physical availability but also their terms of purchase. Having accepted contractual payments obligations before any production and sale is actually made, the firms have then a potential demand for cash as a store of liquidity to allow them to make good their debts in case their expectations about markets are disappointed.

2. Firms also have to decide on their capacity of production, which implies the formation of expectations for distant time-horizons. Such decisions are affected by the increased uncertainty associated with processes that extend far into the future. The amount of resources involved in an investment decision and the long time interval during which the firm will be imprisoned by illiquid assets make this decision a crucial one. As a result of the high stakes involved and the fragility of the informational bases

on which a decision to invest is made, investments tend to fluctuate, this being the primary cause of the global instability that characterizes a modern entrepreneurial economy. Fluctuations in effective demand are rooted in shifts in asset demands towards other forms of wealth, such as liquid assets and money.

3. Consumers are mostly constrained by their income, received from the sale of productive services or by transferences from other agents. Therefore their plans are induced by the actions of firms that are responsible for the employment decisions and, thus, for the actual income that is going to be earned by consumers.

4. Since the expenditure of one agent is the income of another, the dynamics of a monetary economy is dependent on the way demands are decided upon. Demand for investment goods is more volatile than for consumption goods, making of investment the *causa causans* of the path followed by the economy. Investment expenditures, in addition, determine income of investment goods producers, but also of consumer goods producers that supply goods for the workers of the former. In a monetary economy, income and production in both industries (investment goods and consumption goods) move in solidarity.

A complete model of a monetary economy has, then, to be able to describe how the essential decisions to invest are made, as the fundamental cause of this kind of economy's dynamics and, secondly, to account for the modes of propagation of these impulses throughout the economy.

The generation of the original impulses is located by Keynes in the market for assets, where wealth owners decide the forms in which they prefer to keep their wealth over time. The decision to invest in real capital assets, in this perspective, is a result of a larger choice in terms of which assets to hold, something that depends on the advantages one recognizes in some assets over others.

Having decided which assets they prefer, wealth owners interact with producers to determine the rate of construction of new real capital assets, that is the rate of investment, which, in its turn, determines the rate of production and the level of employment in the capital goods sector. Fluctuations in employment in the capital goods sector propagate throughout the economy because of the derived decisions to produce consumption goods to serve the newly employed in the production of capital goods and the newly employed in the consumption goods sector itself. This is called the multiplier. Chapters 5 to 7 will explore the first mechanism, the determination of the demand for assets, while Chapters 8 and 9 will explore the propagation mechanisms. Chapter 10 will summarize the argument presenting Keynes's model of effective demand.

ANTECEDENTS

We saw in Part I that a fundamental insight of Keynes's new paradigm is the acknowledgement that in a monetary economy money becomes an asset, something Davidson has called a 'liquidity time-machine'; that is, a means to transport purchasing power over time without having to worry in advance as to when or how that purchasing power will be spent. If money becomes an asset, it will displace in some degree other forms of wealth holding and therefore it will affect their prices and, through them, the amounts in which they are available. Thus a model that is adequate to capture the dynamics of wealth accumulation in such economies has to allow the decision maker to choose between monetary and other assets and to develop the implications of this choice.

Keynes's model of asset choice in *The General Theory* was an adaptation of the theory of forward markets that he had exposed in *A Treatise on Money*, but on which he had been working for much longer, at least since the *Tract on Monetary Reform*, when the framework was applied to the analysis of exchange markets. In a nutshell, the theory says that, for any given durable good, the divergence between its spot and forward prices, that is between the current price for current delivery and the current price for delivery at a specified future date, will reflect the expectation of the market as to the gains to be derived from its possession between the present moment and the specified future date.

This principle was first applied by Keynes in his examination of the purchasing power parity theory of exchange rates in the *Tract*. There he established that the difference between the spot and forward exchange rates between two monies depended, *ceteris paribus*, on the difference between the short-term interest rates that could be earned on loans in each currency. An example may make it clearer. Let us suppose the existence of a free exchange market between

England and the United States, so that any agent with resources in one of the currencies can invest them freely in any of the two countries. Let us also suppose, for simplification, that at a given initial moment the spot and forward (for a six-month delivery) exchange rates between the dollar and the pound are 1:1 and that interest rates for a six-month loan are 5 per cent in New York and 10 per cent in London. All this means that somebody who made a $100 loan in New York would have $105 after six months, while somebody who made a similar loan in London would have $110. It is obvious that, in a free exchange market, all agents would try to make loans in London rather than in New York.

If the forward exchange rate is assumed to remain stable at 1:1, agents holding US dollars will try to convert them into pounds, to be able to make loans in London now. This will cause an excess demand for pounds to emerge that will last as long as the advantage of making loans in England remains. The excess supply of dollars will cause a depreciation in its value relative to the pound, the spot price of the pound in terms of dollars will increase up to the point at which the interest-rate advantage of making loans in England is precisely compensated by the difference in the prices of pounds in terms of dollars between the two dates. When the spot rate falls to US$ 1: 95.46 pence the resource owner will be indifferent between making loans in New York or London. The divergence between the spot pound price of the dollar of 95.46 pence and the forward price of £1 measures the relative advantage of making loans in pounds rather than in dollars. Therefore full equilibrium would require that either spot and forward exchange rates be adjusted or that spot exchange rates and short-term interest rates be adjusted in both countries.

As Kregel convincingly showed, this scheme was used again by Keynes in Chapter 17 of *The General Theory*, with some modifications suggested by Sraffa's (1932) critique of Hayek's *Prices and Production*. Sraffa's essential innovation was to use the spot/forward scheme to describe the process of quantity adjustments of supplies to demands in the case of reproducible commodities. Forward prices represented flow-supply prices. When a market was characterized by excess demand pressures, competition among buyers would make spot prices rise above supply prices, signalling through the appearance of windfall profits to producers a relative scarcity of that good, leading to a reallocation of productive resources towards the increase of its production. This idea was crucially important for Keynes's further development of his asset-choice model. In fact, the own-rates of interest model proposed in Chapter 17 of *The General Theory* is a generalization of Sraffa's suggestion for all assets, not only reproducible assets. It was thus a combination of his own early use of the scheme, applied to non-reproducible items (currencies), and Sraffa's utilization to study the mechanisms through which supply adjusted to demand.

OWN-RATES OF INTEREST AND ASSET PRICES

To develop a spot/forward prices model to describe asset choice in a monetary economy, that is, an economy where money is an asset that can take the place of other types of assets in the individual portfolios, Keynes created the concept of own-rates of interest.[1] The own-rate of interest of a given asset is a measure of its total yield, not only in terms of the claims to income it gives rise to but also in terms of the convenience of its possession and the capital gains one may obtain by its sale. It is a measure that is adequate to a monetary economy since it recognizes that some assets may offer rewards other than monetary values, such as the liquidity premium, to be defined below. This view of the returns of an asset opens the way to the consideration of money as an asset even though it does not 'pay' any kind of monetary yield.

Each asset will offer a given own-rate of interest and it is proposed that investors will choose those that offer the highest rates of return possible. The competition between wealth owners to obtain the best assets (those with the highest total yields) will determine the prices of these assets. These prices will signal which assets are relatively scarce and which are in excess supply (scarcity being measured by the ratio between demand and supply prices) and will determine the composition of the total wealth accumulated by a community in the period under study.

To develop this model formally along the lines proposed by Keynes (1964, chap. 17) we need to make clear two conditions beforehand. Firstly, one should keep in mind that this is a model of asset choice. We want to be able to understand how decisions as to the means of holding wealth over time are made and to extract the consequences of these decisions. Assets are 'promises' of future returns in a given form; therefore operations with assets are always and necessarily forward-looking. As a model of decision making, the values for own-rates of interest that are going to be considered are all expected values. Current or past realized values are considered only to the extent that they are used by decision makers to form their current expectations of future yields. In this connection, one should also remember that we are dealing with operations with items that may be long-lived and therefore, depending on the period of time the wealth holder may have to keep that asset before being able to readjust his portfolio, the relevant horizon of expectations may be very distant in time from the present. In other words, at least with respect to those assets that are not easily disposable, their purchase may depend on long-term expectations that, as we saw in Chapter 4, may be very insensitive to currently realized values.

The time-horizon involved in the asset-choice decision is also the root of the second condition for the operation of the model. Different assets typically represent claims over future income to be exercised on different dates. The possession of money gives rights to currently available income. Non-negotiable bonds are claims to income to be available at their redemption date. Stocks are claims to profits to be generated in the future but they can also be converted into current claims if sold in stock markets. Thus, when building a model of asset choice, one has to propose a way of dealing with the fact that time itself is part of the returns of an asset. The duration of an asset and the facilities for its pre-redemption convertibility are an important characteristic to be considered when choosing how to transport wealth into an uncertain future. Claims to equal money returns at different dates do not have the same 'value' for wealth owners.

The standard way of dealing with assets of different terms to maturity and/or profiles of payments is the discounting of their expected returns according to the date of accrual. One does not compare the money returns of assets as specified in contracts but their present values. This procedure, however, was not available to Keynes in *The General Theory* because to discount future returns and obtain present values one has to have discount rates, which are themselves rates of return on some selected asset. Usually the problem is solved by having recourse to an exogenous determination of a 'basic' interest rate by, for instance, the monetary authority. Keynes's model of own-rate of interest, however, cannot appeal to exogenously-determined interest rates because this would clearly involve circular reasoning in a model that tries to determine precisely the nature of interest rates.

To escape this circularity Keynes offered a very ingenious solution, proposing a fundamental concept for the development of Post Keynesian economics. The solution was to consider all assets as possessing an identical period of retention, with all payments being made at the same specified date. This would allow the direct comparison of returns, without need to appeal to discounting methods. The time dimension of assets was not ignored but it was embodied in another variable, the liquidity premium offered by each asset. In other words, one can consider that the higher the convertibility of an asset into another (mediated, in general, by its conversion into money as means of payment), the shorter is its retention period; that is, the time one needs to keep an asset before being able to trade it for something else. Liquidity is precisely the capacity of being converted into money and, thus, into anything money can acquire. Therefore the more liquid an asset is, the higher its convertibility and the shorter the effective period of retention a wealth owner has to consider when making his choices. The ease with which one can dispose of an asset defines its liquidity premium and measures, therefore, one central aspect of its time dimension. If this procedure is accepted, we can dispose of, at this level of analysis, the need for discounting.[2]

Summarizing these two points, we will be working with variables that will be measuring the total returns one can expect to get from the possession of a given asset for a specified retention period that is assumed to be the same for all assets. Differences of convertibility in the interior of the retention period will be embodied in its liquidity premium; that is, the capacity a possessor of a given asset has to trade it for other assets within the retention period.

The total return offered by an asset, as we saw, is called the own-rate of interest of that asset. These returns are calculated through the values assumed by four attributes assets are supposed to share. The first attribute is the rate of quasi-rents expected to be earned from the use or possession of that asset, q.[3] An asset may yield some return from its use or simple possession, like machines giving origin to saleable goods, seeds to crops, bonds to interest, stocks to dividends and so on. The ratio between these returns and the price at which the asset is being purchased (Q/CP) is q, the first attribute of assets.

The retention of assets implies some costs, independently of the use one makes of them. Storing, costs of insurance, losses caused by the mere passage of time, and so on, are carrying costs. The ratio between these expected costs and the current price of the asset (C/CP) is indicated by c.

As we have already discussed, different assets have different degrees of 'tradability'. Some assets are easier to dispose of than others. Naturally, those that are more easily converted into money or other assets directly give to their possessor an important 'return' in the form of flexibility in the face of unexpected changes in the environment. This is called by Keynes liquidity premium, and is denoted by l.

Finally, assets can be bought and sold and therefore a wealth owner can gain (or lose) from appreciation (or depreciation) of the market prices of that asset between the purchase and the end of the retention period. This attribute, denoted by a, is the rate between the change in prices and the current price of the asset ($(EP\text{-}CP)/CP$).

The own-rate of interest of an asset is the sum of these attributes less their carrying cost:

$$a + q - c + l$$

The own-rate of interest measures, then, the total returns expected from an asset, not only in value terms but also in terms of safety against disappointments of expectations. It is the latter attribute that allows us to consider money as an asset and to compare its 'return' with the value returns offered by other assets.[4]

Quasi-rents are calculated net of depreciation or, in Keynes's terms, net of both user and supplementary cost. The uncertainty that surrounds the expectation of returns is already allowed for in the calculation (forming the state of long-term expectations). To have a definite value for q, with an allowance for uncertainty, may not be the best way to represent this kind of variable but it is used here for simplicity in the same way Keynes did in another topic of *The General Theory*:

An entrepreneur, who has to reach a practical decision as to his scale of production, does not, of course, entertain a single undoubting expectation of what the sale-proceeds of a given output will be, but several hypothetical expectations held with varying degrees of probability and definiteness. By his expectation of proceeds I mean, therefore, that expectation of proceeds which, if it were held with certainty, would lead to the same behavior as does the bundle of vague and more various possibilities which actually makes up his state of expectation when he reaches his decision. (Keynes, 1964, p. 24n)[5]

This means that income uncertainties are taken into consideration in this scheme through adjustments in q. If the future performance of a market for a given good or service becomes more doubtful, this increased uncertainty about returns of an investment in capital goods to produce that good or service is reflected in the reduction of the value of q. One should note, therefore, that in this sense, l, the liquidity premium, is not the only variable to catch the impact of uncertainty. The liquidity premium has to do with the uncertainty surrounding the disposability of the asset itself, while q measures the uncertainty surrounding the results of its use.

The same argument is valid for carrying costs, c, and the rate of capital appreciation, a. Carrying costs may be known with less uncertainty since they can consist of expenses contracted beforehand. Capital appreciation, on the other hand, the difference between purchase prices in the present and resale prices in the future, has also to be adjusted for uncertainty, although it is clear that changes in value of an asset have much to do with the facilities that may exist for trading existing items. In other words, capital appreciation is connected with the liquidity of the asset to the extent that, *ceteris paribus*, the more liquid an asset the easier it is to sell it, which means the lower is the likelihood of its possessor having to 'bribe' other wealth owners to buy it.

Be that as it may, the most original of the attributes identified by Keynes is the liquidity premium, a concept that became a cornerstone of Post Keynesian monetary and financial theory. As Keynes stressed: 'There is, so to speak, nothing to show for this [attribute] at the end of the period in the shape of output; yet it is something for which people are ready to pay something' (Keynes, 1964, p. 226).

Liquidity is a bi-dimensional concept. It refers simultaneously to the duration of time required (or expected to be required) to dispose of an asset and to the capacity this asset may have for conserving its value over time.[6] Of course, anything can be disposed of very quickly if its possessor accepts a price low enough to find immediate buyers. On the other hand, the likelihood of finding another wealth owner who evaluates an asset in the same way as its present possessor increases if the latter does not care to have to wait an indefinitely long period of time. Therefore we may say that an asset is as liquid as the time required for its convertibility is short and the expected change in its value is small.

On what, then, does the attribute of liquidity depend? Of course, an asset has a high liquidity premium if the public expects it to be resaleable without significant capital losses at any moment. It is its potential tradability that is being considered. If one is talking about the convertibility or tradability of an asset, for a given state of expectations, one is obviously talking about features of the market for this asset. Liquidity thus depends on the characteristics of the market where a given asset is transacted. The more 'efficient' its market, the more liquid the asset becomes because the safer it becomes, in the eyes of wealth holders, the expectation that resaleability at reasonably sustained prices will be guaranteed in the future. The more efficient spot markets for a given asset are, the stronger is the confidence assigned to the expectation of convertibility without significant losses.

We can think of market efficiency in the sense proposed above in terms of three features: its density, its permanence and its organization. Density has to do with the size of the market, with the number of potential buyers for an item that constitutes a reserve of demand that can absorb quickly and without pressures the supplies that eventually are put out for trade at any moment. Density had to do, then, primarily, with the substitutability between individual items of a given type, both in space and time. The lower the degree of substitutability, the more specific a market for a given item is and the lower the likelihood of finding buyers for it. The substitutability may be established both across items that have some slight difference in character (for instance between stocks of firms in the same industry or class) or in age (as with money issued at different dates). The more indistinguishable one item is from another, the larger the market for the overall class of those assets is, and therefore the easier they are to be traded. Items that are not indistinguishable in this sense (for instance, capital goods for specific uses or of different ages) have thinner markets and are thus not expected to be easily disposed of. They are 'illiquid'.

Permanence refers to time of operation. The more permanent a market is, the more liquid the asset becomes because the higher the probability is that the present possessor will find a buyer if needed.

Money, in this sense, is perfectly liquid because its 'market' is open 24 hours a day. Stocks are less liquid as their markets operate only a few hours a day, a few days a week. The markets for some other assets only operate for still shorter periods of time, during, for instance, trade fairs and so on.

Finally, and perhaps most important, we have to consider the degree of organization of these markets. This point is perhaps most important because markets are institutions; they are not natural phenomena. When they are created, rules are set, standards are defined, acceptable behaviours and procedures are established. To a large extent, density and permanence are defined in this 'creation'; that is, the organization of a specific market. The better organized a market is, the more orderly the manner in which we can expect the day-to-day transactions to develop.

We may identify, however, a more precise sense to define the degree of organization of a market. An organized market is that which avoids excessive potentially disruptive fluctuations in the prices of assets, avoiding thereby solvency crises that could threaten the permanence of that market. To contain the fluctuations in asset prices is the function of market makers (Davidson, 1978b), residual buyers or sellers that absorb excess supplies or demands when they exceed some acceptable margin.

The efficacy of market makers depends on two conditions: (1) the extent to which fluctuations in prices are considered desirable in a given market; and (2) the resources market makers possess to effect the operations needed to regulate the market. In the first condition, we are taking into consideration that some degree of fluctuation in asset prices may be healthy in the sense that it may signal some fundamental forces in operation. Stock prices change at least in part to reflect changes in the actual expectation of profits (and dividends) entertained by agents. Of course some change in stock prices is also due to speculative manoeuvres, but since it may be impossible to distinguish one from the other, it is better to accept some speculative activity as a lesser evil, that is, as the price to be paid to have a stock market that can reflect changes in prospective profitability of firms.

If no fluctuation of any kind was desired, the success of market makers in achieving this complete stability of prices would depend on the amount of resources they had to back their operations and to absorb all excess demands and supplies. At the limit, if a market maker had control over an amount of resources equal to the value of the whole stock of a given asset he would have complete control over its price. The cost of organizing such a market, however, would be prohibitive for most assets. In fact the amount of resources a market maker needs to operate efficiently depends on the expectations of those who take part in that market. Under normal conditions, market makers operate marginally because they are expected to be able to shape opinion in their favour. Of course, *ceteris paribus*, one may think that this power is greater when the public perceives the market maker to be strong enough to influence in a decisive way the course of events. Again, this power would be stronger the greater the amount of resources under the control of the market maker. Most asset markets have market makers endowed with resources generated by private agents. This means that resources are limited and there may emerge pressures that cannot be contained by market makers. In other words, expectations as to the future of a given asset may deteriorate so much that the market maker may be unable to stem the tide. Liquidity premia may fall so low that market makers will be unable to sustain prices. Stock market crashes illustrate this possibility. In some cases, however, the presence of very powerful market makers is conceivable. This is the case, for instance, of the Central Bank when operating as market makers, as with demand deposits. The rate of exchange between this type of private liability (assuming privately-owned banks) and currency (legal tender) is kept stable at 1:1 in modern monetary economies. This is mainly because of the existence of a lender-of-last-resort, a Central Bank, that operates thus as a residual buyer of bank liabilities, if need be, preventing the necessity of holders of bank deposits selling them for currency at a discount if some kind of excess supply of demand deposits came to be felt. The role of Central Banks (or equivalent institutions) as market makers has rendered runs on banks obsolete.

When Central Banks act as market makers preventing any degree of fluctuation in asset prices in terms of currency, they are actually indicating that these assets, even if privately issued, are perfect substitutes for legal tender and must therefore be considered as constituting the stock of money of this economy. In this conception, anything that is fully backed by monetary authorities, guaranteeing full convertibility and constant exchange rates, becomes part of the stock of money of the economy.

On the basis of the preceding discussion, we realize immediately that liquidity is a matter of degree. We have fully liquid assets, the stock of money, but the remaining assets also have some liquidity, depending on the features of their markets for existing (second-hand) items. To make this attribute analytically manageable, how-ever, instead of working with a continuous scale of liquidity we will appeal to a three-fold classification of assets according to their degree of liquidity, suggested by Hicks (1967, p. 36). The first group of assets are fully liquid, including currency and its perfect substi-tutes. The second group are the liquid assets, those for which there exist second-hand markets, but where market makers are unable or unwilling to sustain fixed prices for assets. Thus possessors of these assets trust that they will be able to sell their stocks of assets if necessary but they are uncertain as to the price they will actually get for them. Finally, we have illiquid assets, those for which no orga-nized markets exist and that, therefore, cannot be maintained as stores of value, given the uncertainty surrounding their resale possi-bilities. A stylized aggregation of assets that is going to be analyti-cally useful below would call the first group 'money', the second 'bonds' and the third 'capital goods'.

One last remark, before we proceed to some manipulations of the own-rate of interest model, also pertains to the attribute of liquidity. As Kaldor (1980) has observed, the liquidity premium defined by Keynes is a troublesome variable, because if one thinks of how it should be measured one realizes that the reference value for its scale is a maximum, not a zero, as is necessary. We do not have a starting point to create a measurement scale. Kaldor's solution to this dilemma is relatively simple. Keynes defined the maximum liquidity premium as being that attributed to money, because of its converti-bility properties. All the other assets share that attribute but in a descending scale. We have thus a negative scale of liquidity that can be transformed into a positive scale if we consider that maximum liquidity is just the equivalent of minimum risk (as denominated by Kaldor, not to be confused with probability risk, used in neoclassical models). If we create, then, a new variable, r, the value of which is given by the conversion formula

$$r = -1$$

we may define a new measurement, that of risk, in which the starting point is 0, corresponding to the risk of money. The remaining assets will have then an attribute of risk established in relation to the zero-risk of money. The own-rates of interest then become

$$a + q - c - r$$

This formula allows the comparison and choice between assets that offer some form of income $(q - c)$, capital gains (a) or simply the safety and flexibility conferred by liquidity (l). The values of these attributes will depend, of course, on the state of long-term expectations. Typically, however, one would expect income to be the main attraction of capital goods since, being very illiquid, they are not expected to be held for resale. Some goods can be held for resale, most likely standardized raw materials, agricultural goods, oil, but also gold, silver and other precious metals, and so on. These goods can only be held for their possible capital appreciation, although some of them, like gold, may exhibit a considerable liquidity premium. Money, in its turn, has only the liquidity premium to account for its demand as a store of value (although under some circumstances some forms of money may yield interest). Bonds and other financial assets are held both for the income they generate and for the possibility of capital appreciation. A crucial idea is that, in equilibrium, these attributes must balance each other. Since money, for instance, has only liquidity to its credit, in equilibrium the monetary yields expected to be given by the other assets must equal their relative illiquidity when compared to money, in order to equalize marginal advantages.

RESULTS OF THE OWN-RATES OF INTEREST MODEL

We are now in a position to operate the model to see how it allows us to portray the choice of assets and its implications for the process of capital accumulation. The basic assumption is that a given state of long-term expectations is defined by a set of values for the expected variables EP, Q, C and $r.CP$ (that is, the value of the allowance for risk projected by agents). If one starts from a state of expectations newly formed, there is obviously no reason why these expectations should define a situation where the own-rates of interest for all assets calculated at the prices current at the moment of opening of the markets should be uniform. If they are not uniform, agents will perceive new opportunities of returns associated with different compositions of portfolios with respect to their current portfolios formed on the basis of a state of expectations that has now been superseded.

Let us assume, with Keynes, perfect competition in the assets markets, with no kind of segmentation.[7] This implies that agents that are unhappy with their current portfolios in the face of the new expected returns will be free to adjust them in order to maximize their expected total returns. Assets with lower expected returns, measured at their current prices, will be sold, the converse happening to those assets with expected higher yields. The model tries to find out what happens to asset prices in this situation, and what are the long-term consequences of these movements.

The first step is solved by assuming that stocks of the several assets are given. In this case, if the new state of expectations implies different total returns (different own-rates of interest) at current asset prices, the demand for each asset will be different from its supply. Naturally, all assets are in the possession of some agent that will try to trade those with lower yields for those with higher returns. Excess supplies of low-yield assets will emerge, lowering their current prices, and the converse will happen with high-yield assets. Prices will move until the relative advantages of one asset over any other disappear. In terms of the own-rate of interest formula, for those assets offering better prospective returns, current prices (the denominator of all elements) will rise until a and $q-c$ are so reduced that the extra gains that are anticipated disappear. Of course the opposite happens with the low-yield assets: current prices fall so that the values of a and $q-c$ are raised.

If stocks of the various assets are constant, a change in relative spot or current prices is the only equilibrating mechanism between demand and supplies. However, if the state of expectations is believed to last, the new prices will cause changes in the availability of assets to make them adequate to the demands of the public.[8]

In our discussion we specified two prices for each asset: the current or spot price (the price which has to be paid in the present for the immediate acquisition of an asset) and the expected price (the price that is expected to be charged at a given future date when the retention period is over and the agent is free again to reorient his accumulation strategies). If there exist forward markets for a given asset, we may expect these expected prices to coincide with forward prices; that is, prices that would be contracted at this moment for delivery and payment at the specified future date. Moreover, we would also expect that for reproducible goods such as, say, capital goods, these forward prices would coincide with their flow-supply prices. This is so because, if forward prices were lower than flow-supply prices, no production (and thus no flow supply) would be realized. On the other hand, if forward prices were higher than flow-supply prices it would pay to order now additional production of these items and to sell them now at forward markets, deriving a profit from the difference in prices for the same good. This arbitrage operation would be repeated until the difference had disappeared and it just reflects the notion that under competition a good cannot have two prices at the same location and date.

The preceding discussion means that we can consider spot prices as demand prices, since they indicate what buyers of assets think the asset is worth at this moment and expected or forward prices to be flow-supply prices, measuring what would be the cost of an additional production of those assets. A divergence between them, that is, between demand and supply prices, indicates their relative scarcity, as Sraffa (1932) had shown. If spot prices are higher than forward prices, we have a situation in which buyers are willing to pay now more than the asset costs to be reproduced, because this would imply waiting until the new units were available. As Keynes (1923) had shown with his interest rate parity model, this divergence will be felt if there are immediate advantages in possessing the asset now instead of waiting until the future date when new items are available.

For the producer of the assets that are scarce, the divergence between demand and supply prices is a signal that it is profitable to increase their availability, since there is a fringe of unsatisfied buyers willing to pay for them more than they cost. More of these assets will be produced and made available and, thus, more wealth will be generated.

When spot prices are higher than forward prices, then, we have a stimulus to the production of new units of that asset. This was called by Keynes 'backwardation' and indicates a situation in which there is a 'premium' for the immediate possession of an asset, represented by the gains one expects to derive from having the asset now instead of waiting until a future date. This divergence between demand and supply prices for the asset will represent an incentive to the production of additional units. If the assets in question are, for instance, capital goods, a new production will take place and aggregate investment will be increasing. The opposite happens with assets that offer lower expected yields. Their spot prices will fall and if they fall below their forward or flow-supply prices some disincentive to their production will emerge and a contraction in their availability will ensue. This was called 'contango' by Keynes.

One should notice that, contrary to a widespread belief that Keynesian macroeconomics had nothing to say about relative prices,[9] the whole model is based on a theory of relative prices of assets.[10] It shows that decisions to purchase particular kinds of assets are not independent of the other choices available, making it possible to study the behaviour of aggregate investment as a result of the choices of private agents comparing the various forms of accumulating wealth that are available. But the model also allows us to realize that money is also an option of storing wealth that is especially efficient to face the uncertainties of the future, given its liquidity premium. When expectations are optimistic, and uncertainty is low, the liquidity attribute is not as important as the possibility of having monetary gains. The own-rate of interest of money then, at the current spot prices, becomes lower than the own-rates of those assets that are expected to yield gains in a or in $q - c$, such as capital goods. People will try to give up money to obtain investment goods, the spot prices of these will rise and new production will be stimulated. Conversely, if uncertainty is high, the liquidity premium of money will probably be higher than the monetary yields offered by other assets, such as investment goods. People will try to keep liquid portfolios, depressing prices of capital goods and leading to a contraction in the capital goods-producing sector.

The model of own-rates of interest is thus the heart of Keynes's and Post Keynesian macroeconomics because it is the general model from which the more specific theories of liquidity preference and the marginal efficiency of capital will be derived. In fact the latter are just applications of the basic model of asset choice and cannot be adequately studied in isolation. The role of expectations and uncertainty is highlighted and a particular vision of capitalist dynamics is defined.

In the following two chapters both liquidity preference and the marginal efficiency of capital will be discussed against this background, meaning that they will not be studied in reference to markets in isolation but, on the contrary, in terms of the way a particular state of expectation unfolds in each specific submarket.

They should be seen as exploring in further detail the operation of the model of the own-rates of interest rather than alternatives to it.

SUMMING UP

In this chapter we have proposed that the starting point and foundation of Keynes's and Post Keynesian macroeconomics is the model of own-rates of interest presented by Keynes in Chapter 17 of *The General Theory*. This model combined some previous insights of Keynes, especially those developed in the discussion of the interest rate parity theory in the *Tract*, and from other authors, notably Sraffa, in his 1932 critique of Hayek.

The fundamental idea is that the divergence between expected yields from different sources in a given period is reflected in the way agents evaluate the desirability of possessing that source in the present related to its possibility at a later date. Thus the ratio between spot and forward prices measures the attractiveness of an asset and reflects the market preferences for the different ways of accumulating wealth.

In addition, the same divergence indicates for producers the degree of relative scarcity of a given asset and, thus, the profitability of the production of new units, expanding or contracting the stocks of assets, including capital goods.

It is finally suggested that, since Post Keynesians propose that changes in investment are the main forces of movement in modern monetary economies, and changes in investment result from the solution of the model, one should see this approach to capital accumulation as the theoretical heart of Post Keynesian macroeconomics, showing that liquidity preference and the marginal efficiency of capital are specific applications of this general approach rather than the focus of novelty by themselves. The operation of the own-rates of interest model specifies the sense in which money is not neutral in the short as in the long period in a Keynesian notion of monetary or entrepreneurial economy.

NOTES

1. The first concept introduced in Chapter 17 of *The General Theory* is actually the own-rate of own-interest. The latter is defined as a measure of the total yield of a

given asset measured in terms of that same asset. In other words, the own-rate of own-interest is a measure of something like the 'intrinsic' yield of an asset, like the capacity of a machine to produce some good or service, of a consumption good to yield a service, or of seeds to produce new crops. It is a concept of yield that takes the asset in isolation from other assets and does not consider, therefore, 'yields' represented by a change in its value relative to other types of assets. In other words, the own-rates of own-interest establish that assets have yields that are not just their own value appreciation but that can result from their use as instruments of production or claims on future income. In what follows, we are interested in the more general concept of own-rates of interest that, besides considering the intrinsic yields of each asset, also include gains (or losses) from changes in prices relative to the prices of other assets.

2. A more complete definition of liquidity should include not only the resaleability of an asset but also its capacity to serve as a collateral for borrowing from a bank or other financial institution. This does not change the question, however, because it only transfers to the lender the same dilemmas and uncertainties considered above. The lender is substituting a security for money in his portfolio and he will require a compensation, the interest rate paid by the borrower, to pay for the increased illiquidity of his assets now. He still has to consider, thus, whether the asset he is holding as collateral is or is not convertible into money. The relation becomes more clear but its content remains the same.

3. We will follow in this chapter Keynes's own convention in *The General Theory* of using capital letters to represent absolute values and using lower case for rates and ratios.

4. We have to consider the question of substitutability between assets with some care. As Davidson (1978b, p. 64) has pointed out, both Friedman and Tobin seem to assume that any asset can be a store of value, which is equivalent to assuming the existence of spot markets for all and every asset. Post Keynesian theory differentiates sharply those assets that can be held as liquidity reserves, such as money, from those that have no liquidity premium (or, if they do, one which is much less than their carrying costs, making it irrational to retain them as liquidity reserves. Among the latter, we have capital goods, for which there are no organized spot markets. For this reason, Davidson warns against taking the substitutability question lightly (1978a, pp. 19, 61) pointing to the different attitudes of savers, who search for liquidity, and investors, who search for profitable placements (ibid., p. 66). At a more abstract level, however, one has to consider that liquid and non-liquid assets are alternatives to be considered by wealth owners. When the liquidity premium of liquid assets is much higher than expected profits (as on the eve of a deep recession), even investors will consider remaining liquid for a while. The converse is also true. The concept of own-rate of interest allows one to show this fundamental unitary vision of capital accumulation that allows money to be an asset. As Kregel has noted, the own-rates model is 'applicable to all durable assets in the system and provides a perfectly general theory of the demand for durable assets and their returns' (Kregel, 1984, p. 103). Keynes emphasized many times that choice among assets was involved in the determination of interest rates and demand for money and for other kinds of assets (for example, *CWJMK*, XIII, p. 221; XIV, p. 102).

5. This point has to be handled with care, given the discussion of uncertainty in Chapter 4. In any case, we are not dealing with certainty equivalents that an external observer would identify, if he knew the probability distribution function, but with the result the decision maker imagines to be an adequate epitome of his state of long-term expectations, which could represent, say, a pair of Shacklean standardized focus gains or losses.

6. This argument is taken, with slight alteration, from Chick (1983a).
7. This assumption is frequently the object of criticism. See Harcourt (1983). Nevertheless, at this level of abstraction, the criticism may be misdirected, since the basic model can be amended to allow limited access of some agents to some markets, much in the line of the argument of Sylos-Labini in favour of the possibility of amending Sraffa's production prices, also constructed for perfect competition, to allow for barriers to entry. One should also notice Harcourt's last footnote to the paper above.
8. A clear and didactic graphic presentation of this model is given by Davidson (1978a, chap. 4).
9. A belief held even by non-orthodox theorists like the neo-Ricardians who want to combine Keynes's principle of effective demand (seen as the statement that it is aggregate income, not interest rates that balances intended saving and investment) with Sraffa's independently-derived model of relative prices. Since some of the goods in the Sraffa economy are assets, it is hard to see how the two contributions can really be combined. On the idea that relative prices are important in Keynes's analysis, see Minsky (1982, pp. 79, 94) and Kregel (1984). This proposition is explicitly made by Keynes himself. See *CWJMK*, XIV, pp. 102–3.
10. In a brilliant but relatively unknown paper, Townshend actually showed that Keynes can be read as proposing a general theory of relative prices adequate to the analysis of all goods and based on the notions of uncertainty and liquidity. Unfortunately, even among Post Keynesians, these ideas have not yet been developed. See Townshend (1937).

6. Liquidity Preference and Money

Liquidity preference has traditionally been understood to refer to the demand for money, in a narrow sense, something to be directly contrasted to the orthodox quantity approach. Most of the time, it refers to no more than an alternative specification of the demand function in which interest rates are specified among the independent variables as much as income. That interpretation was supported by Hicks in his 1937 paper, 'Mr Keynes and the Classics', for instance, and quickly became the conventional wisdom on this matter.

There is no doubt that *The General Theory* authorizes this interpretation to the extent that liquidity preference is defined in Chapter 15 directly in terms of motives for holding money. On the other hand, there are enough elements in those discussions and in the structure of the book to allow a richer meaning to be developed in line with the view proposed up to this point. To establish the legitimacy of this larger approach one has to notice first that liquidity preference, even narrowly understood, is not a theory of demand for money but a theory of interest rates, by which it is stated: 'Thus the rate of interest at any time, being the reward for parting with liquidity, is a measure of the willingness of those who possess money to part with their control over it' (Keynes, 1964, p. 167).

The aggregative structure proposed in most of *The General Theory* recognizes two assets: 'money' and 'bonds',[1] the first including very short-term assets, for which capital appreciation is not a relevant element, and the latter including all kinds of long-lived assets (sometimes including even capital goods). In this context, there is only one choice for those who may accept parting with liquidity, that is the 'bond', paying 'the' interest rate. Reversing the argument, depending on the level of 'the' interest rate, the public will desire, *ceteris paribus*, to hold a given quantity of 'money', so that liquidity preference becomes an alternative to the quantity theory of money with its sole emphasis on income as the causal factor in the demand for money. When one remembers, however, as Hicks did, that Keynes also considered income to be a determinant of money demand (through the transactions motive to hold money) and also that more sophisticated versions of the quantity theory of money, such as Wicksell's or Marshall's, can also allow some influence for interest rates to play in the demand for money, it is not surprising that the criticisms levelled by Keynes against the classics lost much of their power when conceived merely as an alternative specification of the demand for money.

In Chapter 17 of *The General Theory*, as we have seen, in contrast, Keynes offered a framework to deal with a more diversified structure of assets in which a given amount of each asset is demanded according to its own-rate of interest calculated at the going (spot) asset prices. In this framework, one can generalize the construction offered above to propose that liquidity preference is actually a theory of asset prices (and returns), according to which assets with different liquidity premia have to offer monetary returns to compensate for their relative illiquidity measured against a reference asset. Kahn (1972, p. 80) had called attention to this more general meaning of liquidity preference in a two-asset model. More recently, Minsky (1982, pp. 93–4) and Kregel (1982) renewed the criticism against the narrow interpretation of liquidity preference in terms of merely demand for money, re-proposing it as a theory of asset pricing.

Differences in the degree of illiquidity of the several assets will make up differences in money returns expected from each kind of asset and will determine their current prices.[2] In this sense, a general exposition of the liquidity preference theory would be found in the own-rates of interest model of Chapter 17 of *The General Theory* rather than in the listing of the motives for holding money presented in Chapter 15. Keynes's statement on the interest rate quoted above, for instance, can be put in terms of own-rates of interest as follows. Let the subscripts b and m stand for bonds and money, respectively. Then in equilibrium:

$$a_b + q_b - c_b - r_b = a_m + q_m - c_m - r_m \tag{6.1}$$

By convention we assume $a_m = q_m = c_m = 0$. In fact, r_m should also be null but we will keep it just to make explicit the meaning we give to liquidity preference. Then (6.1) becomes

$$a_b + q_b - c_b - r_b = - r_m \qquad (6.2)$$

or

$$a_b + q_b - c_b = r_b - r_m \qquad (6.3)$$

that is, the money yield a bond has to offer to wealth holders in equilibrium is equal to its excess risk as compared to money, which is precisely the meaning of 'the' interest rate given by Keynes above. If one remembers that the own-rate of interest is equivalent to the marginal efficiency of a given asset, defined for the same conditions,[3] we can see that the traditional Keynesian statement that in equilibrium the marginal efficiency of capital has to be equal to the interest rate is another variant of the same condition. If we take the subscript k to stand for capital we have

$$a_k + q_k - c_k - r_k = a_b + q_b - c_b - r_b \qquad (6.4)$$

which, through rearranging, becomes

$$(a_k + q_k - c_k) - (a_b + q_b - c_b) = r_k - r_b \qquad (6.5)$$

That is, the excess of expected money yields given by capital goods over bonds is equal to the excess of risk that capital goods represent when compared to bonds. One could make the same statement comparing directly capital goods and money and obtaining a 'liquidity preference determination of the marginal efficiency of capital', meaning by that that capital goods will be demanded if prospective profits are enough to overcome the uncertainties surrounding their purchase; that is, their illiquidity or again the risks of wealth loss they represent in case the expectations of wealth holders are disappointed, forcing them to try to sell the asset.

In this sense, if we appeal to a more disaggregated structure of assets, we see that liquidity preference is in fact a more general theory than just an alternative specification of the demand for money function. It is 'the' Keynesian theory of asset returns and, thus, as seen in the preceding chapter, of asset prices. Liquidity, as we saw, is a question of degree and is attached to many different assets. The validity of the model is not threatened by empirical tests applied to narrowly defined 'money markets'. On the other hand, liquidity preference theory does emphasize the peculiar role of money in monetary economies. As will be seen in chapter 11 below, the view that different assets satisfy liquidity preferences in various degrees in different circumstances will be very important to the development of a Post Keynesian theory of inflationary regimes, when money loses much of its attributes. Although the own-rates model is general enough to deal with the whole spectrum of assets of an economy, money and capital goods can be singled out for deeper analysis because they are, undoubtedly, particularly important in this scheme since they identify the two extremes of the liquidity scale that ultimately determines the need for assets to generate compensating monetary yields.[4] For this reason, we will single them out for explicit detailed examination in this chapter and in the next. One should keep it in mind, nevertheless, that, in a Post Keynesian approach, the demand for money as an asset and the demand for investment goods share a common nature not only between themselves but also with other assets. They are all forms of wealth and they will be demanded according to the compensations they give for the risks they represent.

MONEY

We established in Chapter 3 that the starting point of Post Keynesian monetary analysis is the notion of money of account, the unit in which contractual commitments are denominated. The role of money as a means of circulation, and even more so its role as a store of value, are closely related to its power to discharge contractual obligations. Every operation in a monetary economy can be seen as establishing a contract between two parties.[5] Even spot transactions, like an over-the-counter sale of a good, involve a contract through which one party is committed to the immediate delivery of a good and the other to the immediate payment for it. The fact that no paper is signed does not change the nature of the operation that is the free acceptance of mutual obligations. If one party violates the commitment (for instance, by not paying for the good purchased) the other is entitled to seek the help of the state to enforce the accepted obligation. The same is, of course, valid for forward contracts.

Forward contracts usually involve the formal signature of documents specifying the obligations each party is accepting. This happens either because the operations are more complex or because the lag between the date of the agreement and its settlement makes memory unreliable to ensure compliance, even if one rules out moral hazard.[6] In any case, written forward contracts or implicit spot contracts are discharged by something defined in the Laws of Contracts. This recognizes an intrinsically institutional dimension of monetary theory, since

by the mention of contracts and offers, we have introduced law or custom, by which they are enforceable; that is to say, we have introduced the State of the community. Furthermore it is a peculiar characteristic of money contracts that it is the state or community not only which enforces delivery but also which decides what it is that must be delivered as a lawful or customary discharge of a contract that has been concluded in terms of the money of account. (*CWJMK*, V, p. 4)[7]

The means of discharging contractual obligations is the legal tender, something that thus represents the money of account and derives its 'moneyness' from this representation. Thus the legal tender is the generally acceptable means of payment. Whichever performs this role, in correspondence with contractual stipulations, that is, with the obligations set in terms of the money of account, is money. If there are perfect substitutes for legal tender (for instance, because some market maker guarantees fixed exchange rates between some asset, such as demand deposits in commercial banks, and the legal tender) these substitutes will also have the property of discharging obligations and will be money.[8,9]

Being money of account for forward contracts means that, at least for the operations and the period that are covered by the contract, the 'value' of that unit is stable. The larger the proportion between activities regulated by contract and the overall economy and the longer the maturity of contracts, the more stable is the 'real value' of the money of account. Thus the existence of an ample framework of forward money contracts is a support for the stability of the purchasing power of money. On the other hand, to accept the definition of rights and obligations in a given money of account, the parties have to trust that their value in terms of the real goods that are relevant for each party will remain stable. Money is the language that unites agents in a monetary economy. Contracts are its grammar. To work efficiently as a language, money has to behave in a stable (although not necessarily static) manner. In fact there develops a virtuous circle: the more stable the value of money is expected to be, the more likely it will be that agents will enter into contractual obligations denominated in money.[10] If this virtuous circle is achieved, expectations of the future value of money will be inelastic and shocks may be absorbed without threatening the stability of the overall economy.[11]

If the function of money of account is supported by a developed system of contracts that project it into the future, the object that discharges contractual obligations will not only be accepted as a means to liquidate current obligations but also be trusted as a means to discharge future commitments. In other words, the means of payment becomes a very efficient store of value, something acceptable at any time to discharge forward and future spot obligations. It is this property that makes money an asset in a monetary economy; that is, an economy based on a system of forward contracts.[12] As Davidson puts it:

The existence of time-related markets and contracts for performance and money payments is the essence of a money economy, for it is basic to the concept of liquidity. Liquidity in a temporal setting, given the money wage and the resulting price level, is the cornerstone of Keynes' revolution. (Davidson, 1978b, p. 61)

MONEY DEMAND

Post Keynesian monetary theory is a development of Keynes's views on money, and in particular of his central insight that is given by the perception of money as more than just a convenient way to bridge inflows and outflows of resources, as in the old Marshallian monetary theory.[13] As a mere exposition device we will develop this insight in terms of money demand and supply. As will be clear later, however, a distinctive characteristic of Post Keynesian approaches to money is the perception that money may be created as a result of the operation of the economy itself, making a clear-cut contrast between supply of and demand for money to a large extent empty.

The origins of the Post Keynesian monetary theory are found in *A Treatise on Money*, through the distinction proposed by Keynes between two circuits of monetary circulation: the industrial circulation and the financial circulation. The industrial circulation refers to the amount of money necessary to sustain the turnover of goods and services in the economy. It corresponds broadly to the role of money that was considered by the Quantity Theory, focusing on the necessity of means of circulation to allow transactions with goods and services to take place. The amount of money required to perform these functions, naturally, depended on the average retention of money balances on the part of the public; that is to say, the velocity of money. In the *Treatise*, Keynes approached the demand for active money balances, classifying it into two groups: that of households (denominated by Keynes as 'income deposits') and that of firms (called 'business deposits A'). In the first case, one is considering the habits and institutions that govern the making of payments by households, having to do with sales of productive services and spending in consumption goods. In the second, one refers to the circulation of money in the purchase of factors of production and sales of final goods and services.

The novelty with respect to the quantity theory of money was in the concept of financial circulation. Orthodox approaches to money could not ignore the empirical fact of hoarding or the retention of inactive balances. However, as Keynes said some years later (*CWJMK*, XIV, p. 115), to hoard could only be seen as an irrational choice in the context of a cooperative economy of the kind considered by classical economics. Money was seen as only a temporary form of wealth, inferior to any other since it was 'barren', except for the short periods of time for which gains from financial placements could be insufficient to cover the costs of financial transactions. Money was thus a 'convenience', not an asset. The development of the notion of financial circulation, in contrast, allowed Keynes to develop some really novel ideas with respect to the nature of money and of a monetary economy.

The financial circulation dealt with the amount of money used in operations with assets. It included both active balances used to buy and sell assets ('business deposits B') and inactive balances held in the expectation of future changes in interest rates. Those who expected interest rates to rise in the relevant future (and, thus, the price of securities to fall) would prefer to hold money in order to avoid future capital losses. On the other hand, those who expected interest rates to fall in the future would buy securities instead of holding money to enjoy the capital gains. The first group was called 'bears', the second 'bulls'. Current interest rates would move according to the predominance of one or other group until the demand for money and for securities was balanced with the availability of both types of assets.

The most visible feature of the financial circulation was its unrelatedness to the circulation of goods and services. Even though there were channels between them, particularly as regards the influence of interest rates in the purchase of real capital assets,[14] the motives behind financial operations have little to do with income-generating activities, breaking any proportionality relation between the total amount of money in circulation and aggregate income, the cornerstone of the Quantity Theory.[15] The seeds of change, however, were, at a deeper level, the acknowledgement that holding money was an alternative to holding other assets, which was precisely what was to become the focus of Keynes's later concept of monetary economy as one in which money was non-neutral even in the long period. Agents were now comparing gains derived from financial and monetary 'assets'. It was not hoarding, it was speculation. In terms of monetary theory, one can safely say that the basis for the Keynesian revolution was already outlined in the *Treatise on Money*.

In *The General Theory*, unfortunately, Keynes played down this dichotomy between industrial and financial circulations in favour of a more abstract approach in which an undifferentiated 'public' demands money for various 'motives'. Many authors complain about Keynes having left the 'monetary detail in the background', as he said in the preface to *The General Theory* (Keynes, 1964, p. vii). In fact, in the *Treatise*, not only were the concepts of industrial and financial circulations examined in much more detail than was accomplished in *The General Theory*, but important features of that approach were lost or eclipsed in the more abstract 1936 model: for instance, the distinction Keynes made between firms and households, between routine production operations and speculative financial transactions.

The industrial circulation became the transactions motive of *The General Theory*, which means that some room for the validity of the operation of the Quantity Theory was never entirely eliminated by Keynes. From the moment that money could play other roles than a mere convenience bridging two income transactions, the Quantity Theory would never be more than a partial rendering of money's functions. But it had a field of application in the function of money as a means of circulation.[16]

Many developments have been derived from the notion of transactionary demand for money, most of them coming from other schools of thought, something that should not be surprising since this is, as we have argued, a point of confluence with other schools. In particular, the idea of studying the 'technology of transactions' to explore the requirements of money for the circulation of goods and services is most promising. The 'technology' refers basically to the asynchronies that are involved in the operation of an economy that is constituted by several time-consuming activities of production and distribution. There are technical asynchronies connected with the differences in the production cycles of each good or service, that prevent all payments from being made simultaneously.[17] There are also institutional asynchronies resulting, in particular, from the differences in duration of the several types of contracts that are entered into in the economy.

The study of the technology of transactions allows us to treat these asynchronies as data or as variables, depending on the context for which the analysis is made. Progress in the modes of payment, changes in the structure of production, institutional changes (for instance, those induced by inflation or by financial innovation) can be studied and have their effects traced in this approach.

The financial circulation was approached in *The General Theory* through two 'motives' for holding money: the precautionary and the speculative. The precautionary motive received a surprisingly perfunctory treatment in *The General Theory*. In fact, one could argue that it is in relation to the precautionary demand for money that the specificity of Keynes's views on money as an asset should be mainly predicated. When Keynes suggested that money was a defence against uncertainty which would dominate when 'we simply don't know' what may lie ahead, and also that 'money lulls our disquietude' he was obviously referring to the feeling of safety money confers upon its possessor in the face of unpredictable difficulties in the future. This is precisely the precautionary motive: 'To provide for contingencies requiring sudden expenditure and for unforeseen opportunities of advantageous purchase, and also to hold an asset of which the value is fixed in terms of money' (Keynes, 1964, p. 196).

The precautionary motive, in contrast to the transactionary demand and, as we will see, to the speculative demand for money, seems to depend less on expectations proper and more on the state of confidence on these expectations. It relates to the degree of ignorance about the future, money serving as defence against dangers that sometimes cannot even be conceived in advance. Money represents the possibility of quickly reshaping strategies if and when information finally allows the formation of safer or more definite expectations.

The difficulty of being a function of the state of confidence is that of the nature of the state of confidence itself, something elusive and impossible to convert even into a theoretically meaningful variable, let alone something empirically measurable. Being impossible to pin down to some market variable, such as income or interest rates, the precautionary demand for money becomes as intractable as the state of confidence itself. Keynes's hand-waving suggestion was to merge it with the transactionary demand, having both as functions of income.

This choice was very unfortunate because it allowed the more revolutionary element of Keynes's monetary theory to be absorbed into the more traditional statement of monetary theory, which is that money is demanded in proportion to current income. The unpredictable shifts in liquidity preference rooted in the changes in the degree of uncertainty felt by agents are played down, allowing the postulation of fundamentally stable money demand functions comparable to the also stable, institutionally based Quantity Theory.

One of Keynes's closest followers, R. F. Kahn, was also one of the most forceful critics of Keynes's treatment of the precautionary demand for money. In a classic 1954 paper, Kahn explored in detail the operation of this demand (Kahn, 1972, chap. 4). His main contention was that the precautionary demand for money was a twin demand to the speculative demand, not to the transactions demand for money. The speculative demand for money would emerge when an agent expected the rate of interest to move in a given direction in the future (as was the case of 'bears'). On the other hand, one should identify the precautionary motive when the agent expects interest rates (and therefore the capital value of non-monetary assets) to change but does not know in which direction or does not trust his expectation as to which direction they will take. In this case, according to Kahn, agents will keep money reserves depending on whether they are more averse to income risk or to capital risk. Income risk refers to possible losses of income if the agent keeps his portfolio mainly in money, which does not pay interest. Capital risk affects longer-lived assets that have their market values dependent on the levels of interest rates. Agents who are averse to capital risk tend to keep some wealth in monetary form even if they are 'bulls'; that is, even if they expect interest rates to go down and the prices of securities to increase.[18]

Finally, in *The General Theory*, Keynes identified a third motive for demanding money, which he called speculative motive. As a matter of fact, this motive had already been extensively examined in the *Treatise on Money*, when Keynes showed how interest rates (and the prices of assets) were determined. This motive also pertains to the financial circulation, since it deals with the role of money in the turnover of securities.

The speculative motive is based on the idea of normality, discussed in Chapter 2. Refusing the neoclassical notion of a natural rate of interest, rooted in real factors such as time preferences and productivity, as an objective gravity centre around which markets' interest rates move, Keynes suggested instead that every agent operating with assets has a subjective evaluation of a 'normal' rate of interest that is expected to prevail after all short-term fluctuations are taken into account. This normal interest rate works as an anchor to his expectations and to the choice of strategies of accumulation because it indicates likely future movements of market interest rates. In other words, the agent judges the sustainability of the current interest rate and the direction towards which it will probably change by the divergence between this current rate and that considered normal.

The idea of normality is essentially subjective. It depends on how the agent judges his own experience and how he interprets the current conditions as to the extent to which any fundamental change may have taken place that could change the normal values. Therefore different people will evaluate the likely future path of interest rates differently, according to their own idea of normality. For Keynes there is no reason why individually set normal values should coincide. On the contrary, the divergence of expectations is responsible, as will be seen, for the stability that may characterize these markets.

The choice between money and securities is described along the same lines set out in the *Treatise*, presented above. The market interest rate works as the factor balancing the demand and supply of money and of securities. Rises in the current interest rate will transform bears into bulls, and the converse, changing the excess demands for money and securities until agents are willing to hold exactly the available amounts of both assets. The divergence of expectations is a condition of stability because, if all agents had the same expectations, they would all try to sell or to buy, depending on whether they are all bears or all bulls and the price of securities would vary between zero and infinity.

In sum, the speculative demand for money is the demand of bears, of those whose expectation about the interest rate is that it is going to rise. Movements of the market rate of interest transform bulls into bears or bears into bulls until the demand for securities is balanced with the supply of securities.

In the post-publication debates with the critics of *The General Theory*, Keynes introduced a fourth motive for demanding money, which was called finance motive. It was midway between the demand for active balances, such as the transactionary demand for money, and inactive balances, such as the precautionary and the speculative demands. The finance motive was related to out-of-routine expenditures, such as investments, for which some preparation was deemed necessary by agents. It was assumed that, when planning some discretionary expenditure, agents would try to accumulate some liquid reserves in advance of actual expenditure in order to obtain better credit conditions, or to guarantee some autonomy of decision, or for any other motive. During the period in which these balances were being held they could be seen as inactive balances, as with the speculative or precautionary motives, subtracting resources from active circulation unless banks accommodated these additional demands. Nevertheless, they also had a similar nature to that of the transactionary motive, and thus to active balances, since they were held with a view to a specific expenditure at a definite date. As with the transactions demand, money here is a 'convenience', a means of bridging two acts of receipt and disbursement. Once it was spent it would replenish active circulation, allowing another agent to withhold it for the 'financial motive'.

Because of its dual nature, Keynes called the finance motive a 'coping-stone' of his monetary theory, a connection between two components that were being described in a sharply differentiated way. In any case, an efficient monetary system should be able to satisfy the demand for money for the finance motive as much as the demand for money for transactionary, precautionary or speculative motives. The funds to satisfy the finance motive, however, because of being inactive balances that were periodically transformed into active balances again (when the disbursement was effected), constituted a revolving fund, in the sense that, being put into circulation through the expenditure by its former possessor, it could again be held as inactive balances by another agent with discretionary spending plans. The finance motive has to do with the demand for money and it is in the above sense that the funds are freed for new use when they are spent. Unfortunately, the finance motive has been given by many a totally different interpretation, relative to the liquidity of the balance sheet of investors or banks or whoever else it might be. These are different problems, to be treated elsewhere. The finance motive is concerned with the circulation of money, not financing strategies.[19]

MONEY SUPPLY

A central issue in the recent debate on the behaviour of the money supply has been whether the latter is exogenously or endogenously fixed. To a large extent, the opposition between Keynesian and monetarist economists has been centred around the question of the relative efficacy of monetary policies, contrasting measures to control reserves to attempts to regulate interest rates.

Even some non-mainstream Keynesians have felt the need to identify themselves as endogenists or exogenists, usually as the former, in the understanding that the validity of orthodoxy hinges on the choice that is made as to how money is created. Kaldor (1982), for instance, accuses Keynes of submitting to orthodoxy because of his liquidity preference theory and his consideration of an exogenously given money supply in *The General Theory*. Moore (1988), in addition, claims that Keynes's assumptions as to the properties of money are only valid for more primitive commodity-money systems and not for modern, allegedly credit-money economies.

In what follows we suggest that these views are largely mistaken. Firstly because, no matter how important the issue may be for the evaluation of the relative efficacy of alternative monetary control instruments, no really fundamental theoretical line divides 'verticalists' and 'horizontalists' in terms of essential monetary theory. The opposition between liquidity preference theory and the several versions of the quantity theory of money (including loanable funds models) refers to the way money affects the decisions to produce and to invest, no matter how it comes into existence. One can be an endogenist and, at the same time, very orthodox in fundamental theoretical matters, as Wicksell and Schumpeter have proved. It is much more, if we want to retain the dichotomy, a question of demand for money than of its supply.

In an important sense, however, one can say Keynes has presented an original approach to the determination of the money supply, although certainly not in *The General Theory*. The proposition of Keynes, however, is not of an automatically accommodating monetary system or an entirely rigid one. The crux of Keynes's approach is the consideration that money is partly created by private agents, banks, and that the behaviour of these agents has to be understood with the same basic motivations as any other agent. In particular, one has to consider that banks have their own liquidity preference schedule. It is through the portfolio choices made by banks that we will approach the question as to whether or not money is endogenous or exogenous.[20]

From the start we should mention that an entirely endogenous or perfectly accommodating monetary system seems to be contradictory to the very idea of monetary economy. In fact, Keynes argued, in support of his assumption that money is characterized by low elasticities of production and substitution:

The attribute of 'liquidity' is by no means independent of the presence of these two characteristics. For it is unlikely that an asset, of which the supply can be easily increased or the desire for which can be easily diverted by a change in relative price, will possess the attribute of 'liquidity' in the minds of the owners of wealth. Money itself rapidly loses the attribute of 'liquidity' if its future supply is expected to undergo sharp changes. (Keynes, 1964, p. 241n)

If the availability of money can be subject to 'sharp changes', its future value becomes too uncertain for agents to accept contractual obligations in such a unit. If contract duration shrinks, expectations about the future value of money may become elastic, making the whole system unstable. Of course it is not being argued that the money supply is to remain fixed or even that it can only increase according to a pre-determined rule. What Keynes seems to suggest, however, is that it is necessary to have some identifiable sources of discipline in the monetary system to support confidence in the maintenance of its real value.

The difficulty, however, is that, in a modern monetary economy, most of what constitutes money is created by private agents. Post Keynesians consider money as the set of assets comprising the legal tender and its perfect substitutes; that is, those for which there exists a second-hand market and a market maker able to guarantee immediate convertibility into legal tender at fixed or almost fixed exchange rates. It is this requirement that allows some private debts, such as demand deposits in commercial banks, to become money:

Bank money is, of course, simply evidence of a private debt contract, but the discovery of the efficiency of 'clearing', that is the realisation that some forms of private debt can be used in settlement of the overlapping myriad of private contracts, immensely increased the efficiency of the monetary system. Three conditions are necessary in order for such a private debt to operate as a medium of exchange: 1. the private debt must be denominated in terms of the monetary unit; 2. a clearing institution for these private debts must be developed; and 3. assurances that uncleared debts are convertible at a known parity into the legally enforceable medium of exchange. (Davidson, 1978a, pp. 151–2)

According to Keynes, one has to consider two elements in the process of money creation: the creation of reserves by the monetary authorities and the creation of deposits by banks.[21] The creation of reserves depends on the investment policy of the Central Bank. Even if there are more or less compulsory channels to force the creation of reserves, such as, in some cases, the operation of the discount window, there are other instruments at the disposal of the Central Bank, the Open Market, that are assumed to be very effective. As Keynes once wrote: 'This method . . . seems tó me to be the ideal one . . . it enables the Bank of England to maintain an absolute control over the creation of credit by the member banks' (*CWJMK*, VI, p. 207).

For any given policy of the monetary authorities, the actual creation of money will depend on the behaviour of banks. The portfolio choices of banks are oriented by the need to combine profitability with liquidity. According to the conditions in which existing asset possibilities offer those two attributes, banks will choose an investment policy which will ultimately determine the money supply. This is so because money is created by banks when they create deposits that are used to buy assets from the public as, for instance, when a loan is made. Banks can direct their resources to the financial circulation (when they buy government bonds and bills, for instance) or to the industrial circulation (if they finance the working capital of firms).[22] Depending on the choices made by banks, not only can the money supply vary but also the relation between the availability of money and aggregate demand can be different, since resources directed towards the financial circulation do not directly affect the demand for goods and services, as discussed above. Thus the final effect of a policy by the authorities on the money supply depends on private decisions as to what to do with the reserves that a Central Bank may decide to create. This is a factor of endogeneity, although it would be hardly conceivable as leading to a horizontal supply curve of money.

When Keynes wrote the *Treatise* the choices open to banks referred basically to the investments they could make. Modern banks have more varied and complex choices, since they can also actively search for resources in what is called liability management. The essential point, however, remains: the money supply, and in particular the availability of money for industrial circulation, depends on portfolio choices by banks, that is to say, on their liquidity preference.

In a sense, this approach suggests that the very dichotomy between demand and supply of money is too narrow. It is the same fundamental factor that is in operation in both sides of the market: liquidity preference. This approach allows us also to overcome another difficulty, pointed out by Chick (1983a, p. 188). Keynes based his principle of effective demand on the deflationary effect of the shift of the demand for assets towards irreproducible money. The public, however, does not keep physical 'pieces' of money but holds deposits at banks. This does not, per se, have to be deflationary, since banks can themselves re-lend the resources that are deposited with them, activating the demands of other agents. Keynes actually not only recognized this possibility but emphasized it when he formulated his Clearing Union proposals by the end of the Second World War. Calling it 'the banking principle', Keynes presented the idea thus:

No depositor in a local bank suffers because the balances, which he leaves idle, are employed to finance the business of someone else. Just as the development of national banking systems served to offset a deflationary pressure which would have prevented otherwise the development of modern industry, so by carrying this analogy into the international field we may hope to offset the contractionist pressure which might otherwise overwhelm in social disorder and disappointment the good hopes of our modern world. (*CWJMK*, XXV, p. 75)

In this sense, it is not the household sector that can ultimately generate effective demand failures but firms that may prefer liquid assets to physical capital goods and banks that can choose to direct financial resources to the financial circulation instead of towards the needs of industry. In the words of Minsky, 'the essential liquidity preference in a capitalist economy is that of bankers and businessmen' (Minsky, 1982, p. 74). The banking principle is not enough to rule out the possibility of deficiency of effective demand.

The need for liquidity, of course, changes with the phases of the economic cycle. The perception of risks and the demands for safety are changed and not only for banks. Households and firms also become more 'bullish' in the upswing (and more 'bearish' in the downswing), allowing the banks that issue them deposits to accept higher degrees of illiquidity. In this sense, also, one may see an element of endogeneity in the creation of money.[23]

Both verticalist and horizontalist views seem to miss most of these points, because of their oversimplification of the way both the monetary authority and the banks operate. In particular, the horizontalist view, the extreme endogenism, not only fails adequately to conceive of banks' behaviour but also ignores the existence of a financial circulation, in the sense proposed above. One only sees money being created as credit to purchase goods as if the finance of working capital was not only the main function of banks but actually their only one. Kaldor (1982) explicitly considers only the demand for credit as the way money is created (p. 22). A Post Keynesian monetary theory that keeps its roots in Keynes's monetary thought, in contrast, realizes that banks are not only endowed with their own liquidity preference scale but also that they find themselves at the crossroad between the industrial and the financial circulations. Monetary policy can affect aggregate demand by changing the relative attractiveness for banks of applications into one or the other circuits. It is not the general public that matters, but the banks' portfolio choices.

Restricting their discussions to the industrial circulation, the extreme endogenists are able to tell only a partially correct story. It is true that it may be useless for the Central Bank to create reserves if a bank cannot find borrowers, but it is only with the industrial circulation that the demand for money is independent of the supply. The creation of money in the financial circulation affects both supply and demand, because it changes interest rates and, thus, the relative attractiveness of the several placements. In the latter form of intervention there is no reason to suppose the Central Bank to be powerless to affect the amount of money in circulation.[24] Moreover, through their effect on interest rates and, thus, on productive investments, monetary changes initiated by the monetary authority can find their way into the industrial circulation as well.

Before leaving the subject, one should add that, in this approach, money is not the same concept as credit or as 'liquidity', as understood in the Radcliffe Report. Money is believed to be the foundation for the liquidity of all other assets, that have to be converted into money to represent a claim over other forms of wealth. For the same reason, banks are not similar to other financial institutions, at least as long as the latter do not possess clearing systems and lender-of-last-resort facilities. To emphasize these points is important because they relate to the possibility of endogenously creating liquidity through financial innovations. As Minsky pointed out, financial innovations actually reduce liquidity instead of extending it (Minsky, 1982, chap. 7) and should be considered, for the present discussion, as presenting no problems other than those posed by other decisions made by agents to trade liquidity for profits.

SUMMING UP

In this chapter we have showed that, contrary to common usage, liquidity preference is not just a theory of demand for money, but a model of determination of asset returns and asset prices. The fundamental statement of the model is that an asset to be purchased must offer the perspective of monetary yields sufficient to cover for its relative illiquidity with respect to the reference asset.

Nevertheless justification was found for special attention being given to money and to capital goods as they represent the extreme points of a liquidity scale, from an asset that in principle does not have to offer monetary yields because of having maximum liquidity to the most illiquid asset the demand for which is only feasible if heavy returns are expected.

In the rest of the chapter the nature of money and the motives for its being demanded were discussed and it was shown that the creation of money by banks could be understood as a result of the same determinants responsible for the overall public demand for money.

NOTES

1. That 'money' in *The General Theory* is an aggregate that may include more elements than its more precise meaning allows for is clear from footnote 1 to Keynes (1964, p. 167) where money is suggested to include up to three-month bills. On aggregation in *The General Theory*, see also Leijonhufvud, 1968.
2. Robinson's classic study on the rate of interest (Robinson, 1979) extends Keynes's concepts into a model of the structure of interest rates rather than 'the' interest rate.
3. That own-rates of interest and marginal efficiencies are equivalent concepts is made clear by Keynes himself in his paper to Fisher's Festschrift, reproduced in *CWJMK*, XIV, pp. 101–8. Also, 'I regard the rate of interest as being the marginal efficiency (or productivity) of money measured in terms of itself' (*CWJMK*, XIV, p. 92).
4. In the next chapter we will discuss the demand for capital goods, showing that this general approach is not contradictory to the notions of uncertainty that surround distant time horizons or to notions such as conventional behaviour or 'animal spirits', that seem to minimize the role calculations can exert in the choice of assets.
5. For a definition of elementary spot and forward contracts, see Davidson (1978a).
6. Non-written forward contracts can be broken more easily but this does not mean that they cannot be important in some particular situations, such as, for instance, Okun's implicit contracts relative to job promotion. See Okun (1980).
7. The importance of the state in the determination of what should act as legal tender is emphasized not only in the *Treatise* but also in the *Tract on Monetary Reform*. See also Davidson (1978a).
8. The importance of the existence of clearing systems and lender-of-last-resort facilities to the banking system is discussed in the last section of this chapter.
9. The Keynesian concept of money, thus, is theoretically well defined according to its explicit functions instead of the 'ad hocery' characteristic of, for instance, Milton Friedman's approach to the definition of money.
10. On the need for stability to make it possible to build a system of contracts see Davidson (1982, pp. 146–7).
11. Expectations are inelastic if, in the event of a current change, they react less than proportionally to the size of the change. Inelasticity of expectations is an important stability requirement in some models. See Hicks (1946).
12. See Wells (1983, p. 524). See also Robinson in *CWJMK*, XIII, pp. 646–7.
13. The Marshallian quantity theory and its developments, including those by Keynes in his early monetary writings, are discussed in Kahn (1984).
14. Keynes was unable to explore these channels in the *Treatise* because of his failure to distinguish between financial placements and capital goods. See Kregel (1988).
15. See *CWJMK*, V, p. 222.
16. It is important to keep in mind that the Quantity Theory is incomplete rather than completely wrong because in situations where the other attributes of money disappear, and it ceases to be an asset, as in hyperinflations, the Quantity Theory, although in a modified version to take into account endogenous changes in velocity induced by inflation itself, becomes an important conceptual instrument of analysis. Keynes's frequent allusions to the possibility of a 'flight from money' in extreme situations suggest that he never abandoned his early views on the ways a hyperinflation operates. What was abandoned was the idea that the hyperinflationary regime is in any sense a fair stylization of the normal

operation of a monetary economy. These insights are also valid for a critique of analyses such as Cagan (1956) or Sargent (1981) that see hyperinflations as laboratory experiments for the Quantity Theory since changes in the value of real variables are dwarfed in the face of monetary changes, making it possible to 'isolate' monetary mechanisms from real mechanisms. In an extreme situation like this the 'real' mechanism is impaired as much as the monetary, with feedback effects from one into the other, preventing the notion of isolation of variables in any sense.

17. The simultaneity of payments in general equilibrium models is obtained because they deal with either existing goods or with promises of future goods. Production was either completed before the transactions began or will begin after transactions are completed.

18. Kahn's discussion of the precautionary motive and the types of risk-aversion are an alternative to Tobin's 1958 reinterpretation of liquidity preference in which the idea of probabilistic risk is introduced in order to obtain the result that agents will tend to diversify their portfolios. In both works one gets the result that at least some agents will keep money and securities in the portfolios. Tobin obtains it, however, by sacrificing Keynes's notion of uncertainty. Kahn, in contrast, although recognizing, like Tobin, that the speculative demand for money is not an adequate portrayal of the functions of money as an asset, prefers to solve the problem within the concepts offered by Keynes himself.

19. See *CWJMK*, XIV, pp. 208–9. For some interpretations see Davidson (1982, p. 124–5); Chick (1983a, pp. 198–200).

20. Similar points are made by Chick, 1983a, p. 236; Kregel, 1984–5; Chick, 1979, pp. 19–20.

21. That reserves may constitute a limit to expansion of deposits in Keynes's view is seen from *CWJMK*, V, p. 3; VI, p. 201.

22. On the role of banks in financing working capital see *CWJMK*, XIII, pp. 84–6; XII, chap. 3.

23. The point that cyclical changes affect the need for liquidity of banks and the general public at the same time is made by Keynes in *CWJMK*, XIII, pp. 87–8 and Robinson, 1979, pp. 20, 62.

24. These two methods are called respectively 'income-generating finance' and 'portfolio change' by Davidson, 1978a.

7. Own-rates of Interest and Investment

We showed in the preceding chapter that the Post Keynesian theory of the demand for money is a particular case of the asset-choice model presented by Keynes in Chapter 17 of *The General Theory*. So is the marginal efficiency of capital theory of investment. In fact, marginal efficiency and own-rate of interest are equivalent concepts and Keynes himself used them interchangeably in many contexts since they both measure the yields that are expected to flow from the use or possession of an asset, allowance being made for the uncertainties involved in this kind of operation.

The central argument, we should remember, is that any asset is a claim over future income. It has to be converted into goods in the future, either for enjoyment or for further accumulation. Some assets are converted into income by being sold. Others are converted by being used up in the creation of income. This is measured by the rate of depreciation plus any form of scarcity rent it may generate. The hypothesis is that the money value of the returns expected from an asset during a given retention period must be such as to compensate the risks it embodies by being a specific form of accumulation of wealth in comparison to a general (and, thus, safer) form of wealth, that is money itself. This was the hypothesis for bonds in the last chapter and it is the same hypothesis for investment goods in this chapter, though not through any liquidity premium as a store of value but as an income-generating asset. In equilibrium, which is understood here as referring to a situation in which wealth owners are satisfied with their portfolios, given their expectations of returns for the various assets, returns of all assets, adjusted for their specific uncertainties, are equalized.[1]

This is not to deny that, in a less abstract analysis, important

117

peculiarities cannot be identified through the examination of assets of a specific nature. We conducted this kind of examination in Chapter 6, with relation to money. In this chapter we will do the same with reference to investment goods, but one should keep in mind the general approach from which the following discussion springs.

THE INVESTMENT DECISION

Keynes's presentation of a theory of investment has been criticized by friends and foes alike. Some pointed to possible mistakes in the handling of the stock/flow relationships when defining the concept of marginal efficiency of capital (that they would prefer to see as the marginal efficiency of investment). Others stressed possible contradictions between the propositions of Chapter 11 of *The General Theory*, where Keynes offers a definite rule of calculation of expected returns, and Chapter 12, where Keynes defends the importance of the notion of animal spirits under the argument that calculation is not possible when uncertainty about the future prevails.[2]

In the discussion that follows the position is assumed that the fundamental insights for a Post Keynesian theory of investment are those offered in Chapter 12 of *The General Theory*. The role of the marginal efficiency concept is to offer a theoretical measure of returns, in the same sense as the own-rates of interest, to allow the exposition of the argument to be developed with formal rigour.[3]

Even though Keynes had accepted the marginal productivity theory of wages,[4] he denied the same validity to a marginal productivity theory of profits or of interest. In fact he argued that capital assets earned a scarcity rent rather than a payment for services. This scarcity, which could be overcome if enough investment was made, was kept for reasons rooted not in the productive infrastructure of the economy but in the very institutional structure of a monetary economy that made the investment decision subordinate to an asset-choice process:

It is much preferable to speak of capital as having a yield over the course of its life in excess of its original cost, than as being productive. For the only reason why an asset offers a prospect of yielding during its life services having an aggregate value greater than its initial supply price is because it is scarce; and it is kept scarce because of the competition of the rate of interest on money. If capital becomes less scarce, the excess yield will diminish, without its having become less productive – at least in the physical sense. (Keynes, 1964, p. 213)[5]

Some authors have seen in this quotation some approximation to a labour theory of value and to Marx. This is not the only part of *The General Theory* where Keynes makes some friendly remarks on a labour theory of value (see, for instance, the chapter on the choice of units) but it is a mistake to take it as closeness to Marx. The idea that earnings of capital goods owners are due to scarcity is closer to Marshall's concept of quasi-rent than to Marx's theory of exploitation, a theory that Keynes, by the way, always treated with contempt. On the other hand, an approach to value concerned with measurement alone, such as Smith's labour-commanded theory of value, is much what Keynes had in mind (see, again, his choice of units discussion in Chapter 4 of *The General Theory*, perhaps the closest one can be to Adam Smith's version of the labour theory of value) in contrast to a model of exploitation such as Marx's.

Be that as it may, if marginal productivity was not an adequate basis for a theory of capital rewards it was even less adequate to a theory of investment. As we saw, it is not the physical returns that count but the monetary returns, something which involves market uncertainties that are greater the longer is the period ahead for which one is making investments. In an uncertain world, one cannot assume that the future will be like the past and, thus, current results cannot be simply projected into the future as the basis for an investment decision. It is the future that has to be telescoped into the present, not the other way around:

The mistake of regarding the marginal efficiency of capital primarily in terms of the current yield of capital equipment, which would be correct only in the static state where there is no changing future to influence the present, has had the result of breaking the theoretical link between today and tomorrow. (Keynes, 1964, p. 145)

The decision to buy capital goods does not include only long-lived items, such as machines or building plants. The relevant dividing line is traced, in a first step, separating assets that are producible goods from promises of payment, paper assets (including money). In a finer examination, different classes of goods have to be distinguished, according to their durability, value, degree of liquidity and so on.

Keynes took three types of capital goods into consideration: fixed capital, working capital and liquid capital. All of them are grouped as capital goods because they share an important characteristic: they are producible, which means that, if there is a stimulus to increase the availability of such assets, there will follow an increase in the rate of production of capital goods which, in turn, should lead to an expansion of employment, giving rise to secondary effects such as the consumption multiplier, to be examined later.

FIXED CAPITAL

Fixed capital goods are defined as long-lived items (that is, those that survive more than one production period).[6] This means that they have to be purchased with a view to a horizon longer than the immediate future. Their initial supply price is usually high (which makes it recoverable by the investor only after an extended period of time) and sometimes they can only be bought in sets of integrated units, which augments the amount that is necessary to spend to obtain them. In other words, indivisibility problems are often characteristic of fixed capital investments. Finally, these items tend to be specialized (although some types of equipment may be the object of more general demand) in some functions and also differentiated according to their age, as a result of continuing technical progress. As a result, they are generally highly illiquid, which means that, if the investor's expectations are disappointed, the capital losses following attempts to re-sell these items may be very heavy.

Given all these features, the decision to invest in fixed capital goods is, in principle, the riskier strategy of accumulation open to agents. Since they cannot be held as stores of value (given their illiquidity) their eventual purchase must be induced by very optimistic expectations as to their future quasi-rents, such as to overcome all their disadvantages.[7]

Given the time-horizon involved in this decision, the inducement to investment in fixed capital goods is the state of long-term expectations. These expectations are very complex because they are largely (but not entirely) autonomous in relation to current events. On the other hand, as discussed in Chapter 2, they are not related in any sense to the notion of long-period equilibrium values, which is, a notion adequate for an external observer of the economy, not for an internal participant. To determine long-period equilibrium values one has to know all (or at least all the relevant) elements influencing the result, and suppose them to remain constant while some convergence process operates in a given run of time. For the investor, uncertainty means precisely the opposite: not all relevant variables are known and even if some could be known, nothing guarantees they will remain constant.[8]

To discuss long-term expectations, one has to consider two elements: how the calculation of future rewards under conditions of uncertainty is made, and how confidence in these calculations is built. Let us recall from Chapter 4 how expectations are to be formed. The decision maker starts from a given set of known data, obtained from various sources such as technical blueprints, market research, institutional constraints and so on. The potential investor may know, then, from the start what the methods of production being considered are capable of achieving (after all, an engineering problem), if there are cultural or other types of restrictions against the use of the resulting good (such as, say, the production of alcoholic beverages in Muslim countries), if there are restrictions to entry in the market (such as cartel arrangements) or if there are institutional restrictions (safety regulations, zoning restrictions or quality standards, for example). All these factors are obtained as what we could consider, with Keynes, direct knowledge from which to start to build the probability statements that will serve to support an investment decision.[9]

Obviously, these data are not enough to orient investors with certainty. By themselves they are not enough even to lead to any conclusion, let alone certain conclusions. Information about current efficiency of production methods tells little about the possibilities of future innovations in processes and even less about possible product innovations that could kill the whole market.[10] Customers may change their minds. The size of markets may change because of larger events (for instance, economic policy changes). Rules of competition may be altered. About all these, and many other uncertainty-generating factors could be listed, the decision-maker has no safe information whatsoever. These are the missing premises he needs, however, to arrive at a decision. He will have to complement what he knows with what he imagines, with what Shackle called 'figments of imagination' to construct scenarios in terms of which he may able to decide.[11]

The problem then changes its form. The decision maker knows that he is forming expectations based on uncertain foundations and also that he would probably be unable to calculate how uncertain those expectations are, since he may feel that besides the data he imagined to fill the gaps in his knowledge many other values were also possible, even if he could not imagine them. In other words, the investor may be conscious that his power of constructing possible sequels in advance of his decision is limited and that entirely unpredictable (even inconceivable) developments can occur that would completely invalidate all his conjectures.[12]

So the decision to act based on these consciously known, imperfectly informed expectations will depend on how confident the agent is about them; in other words, on how significant is the weight of the evidence from which the expectations were formed. This is where 'animal spirits' come into play. Consideration of animal spirits is not contradictory per se with calculations. It refers to the course of action that will be chosen on the basis of these calculations. Its relevance is in making it possible for an agent to act even if the weight of the evidence he possesses is small. If he is confident about his power to identify sequels and relevant influences in the future, he will act even if the objective knowledge basis on which the decision is sustained is slight.

As a result, we should expect two agents with the same objective knowledge basis to form different expectations if they appeal to different 'figments of imagination' to complement it. But even if they did appeal to the same missing premises they might act differently, depending on the weight of the evidence that sustains their predictions and the degree of confidence they have in their own powers of prediction; that is, depending on their 'animal spirits'.

All this discussion points to an important feature of a Keynesian theory of investment, the functionality of reducing uncertainties to stimulate the acceptance of the considerable risks it involves. The more predictable the future, the larger is the knowledge basis for a prediction to be made and the safer an investment decision becomes, reducing the need for the almost supernatural entrepreneur that is implicit in the 'animal spirits' argument.[13] Alternatively, the lighter the penalties suffered by an agent who has taken the wrong decisions, the more likely it becomes that more agents will be able to accept the risks.

Reducing future uncertainties is one of the main roles of an economic policy designed along Keynesian lines. Long-term fiscal policies should be designed, for instance, to remove the uncertainties related to the cyclical fluctuations of the economy. This would signal to potential investors that aggregate demand would be stabilized (at full employment) so that they could take that information into their calculations.[14]

A second way of reducing uncertainties was taken by civil society itself, through the development of institutions that permitted a socialization of risks. Forward contracts, as we saw, are the most important and widespread of these institutions. The transformation of the nature of some especially risky decisions, such as the investment decision, is another of these institutional innovations.

Keynes mentioned the stock exchange as a device to reduce the illiquidity that plagues fixed capital goods. The latter, of course, are still illiquid but property claims on them can become negotiable, allowing any individual to think that, in case of need, he will be able to get rid of those assets through the sale of the stocks he owns. Moreover, stocks are divisible while fixed capital is not, allowing piecemeal operations that reduce the value of commitments anyone is required to maintain when making fixed capital investments. All these devices allow the 'common' individual to take part in strategies of accumulation that otherwise could only be assumed by 'real' entrepreneurs, those endowed with strong 'animal spirits'.

There is a dialectical effect, however, to be identified in these developments. Institutional arrangements and other kinds of support increase the safety with which all kinds of speculative deals, including investments, are made. Two consequences follow. Firstly, there emerges a general incentive to bolder speculative operations, since even more risk-averse agents can feel now that institutional safety nets are enough to warrant adventurous initiatives.[15] Riskier or more fragile deals become acceptable if there is some institution in the rearguard to contain the losses. Secondly, and related to it, less informed or able individuals begin to participate in the market who are characteristically more volatile and unstable in their expectations and actions since they do not always understand the ways of the market. They can be manipulated and exhibit the so-called 'mob-behaviour' that much amplifies any disequilibrium that may emerge.[16]

The paradoxical result is that institutions devised to increase the stability of the economy end up by also increasing its volatility. This is not the result of imperfect design. Rather, it is the unavoidable consequence of living under uncertainty. There are no unmixed blessings, nor is there any sure recipe for efficiency. The same practices and institutions that serve to promote growth also serve to amplify a crisis. The whole point is not to avoid the contradiction but to devise institutions that, on balance, allow enterprise to prevail over the casino and to remain forever alert for unexpected developments.

The introduction of institutions such as the stock exchange, that make illiquid investments liquid and allow the participation in the market of individuals who are not informed or prepared to understand it, gives rise to a very interesting phenomenon, which Keynes called conventional behaviour. A convention is a shared belief that is sustained basically by its own bootstraps; that is, it survives mainly because people see in its survival a sign of its adequacy. Facing an uncertain future, agents may feel that an efficient strategy may be to suppose that the future will repeat the past and present. That other people do act on this belief is seen as confirmation that the convention is reasonable because others may perhaps have some information which leads them to behave that way. Conventional behaviour is a way of acting when there is no better basis for judgement. It may be more or less solid if it reposes on old customs, laws or other institutions. Other conventions are more fragile, based only on current observation. In any case they work as an important factor of continuity as long as agents have no reason to suppose that the past 'normality' will be broken and new strategies will be required.

In Chapter 12 of *The General Theory*, Keynes applied the notion of convention to the behaviour of investors – people who evaluate the future as just a continuation of the past. Convention, however, is not a substitute for the state of long-term expectation as a determinant of investments in fixed capital. Unless they are anchored in some fundamental feature of society, conventions, or, at any rate, conventional beliefs about the behaviour of the economy, tend to be short-lived, given the empirical experience of agents with change. A conventional belief is useful for the study of, say, the behaviour of stock prices; that is, liquid assets that are bought to be resold at any desired moment, at prices that can be conventionally assumed to be a projection of current prices. Fixed capital goods, in contrast, are not purchased to be resold in the short term. They are bought to be kept for an extended period for which no conventional belief can be reasonably sustained and which no sensible investor could hold. So conventional behaviour is not a theory of long-term expectations. If anything, it is a mode of formation of short-term expectations that can become the inducement for financial placements, such as the purchase of stocks.

Up to this point we have discussed the inducement to invest. Current conditions have, in principle, little influence over this kind of reasoning, except for the actual knowledge basis on which the decision is made and, perhaps, for the influence that current events may have on the state of confidence.[17] The most important channel through which the present can influence the investment decision, however, is the financing of investments.[18]

When talking about finance we may think of two elements: the role of the rate of interest and the question of the availability of funds. The availability of funds is a two-fold question. On the one hand, it refers to the disposition of financial institutions in providing the necessary means to implement a given investment plan. According to Keynes, banks do not usually satisfy all demanders of funds, either because they do not want to reduce indefinitely the liquidity of their assets or because the demander may not qualify to obtain loans (Kahn, 1972, p. 146). There emerges then a 'fringe of unsatisfied borrowers' for whom loans are rationed. But availability does not refer only to volume but also to the terms on which these funds are offered. In Chapter 9 we will discuss the problem of the modes of financing expenditures, in particular the distinction between finance and funding that has an important role in the Post Keynesian theory of investment.

At a more general level of discussion, the leading role among financial variables would be assigned to the interest rate. The influence of the interest rate is felt at first as a crucial element for the evaluation of the demand price of the asset. The demand price of an asset is the present value of its expected yields. To obtain it, one has to discount future receipts to make them temporally equivalent and comparable. It represents the value that a potential buyer is willing to pay for an asset, the amount of money now that the buyer considers equivalent to the income stream promised by the asset over time. To obtain the demand price DP one discounts expected receipts Q at the appropriate rate of discount d:

$$DP = \sum Qt \,/\, (1 + d)^t$$

The discount rate is obtained from the market rate of interest on some risk-free asset (such as a Treasury bill or bond, depending on the relevant retention period), adjusted for the specific risk represented by the asset in question when compared to the risk-free asset. This influence of the interest rate, that does not depend on the investor being financed by external sources, is stronger the longer the retention period and the smaller the allowance to be made for uncertainties specific to the asset being considered. The combination of these conditions shows that not many types of investments are very sensitive to interest rate movements. Long-lived capital goods would fulfil the first requirement but could possibly fail the second, because the longer is the relevant period of retention, the greater are the uncertainties felt by agents and, thus, the greater the weight of specific uncertainty factors in relation to the risk-free interest rate. The converse is also valid. Short retention periods, on the other hand, reduce the weight of asset-specific uncertainties but reduce the importance of the denominator of that formula, as is the case with low values for 't'.

In conclusion, despite its theoretically general validity, the actual influence of interest rate movements on the value (demand prices) of assets may be relevant only for those capital goods that simultaneously last longer and have more or less definite markets. For Keynes, investments in utilities or housing had this nature and represented the channel through which changes in interest rates would affect the pace of investment. To the extent that these investments have been nationalized in a large number of countries, one would expect this influence to be less important now than it could have been in the 1930s.[19]

If we take the interest rate to represent the actual terms of loans, the influence may remain strong at least to the extent to which external funds are effectively sought by investors. Interest costs may be important but do not constitute the only channel through which the terms of credit can influence the availability of resources and, thus, investment. If the terms of credit include the use of collaterals as a guarantee on the part of borrowers for the loans they obtain, changes in interest may play a more important role in the decision to invest through the reevaluations they cause of reserve asset prices.[20] A rise in interest rates depresses the value of assets used as collateral, which may reduce the supply of loans if the borrower has no additional assets. This is considered by some Post Keynesian authors, such as Minsky, as one important channel for a restrictive monetary policy, despite the risks it brings of a collapse of asset values and of a debt deflation.

Be that as it may, one could expect that, *ceteris paribus*, the terms of credit would worsen when the demand for credit by any given borrower increased. This would happen because both the lender's and the borrower's risk increase when indebtedness increases. The borrower's risk is given by the probability of insolvency in case of a disappointment of expectations causing an incapacity to honour contractual obligations. The lender's risk increases because the higher concentration of resources on any given borrower strengthens the solidarity between both, making the fate of the lender dependent on that of the borrower. These notions of lender's and borrower's risk, suggested by Keynes (1964, pp. 144–5), are foundations for the principle of increasing risk of Kalecki (1971, p. 106), that would suggest then a positively-sloped supply curve of credit for any given agent.[21]

Minsky's presentation of the principle of increasing risk allows us to give a graphic representation of the determination of investments that does not rely on decreasing returns in the production of capital goods that bother so many Post Keynesians. Let us consider Davidson's graphic representation of the investment process. In Figure 7.1, S stands for the stock supply or assets, s for the flow supply; D is the stock demand and d is the flow demand for replacement of used up capital goods as a fixed proportion of the desired stock of capital goods. In the case shown, we have the spot price (given by the intersection between the current demand for stocks and the available stocks) above the forward price; that is, that price that equilibrates demand and supply when new items can be produced. The definiteness of the result is allowed by the assumption of decreasing returns in the production of the asset, since the negative slope of the demand curve can be explained by reasons other than decreasing productivity. We have already mentioned that different combinations of identical factors of production are the neoclassical way of obtaining decreasing returns, but they are not the only one, nor is it the case that they are empirically more likely to take place. But even if we think of perfectly constant returns in the production of the asset (a horizontal s-curve) the scheme can still be closed if the principle of increasing risk is employed.

Minsky introduces the principle as in Figure 7.2. Supposing that

Figure 7.1

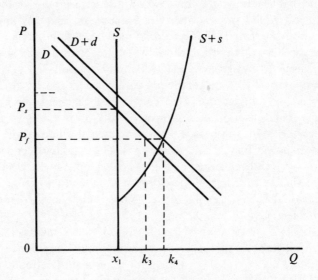

Figure 7.2

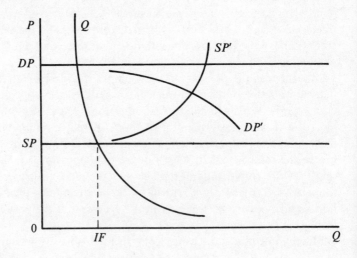

Figure 7.3

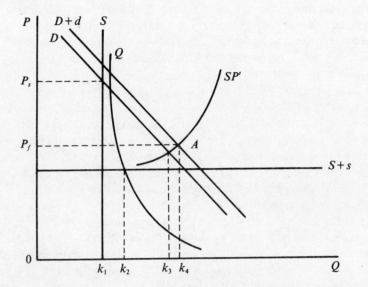

an investor can buy an indefinitely large number of units of this asset
at the current supply price and that he can also use them without
fear of saturating his own market, both the demand price curve (*DP*)
and the supply price curve (*SP*) would be horizontal. No equilibrium
could be achieved and investment would tend to infinity. However,
let us consider the principle of increasing risk. It just states that an
increasing appeal to outside funds depresses the value of the asset as
evaluated by the holder and, on the other hand, can only be satisfied
if the holder is willing to pay the increasingly worse terms of credit
that are imposed by the suppliers of funds. The *DP* curve is then
modified into *DP'* and *SP* into *SP'*, starting from the point at which
appeal has to be made to outside sources of finance. An equilibrium
is eventually reached at point *A*.

Combining both approaches, we have Figure 7.3, where the decreasing returns of production are replaced by the increasing risk.
Equilibrium is reached at point *A*, where a limit to investments in
that particular asset is given by financial considerations rather than
by marginal productivity factors.[22]

WORKING CAPITAL AND LIQUID CAPITAL

Fixed capital goods are not the only possibility for investment, although they are the most important in the sense that, being largely autonomous with respect to current events, they are mainly responsible, according to Keynes and Post Keynesians, for the fluctuations of a monetary economy.

There are two other types of capital goods, however, still to be considered. The first group includes goods-in-process as well as goods held in inventory to guarantee the smoothness of production processes. These are short-lived goods, usually divisible and some of them even having some positive liquidity premium. They constitute the working capital, that part of the output that is not yet available for final use, either because of technical delays in the production process or because of the necessity of keeping technical reserves of some raw materials in order to avoid interruptions or failures in that process. The nature of the working capital is defined by its technical role in the productive process and it is in part a function of its duration. It is held in proportion to the volume of production that is being undertaken and is thus dependent on the state of short-term expectations.

The importance of taking the working capital into account follows from three characteristics: (1) they determine the speed with which production processes can be resumed after some paralysation or can be accelerated; (2) they amplify fluctuations in production; and (3) they constitute an additional channel through which monetary policy can affect output.

The first characteristic, to which Keynes calls attention in his *Treatise on Money*, is due to the need to consider that production takes time. Any recovery or increase of demand will always face a lagging supply response because goods have to be processed before they are completed. Moreover, higher rates of production may require higher technical inventories of raw materials, another factor to delay supply adjustments to a changing demand.

The second feature refers to the fact that any change in production requires a proportional change in the working capital. Thus any change in output induces a new investment, causing a larger effect on the economy than the original one. In fact we could think of the investment in working capital as operating according to the accelerator model. In this case, if, say, an investment in fixed capital causes production to increase, through the multiplier effect, the resulting increase in production will feed back into investment, this time in working capital, creating new repercussions on income and employment. Hicks (1954) called a mechanism of this kind a 'supermultiplier'. The combination of the multiplier with the accelerator as a result of some autonomous investment in fixed capital also reminds us of Schumpeter's 'secondary wave' (Schumpeter, 1939).

Finally, investments in working capital have also to be financed. Given the short-term nature of the goods involved they are usually financed by short-term bank credit. This feature opens the way for a second form of influence of monetary policy instruments upon the investment process. When discussing fixed capital investments we were naturally referring to the long-term rate of interest. In the case of short-lived working capital it is the short-term interest rate that matters.

Liquid capital is also constituted by inventories of raw materials and finished goods. Unlike working capital, however, it does not keep any kind of technical relation to production. On the contrary, liquid capital is held for strictly speculative reasons. Those who hold liquid capital speculate that prices of those items will go up. Those who liquidate inventories bet that prices will go down.

Liquid capital used to be (and it still is for some authors) the main focus of models of the business cycle. In the *Treatise on Money*, Keynes tried to dismiss this notion, emphasizing the importance of fixed and working capital. In times of highly unstable prices, however, liquid capital may become an important outlet for investable funds if an agent's expectations about the difference between the price of a good at a certain future date and spot prices are high enough to induce speculators to pay its carrying costs.

SUMMING UP

In this chapter we have extended the own-rates of interest model to examine in detail the decision to invest, that is, the purchase of assets located at the opposite extreme to money in the liquidity scale.

Investment, as opposed to financial placements, refers to the purchase of capital goods. One usually thinks of fixed capital goods when discussing investment, but Keynes considered two other categories of demands in the same group – working capital and liquid capital. Although they involve goods that are very heterogeneous in nature, they all have in common the repercussions on employment that a decision to produce them implies.

Fixed capital refers to long-lived, expensive, non-divisible, illiquid items that cannot act as stores of value since they do not have relevant second-hand markets. The demand for them depends, then, on there being expectations that are optimistic enough to induce agents to face all the uncertainties of such a commitment. The purchase of fixed capital goods depends on the state of long-term expectations, which are very complex, combining current information, conjectures and judgements of the weight of the evidence on which the expectation relies. The importance of the latter kind of judgement justifies the attention one needs to give to such intractable factors as the state of confidence and 'animal spirits'.

Working capital, on the other hand, is important mainly for its amplifying effects on production and income. It is an induced form of investment, not a cause of fluctuations. Liquid capital can be autonomous and thus the cause of economic changes. However, it is supposed to be connected to relatively small and short-lived movements of output.

This chapter, together with Chapters 5 and 6, described the sources of dynamic impulses in a monetary economy. Different states of long-term expectations trigger adaptations in portfolios that have an impact upon the demand for money, for capital goods and for other assets as well. The attempts by agents to adjust their holdings to the new state of expectations induce changes in the rates of production of reproducible assets that will have further repercussions on income and employment. To describe these repercussions we need to identify the propagation mechanisms of a monetary economy. The most important one is the multiplier. Thus, after discussing the causes of shocks to the economy, represented by changes in the state of long-term expectations, through the examination of the demand for money and for capital goods as applications of a general theory of asset choice and accumulation, we turn now to the discussion of propagation mechanisms with the examination of the propensity to consume.

NOTES

1. At this level of generality, this statement is valid both for more conventional models comparing the marginal efficiency of capital to the money-rate of interest or for Shacklean models where the choice of assets is obtained from gamblers' indifference maps. See Shackle (1952).

2. A third motive of dissension has been the notion that the curve of returns of investment is negatively sloped, something which, for some, especially neo-Ricardians, smells like the marginal productivity theory of investments. However, this identification is not supported by evidence from Keynes himself but by an appeal to other, neoclassical, theories of decreasing returns. See Garegnani (1978/9). There is a problem with the argument, however, because in the neoclassical traditions decreasing returns result from the decline in the marginal productivity of capital, when the intensity of capital is increased. Keynes's theory, on the other hand, is not referred to an increased amount of capital imposed upon a given quantity of labour. His notion of decreasing returns is compatible with the maintenance of constant capital/labour ratios (since employment is also supposed to expand when investments are made) and with empirically-based arguments such as those employed by Sylos-Labini (1966) according to which, from some point on, decreasing returns are likely to emerge in manufacturing because of the employment of less efficient or older machines, less skilled workers and so on, something that had nothing to do with the neoclassical concept of decreasing returns. For that reason, this criticism will not be considered here. We will also ignore arguments such as Deleplace's (1988) according to which, if Keynes had considered the effects of an investment decision, he would have taken into consideration further changes in the own-rates themselves, inducing new decisions and so on. This argument clearly relies on a confusion between ex ante and ex post variables being invalid to support a decision-making model as we proposed the own-rates model to be. A more important criticism was made by Asimakopulos (1971), according to which Keynes himself was guilty of some confusion between ex ante and ex post elements in his model to the extent that he considered increasing flow-supply prices for reproducible assets in the set of data considered by each wealth holder, information that would be inaccessible to each individual except ex post factum.

3. Kregel (1988) has suggested an important role for the concept of marginal efficiency of capital in the development of Keynes's own ideas about asset pricing. In the *Treatise on Money* debts and capital goods were grouped and the price of non-monetary assets was determined as being directly the reciprocal of the market rate of interest. This procedure was sharply criticized in the discussions of the Cambridge Circus and by Kahn in particular. In *The General Theory*, as a result, Keynes distinguished between a liquidity preference theory, in a narrow sense, to determine the price of debts, and a marginal efficiency of capital, to determine the prices of assets.

4. In the 'first postulate' of classical employment theory, Chapter 2 of *The General Theory*. This acceptance was later challenged by Dunlop and Tarshis, to whom Keynes hesitantly conceded that returns could be constant in the relevant range, depriving the first postulate of validity. With constant returns, oligopoly made its appearance, changing the model into a mark-up model. We will return to this point in Chapter 10.

5. Minsky (1975) has argued that the business cycle is actually the form through

which the capitalist system reconstitutes the relative scarcity of capital with respect to other types of assets of production factors.

6. The difficulties created by the durability of fixed capital were discussed in Shackle (1970, p. 78).

7. One could argue, following modern oligopoly theories, that expected profitability may no longer be an important inducement to invest, at least to oligopolies in mature economies. The argument is that megacorps are interested in maintaining existing market shares rather than maximizing profits. Investments will then be made defensively, no matter what the expected profitability may be. This may be a sensible argument but for very restrictive conditions, such as maturity, in the sense of Steindl (1976), where innovation is practically ruled out, competitors are all too strong to be dislocated by any competitive strategy, and markets grow at a vegetative rate. In the long term, however, as Steindl himself has acknowledged, one cannot dispose of the effects of technical progress and maturity may become a less important restriction. When deciding on new markets and new products one would not expect that kind of passive and defensive strategy postulated to maturity. Penrose's models of the growth of the firm would be more relevant than Steindl's stagnation model. For a detailed examination of these ideas in a Post Keynesian framework, see Feijo (1991, chaps 2 and 3).

8. For instance, the main factor of uncertainty for an investor is probably related to the nature of the markets he will face when the investment has been completed. One cannot know in advance what future markets will be like. Even if some market research is made in terms of customers' inclinations, these are merely information about current inclinations. Nothing prevents customers from changing their minds before the investment is recovered.

9. In a 1934 draft of *The General Theory*, Keynes listed some possible influences on long-term expectations:

> Upon what will these expectations be based? Upon prospective estimates of four factors: (i) the scarcity or abundance of the type of asset in question, i.e. the supply of assets capable of rendering similar or equivalent service, (ii) the strength of the demand for its product compared with the demand for other things, (iii) the state of effective demand during the life of the assets, taken in conjunction with the shape of the supply function of the assets' product, and (iv) changes in the wage unit during the life of the assets. (*CWJMK*, xiii, p. 451)

10. Future technological paths are not entirely unpredictable, since it is possible to identify technological paths along which an original concept is developed into ever more adequate innovations. See Rosenberg (1982). In any case, uncertainty is not removed since not all developments can always be mapped in advance (except, perhaps, in the final stages of a given path, in declining industries) and, most importantly, there is nothing to prevent an entirely new path developing unexpectedly, redirecting a whole industry's trajectory.

11. It is really immaterial for this discussion whether the decision maker arrives at a given definite value, as is the case with the marginal efficiency of capital, or at ranges of possibilities, as is the case with Shackle's potential surprise model. The point is to postulate that the investor is able to compare and to rank the alternatives.

12. As Shackle has identified them, we should be concerned both with counter-expected events (those that were pre-identified but that had their plausibility judged to be low) and with unexpected events (more destructive in their effects because they were shown to be possible even though the theory entertained by the decision maker could not conceive it). See Shackle (1952).

13. Schumpeter also had this idea of the entrepreneur as somebody endowed with very special leadership characteristics. See Schumpeter (1934, 1939).
14. This is the main role of economic policy in Keynes's approach. See Chapter 12, below.
15. This is the basis for Minsky's famous aphorism 'stability is destabilizing', that Lerner (1978), however, identified as Marxist rather than Keynesian.
16. Investment is always volatile (see *CWJMK*, XIII, pp. 354–5) but mob behaviour can aggravate this volatility. For a very interesting historical description of mob behaviour in financial markets see Kindleberger (1978).
17. This excludes the theoretical acceptability of accelerator-type investment functions for fixed capital. See Robinson (1979, p. 132). Davidson is also very critical of the use of profit rates in investment functions. See Davidson (1978a, pp. 57–8, 134). There may be situations, however, where the use of accelerator models can be justified. See Feijo, 1991; Carvalho and Oliveira (1991).
18. It was a lifelong view of Keynes that investment required favourable expectations and efficient banks. See, for instance *CWJMK*, VI, p. 133, among as many examples as one may wish.
19. The reasons for the special sensitivity of investment in utilities in contrast to the insensitivity of investment in the manufacturing sector are discussed in *CWJMK*, XIII, pp. 234, 364. See also Kahn (1984, p. 148) and Shackle (1970, p. 96).
20. This effect was noted by Keynes. See Keynes (1964, pp. 172–3).
21. Which does not necessarily imply that the market supply curve of credit is positively inclined.
22. The additional information is given by the figure:

$$\text{Gross investment} = 0k_4 - 0k_1$$
$$\text{Replacement demand} = 0k_4 - 0k_3$$
$$\text{Net investment} = (0k_4 - 0k_1) - (0k_4 - 0k_3) = 0k_3 - 0k_1$$
$$\text{Internally generated funds} = 0k_2 - 0k_1$$
$$\text{Borrowing} = 0k_4 - 0k_2$$

8. The Propensity to Consume and the Multiplier

Changing views of the future have a direct impact on the strategies of wealth accumulation chosen by agents. These strategies, in turn, determine the temporal path of the economy, as long as that specific state of expectation prevails. The attempts by capital assets producers to suit the demands of wealth holders will change current levels of income and employment, depending on whether the current state of expectations favours the demands for reproducible over irreproducible assets and to what extent this happens.

According to Keynes, once the impact of the new state of expectations on the structure of asset demands is known and the level of primary employment is determined (that is, the level of employment in those sectors that produce those assets for which the additional demands of wealth holders are channelled) a series of repercussions will take place in a monetary economy that are peculiar to this kind of economy when compared to cooperative economies. The most important of these repercussions has to do with the inducement to increase consumption expenditures that is rooted in the increase in primary employment. This type of phenomenon is called the multiplier and, as Alvin Hansen (1953) noted long ago, is the mechanism operating in a monetary economy alternative to the Say's law mechanisms that operate in cooperative economies.

Keynes's analysis of the role of consumption and the multiplier is important to illustrate the hierarchy that is characteristic of a monetary economy because it shows that households' decisions to consume are actually constrained by firms' decisions to invest. In a monetary economy, spending decisions by households, unless financed by credit, depend on income being earned by the proprietors of factors of production, particularly labour. The purchase of

136

the services of these factors is decided by firms according to their short- and long-term expectations. Therefore consumption is not an alternative to investment but a complement to it, because it is the decision of firms to increase the production of investment goods that will lead to an increase in the income earned by households, thus sustaining their increased consumption expenditures.[1]

Although the analysis of the propensity to consume and the multiplier is not the starting point of an analysis of the dynamics of a monetary economy, it is a very important element of the understanding of its propagation mechanisms and as such is very distinct from what one would expect to happen in cooperative economies. That is the reason for the prominent place given to the multiplier in Keynes's and Post Keynesian analyses, since it strengthens the claim for the development of a conception of economic society that is different from that which is the subject of classical economics and works according to different rules.

THE PRE-KEYNESIAN APPROACH TO CONSUMPTION

In a cooperative economy consumption and investment are alternative uses for the current output. Actually they are identical in nature, since investment is nothing more than provision for future consumption, so the difference between consuming and saving (which is the same as investing) is just the date for which the act of consumption is planned.[2] As much as consumption and saving are alternatives from the point of view of an individual, consumption and investment are alternatives from the macroeconomic or, better, aggregate point of view.[3]

Ricardo's famous version of Say's law (*Principles*) states that no general saturation of demand is conceivable since one only produces because there are unsatisfied demands: 'No man produces, but with a view to consume or sell, and he never sells, but with an intention to purchase some other commodity, which may be immediately useful to him, or which may contribute to future production' (Ricardo, 1971, p. 291).

If a point of saturation was eventually reached, no additional production would be undertaken because ultimately in a cooperative economy production is conducted by household producers concerned with their own satisfaction. A general glut could not take place because, if all demands were satisfied, additional production would simply not take place.

In the neoclassical elaboration of Say's law, through consumers' satisfaction maximization analysis, some more precise conditions were added in order to use it as the foundation for a model of capital markets. Firstly, it was supposed that individuals could order their preferences in a definite way. Actually this was (and is) a general requirement for the development of consumers' preferences analyses. In addition to this, however, an ad hoc form for the preference ordering was proposed, according to which present consumption was to be preferred to future consumption.[4]

Under these conditions, individual agents would try to maximize their satisfaction, 'given' their income (which was already determined by Say's law mechanisms) by choosing between present goods and also between present and future consumption. This reasoning, as already seen, was valid both for the individual and for the whole economy. The individual had his income determined by the sale of factors' services. The economy had its income determined by Say's law.

The choice between present and future consumption was oriented by the rate of exchange between them, as with any other pair of goods. Substitution effects would operate to induce consumers to concentrate expenditures on the relatively cheaper goods. The rate of exchange between present and future consumption is given by the real rate of interest, that measures how much of a given basket of goods has to be given out in the present to obtain another given (assumedly larger) basket of goods at a future specified date. The higher the future rewards, that is the cheaper the future basket with respect to the current basket, the higher the amount currently saved. One could draw, then, a savings schedule relating the value of desired savings to the various possible levels of the rate of interest. This was the supply curve of resources for transformation into future goods. Thus it was not just a savings curve – it was also a supply of capital schedule.

The obtention of future larger baskets of goods, on the other hand, depended, of course, on the actual possibilities of transforming current into future goods; that is, on technology. Depending on the productivity of capital, savers' preferences could or could not be satisfied. Neoclassical analysis assumed that technology would show decreasing returns to the intensity of factors. In other words, the higher the amount of capital employed by a given number of workers, the lower would be its (marginal) productivity. It was thus possible to draw another schedule relating the amount of capital to be added to production (investment) to the return it could pay. This negatively-sloped function was a demand curve for capital.

Naturally, a sustainable position for this economy would be reached when intertemporal preferences could be reconciled to technical possibilities or, in a more technical way, if the rate of exchange between present and future goods desired by savers was compatible with productivity of that amount of desired savings. The rate of interest would then be equal to the marginal productivity of capital, balancing demand and supply of capital. It would regulate the uses of current output, between consumption and investment (that is, between present and future consumption), but not its volume, which was given.

At this point let us stress the main features of the pre-Keynesian approach. Firstly, as is clear, all relevant variables are real. We have preferences of consumers and technical possibilities. The introduction of money and banks into this scene does not change its fundamental dynamics, as Wicksell has shown. Transitory disequilibria may emerge that do not affect the equilibrium position. Money is at best neutral. Secondly, we have the emergence of a 'natural' rate of interest that is rooted in the 'real' economy, determined by material choices and possibilities. It is then an anchor, the only one to allow the correct conciliation between what is wanted and what is possible. Tampering with market rates of interest can only be conducive to disorder and disturbance. The third characteristic of this analysis is its dependence on the exogenous determination of total output, usually obtained through some application of Say's law. To solve an individual consumer's maximization problem requires the knowledge of his constraints, since demands are assumed to be insatiable. The model simply transfers to the aggregate the same exogenously given constraint on the individual. Fourthly, although it is rarely made explicit, there are some heavy informational requirements involved in making possible the solution of intertemporal maximization problems. Consumers obviously cannot be choosing between two amounts of money, because money has no intrinsic utility. One has to be choosing between definite baskets of goods at definite dates for which it is necessary to have full information, otherwise the problem cannot be solved and demand curves for future goods (the supply curve of savings) cannot be derived. This scheme is incompatible with the existence of uncertainty, in the Post Keynesian sense, that, as will be shown, will revert the whole chain of determination. It is also, of course, incompatible with the existence of money as a liquidity time-machine that allows consumers, even if they have definite intertemporal preferences at any given moment, to avoid commitments with future baskets of goods, postponing their choices. Finally, consumers and investors are treated symmetrically in this model. They represent the opposing blades of the Marshallian scissors of the capital market, independent from each other and equally powerful to determine the outcome of its operations. There is no hierarchy in this market.

CONSUMPTION EXPENDITURES IN A MONETARY ECONOMY

Two chief characteristics of consumption behaviour will define the Post Keynesian alternative approach to the cooperative economy. On the one hand, the consideration of uncertainty will change the modes of decision between consumption and savings on the part of individuals. On the other hand, the budget constraints under which these individual decisions will be made will be endogenous to the macro model of the relations between consumption and investment, replacing Say's law with the principle of effective demand, according to which, as it was once put by Lerner, 'Each individual is constrained to save the amount that he does by the size of his income; and the size of his income is determined by other people's expenditures on the goods that he produces' (Lerner, 1947, pp. 621–2).

To consider uncertainty in the sense of Keynes implies changing the approach as to the motives behind the consumption/saving decision. A consumer who is uncertain about his future needs, future sources of income or future opportunities may decide to set aside some part of his income in order to smooth his path over time. To save is to make a buffer against an uncertain future, induced by precaution rather than by intertemporal preferences. Savings that are induced by precaution take primarily the form of liquid assets, stores of value that can be easily converted into means of payment. Consumers are searching for safe 'liquidity time-machines', to use

Davidson's expression (Davidson, 1982, p. 29). To persuade them to retain wealth over time in less liquid forms, some kind of compensation for the risks brought about by the holding of less liquid assets has to be offered to them: this is the liquidity preference theory of the rate of interest. Consumers are persuaded to keep their savings in forms other than money when these other forms pay them enough to compensate their ex ante feeling of insecurity in the face of an uncertain future.

One should note that to say that precaution against unpredictable events is a reason, or, perhaps, the main reason for saving is not contradictory with the idea that savings can also be made to enjoy perceived or expected opportunities of enrichment. If there are placements that are expected to be profitable and the state of confidence on these expectations is strongly favourable, a consumer may decide to save in order to buy these assets. Therefore changes in interest rates may, in these conditions, induce some increase in the desire to save.

In *The General Theory*, Keynes does not state that savings are insensitive to changes in interest rates, although he does stress that the sensitivity should not be intense. The main criticism against the postulation of a definite relationship between savings and interest rates is that the sign of this relation cannot be established a priori, on the basis of some maximization mechanism that assumes that savings are decided in a context that excludes uncertainty.[5] For Post Keynesians, agents cannot be assumed to have the necessary information for solving the maximization problem and for allowing substitution effects to prevail when rates of interest change, along the lines made explicit in the preceding section. Wealth effects and income effects tend then to prevail over substitution effects.

The decision to consume (and save) depends then on those same kinds of factors that are subsumed in the notion of state of confidence. It is subjective and for that reason it is influenced by those elements that Keynes listed in Chapter 9 of *The General Theory*, such as 'Precaution, Foresight, Calculation, Improvement, Independence, Enterprise, Pride and Avarice' (1964, p. 108).

As we have suggested, the consumption/savings decision can also depend on objective factors when expectations about the future can be formed more definitely. As mentioned by Keynes, changes in interest rates or in fiscal policy are certainly factors that can be known relatively easily. A main objective factor is current income.

The relation of consumption and saving to income is understandable in the context of a monetary economy. Income works as an inducement to save (not as a restriction on consumption) since, when income is increasing and living standards are being improved, larger precautionary savings must be made in order to sustain that newly-achieved living standard against unpredictable changes. We have here an obvious analogy with the idea of planned idle capacity proposed by Steindl. This idle capacity is kept by oligopolies to satisfy precautionary motives and is also proportional to the total capacity of the firm. It is for this reason that income effects, that are related to relatively easily identifiable factors like desired living standards, prevail over substitution effects, that depend on the clarity with which the consumer can solve his satisfaction maximization problems. It is also a reason why immediate reactions to income changes are not necessarily those that will be sustained in the longer term: the income earner has to judge whether the change was or was not permanent so as to change his standard of living and, therefore, his provisions for the future. A form of Friedman's permanent income hypothesis, modified to suit the assumptions of a monetary production economy, is thus compatible with Post Keynesian economics.[6]

The second central feature of the Post Keynesian approach to the propensity to consume is the macroeconomic endogenization of budget constraints on consumers' decisions. As was proposed in Chapter 3, a monetary economy is a hierarchical social arrangement in which those who have accumulated assets or who can issue liabilities to have access to discretionary funds have the decisive influence on the development of economic processes. In a highly stylized way, we could describe the fundamental dynamics of employment determination in a monetary economy as follows: firms decide on how much investment to make in a given period; assuming that capital goods producers are able adequately to estimate the demand for newly produced items that are to come from firms, factors of production are hired in order to produce the new capital goods; for the proprietors of these factors the income or budget constraints on consumption decisions are determined by this new scale of employment; if we are supposing an expansive movement, we will have a derived demand for consumption goods sustained by the higher level of income now available to these agents; when their additional consumption expenditures are made, it is the production of consumption goods that is expanded, for which new factors of production are needed, which relax the income constraints under which the proprietors of these newly employed factors of production decide on their own consumption expenditures. This process continues, with additional repercussions on consumption expenditures, until it is exhausted. This happens because, according to Keynes's 'fundamental psychological law', the marginal propensity to consume is smaller than one, meaning that not all of the increase in income is spent in consumption. As we saw, some precautionary savings tend to be made, which leaks out some income at each turn of the multiplication process.

The multiplier, the theoretical novelty that was much stressed by Keynes in his debates about *The General Theory*, is just the result of the endogenization of budget constraints. Each consumer makes his decisions as if his income was fixed (as it should really be). However, there is a fallacy of composition in considering, as classical economics does, that budget constraints are also fixed in the aggregate. Keynes's analysis of the propensity to consume is the critique of this fallacy.

At the micro level what we observe is each agent trying to make his level of savings adequate to his desired savings/income ratio. When new payments are made, the agent sees himself with a higher income than before for which no consumption destination had already been decided. It is like having a (transiently) unitary savings propensity (cf. Chick, 1983a). The agent will try to reach his desired position by liquidating some of the excess accumulated assets and replacing them with consumption goods. They do this by buying consumption goods and thus creating a new additional income for somebody else who will see himself in the same position as the preceding consumer at the beginning of his cycle. The multiplier is completed when all consumers are in equilibrium; that is, when they are saving only the desired proportion of their income, having got rid of their excess savings through the purchase of consumption goods.

Naturally, the action of the multiplier depends on many factors, the most important of which may be the perception of whether the increase in income is or is not permanent, allowing or not a change in living standards. Perceived windfall changes may affect consumption in any direction. Changes assumed to be permanent warrant changes in living standards. Again one should note that this interpretation, that is also very close to Keynes's own, has the power to absorb insights like Friedman's permanent income or Duesenberry's 'ratchet' effects, without having to accept the maximization paraphernalia that assumes full information.

One point that should be made clear is that the multiplier process is not something that obtains, at its completion, an amount of savings equal to the investments made. These are equal all the time, both in the financial and in the material sense of being non-available output, to use the *Treatise on Money's* terminology (Cf. *CWJMK*, XIII, p. 582; Lerner, 1947, p. 630). The multiplier is a process of redistribution of savings among savers in order to reach a situation in which all the savings are being made by those who wish to save. As long as there is anybody saving more than he desires, he has the choice of spending the excess, taking another step in the multiplying process.

SUMMING UP

In this chapter we have discussed the most important of the propagation mechanisms operating in a monetary economy, the consumption multiplier. Keynes criticized the orthodox approach to the consumption/savings decision by which the amount of savings made was assumed to be an increasing function of interest rates because of intertemporal substitution effects. He also rejected Say's law, which was the support for taking aggregate income as exogenously given. Keynes and Post Keynesians substitute the ideas of uncertainty and endogenous budget constraints for the notions of intertemporal maximization and Say's law.

Entirely different adjustment processes were assumed to operate in a cooperative economy and in a monetary economy. In the former, investment and consumption are alternative uses for current output. This may portray adequately some kind of corn economy, where the same good may perform both the roles of consumption good and of investment good, but it is a very poor rendering of modern, complex monetary economies with specialized goods. Production of investment and consumption goods involves decisions that have to be made in advance: they are not alternative allocations for current output. Thus, in a monetary economy, capital goods-producing firms decide, acting on their short-term expectations, what to produce to satisfy the expected flow of investment demands and this triggers a multiplication mechanism in which factors of production employed in the production of capital goods spend their additional income creating new demands and new income, and so successively until the sequence is exhausted.

One should note that, when the multiplier has completed its task, agents will be in equilibrium, in the sense that each will be saving just the proportion of his incomes he desires. It is a real equilibrium that is not, however, a full equilibrium in the sense that we do not know yet if these savings, that are correctly distributed, are also kept in their most adequate structure. In other words, all we know, at this point, is that agents are saving the amount they desire; we do not know yet if they are holding the assets they desire. The financial side of this operation is the subject of the next chapter.

NOTES

1. Even if consumer expenditures are financed on credit, ultimately the amount of credit available to most consumers is a function of the current income they earn from the sale of factors services.
2. Neoclassical economics is an abstraction of a corn economy, where the same product can be used either as a consumption good or as an investment good. It is appropriately called by Minsky the 'village fair paradigm' (Minsky, 1986).
3. This equivalence between the micro and the macro decisions to consume and save and/or invest will be the point of attack of Post Keynesians on the classical mechanism. See Chick (1983a). This point will be treated below.
4. The ad hoc nature of this assumption is made clear, for instance, by the uneasiness with which Marshall introduced it, by appealing to a supposedly empirical observation of human behaviour and to assumed characters of human nature (Marshall, 1924). As a matter of fact, neoclassical consumer analyses do not generally specify preferences. They claim to take consumers' preferences as given, whatever they are, to show that they act according to them if they are to be rational. Rationality refers to means, not to ends. Something is good if an individual thinks it to be good. No preference structure is more rational than any other. This neutrality with respect to preferences is, however, broken in the case of intertemporal preferences in order to obtain well-behaved savings supply curves that postulate a direct relation between the amount saved and the interest rate. Keynes, by the way, while not disputing that preferences like this may happen, was more coherent with a neoclassical background when he raised the point that other preference orderings were possible as well.
5. According to Keynes the relation between consumption (and saving) and interest rates was very complex. Any attempt to present it in a simple way would falsify the forces in operation. See *CWJMK*, XIII, p. 447; XIV, p. 248).
6. 'When there is an unforeseen change of conditions the propensity to consume temporarily departs from its normal value and there is a time lag before it resumes it . . . It is not that there is a time lag in the operation of the multiplier theory. What happens is that the parameters on which the multiplier theory operates

temporarily depart from what their values would be if all had been foreseen'
(*CWJMK*, XII, p. 804).

9. Savings, Finance and Funding: Financial Institutions and the Sustaining of Investments

As we described in the last chapter, the multiplier obtains an equilibrium situation where all consumers end up saving the proportion of their increased income they desire. If the producers' short-term expectations as to incoming demands are correct, the output of consumption goods will match these demands and the goods markets will be in equilibrium.

There is no reason, however, for this to be a full equilibrium. In our description of the mechanisms operating in a monetary economy, the original act of spending that triggered the multiplier was made feasible through the creation, by the banks, of means of payment. Debts were created, to be held by the banks. On the other hand, consumers were left with new wealth in their hands – the saving they made on their increased income. We should, then, be concerned not only with the flow equilibrium in the goods markets but also with stock equilibria in the assets and debts markets, about which the multiplier mechanism is silent.

It is a fundamental proposition of Keynesian economics in any of its forms that the savings decision should be studied separately from the choice as to the form in which saved income should be stored.[1] As already argued, the savings decision refers to some kind of intertemporal preferences, explainable either by the existence of definite plans for future expenditures or, most probably, by precautionary moves against an uncertain future. Having decided how much to save, the agent has still to decide how to store these savings. The second decision is oriented by the extent to which the saver prefers safety to enrichment; that is, by his liquidity preference. The multiplier (and the generation of savings and its distribution among individuals) attacks the first question. It does not deal with the second.

To go beyond the goods market, we have to consider that to save is to demand an asset of some kind. This demand, as we have seen, will depend on the preferences of agents as to rentability and liquidity, which are expected to vary in opposite directions. In addition, we also have to remember that other operations with assets are taking place in which banks exchange money with firms for debts issued by the latter, that become the assets held by the banks. Firms, on the basis of these debts, in turn buy other kinds of assets (for instance, fixed capital goods). The multiplier would achieve full equilibrium if one could show that in that process not only consumers' demands for additional consumption goods were satisfied but also savers' demands for assets of given characteristics were satisfied by the creation of securities by firms and banks. Unfortunately, the multiplier per se is powerless to give any information on these latter transactions. An equilibrium in the goods markets may coexist with deep disequilibria in assets markets. The kinds of assets that savers search for may be incompatible with the kinds of assets that debtors may want to issue. A stock disequilibrium may survive the obtention of equilibrium in the goods markets and disturb the goods markets themselves later. To discuss these possibilities and explore their implications is the object of this chapter.

SAVINGS AND FINANCE

The relations between savings and finance may perhaps be the area where most misunderstandings of Keynes's ideas have been presented since the publication of *The General Theory*. In particular, the proposition that investment generates its own finance has been interpreted in ways that range from the correct meaning attributed by Keynes to absurd arguments as to some alleged unimportance of financial relations and the forms of indebtedness to the decisions to invest.

To try and dispel these confusions, let us start from Keynes's original treatment of the point in *The General Theory* and in the debates that immediately followed its publication, in particular Keynes's discussions with Ohlin in 1938. In these works, Keynes establishes a theoretically clear-cut distinction between the concepts of savings, finance and funding. These distinctions can be blurred in practice by the diversity of institutions and financial procedures of actual economies, but the phenomena stylized by each of them can be clearly conceived.

In a monetary economy, goods are bought with money, no matter whether the latter is obtained by the sale of some good or service or by the issuance of a debt. To invest is to purchase investment goods and to make this acquisition what is necessary is the availability of money. An investing firm may have accumulated money from past profits or may appeal to external sources of money, such as the general public or the banks, through the issuance of debt. If it appeals to the general public, the firm will be absorbing liquid resources that were being held in some other form, forcing the issuers of the claims being replaced in the public's portfolio to search for other sources of finance. If it appeals to the banks, new deposits will be created without any crowding out of existing claims. Banks can finance, then, new purchases with the creation of additional money. The appeal to accumulated profits or to the general public's asset holdings does not generate additional purchasing power but the replacement of some claim for another. As put forcefully by Keynes:

This means that, in general, the banks hold the key position in the transition from a lower to a higher scale of activity. If they refuse to relax, the growing congestion of the short-term loan market or of the new issue market, as the case may be, will inhibit the improvement, no matter how thrifty the public purpose to be out of their future incomes. (*CWJMK*, XIV, p. 222)

The creation of money to sustain any planned expenditure is called by Keynes finance. As is stressed by Keynes and Post Keynesians, it is nothing but a bookkeeping operation by which a bank buys an asset (the claim against the borrowing firm) by creating a liability against itself (the demand deposits that the firm will use to make its purchases).[2] No real resource is involved; no savings, in particular, take place or have any role in this operation. Finance is creation of the amount of money necessary to make some spending plan possible. It is an operation that precedes in time the actual purchase or even the actual production of the investment goods that will be demanded. We may, if we want to stress the point, conceive that investment goods producers produce to order or that they observe bank credit creation to form their short-term expectations so that actual production will only start after finance has been obtained. If production has not been started, income has not yet been generated and thus savings, that are an allocation of current income, cannot yet exist.

Finance is thus the creation of money by the institutions that have the necessary power: banks or monetary authorities. Savings, in contrast, are allocations of earned income, made by the general public. The conceptual difference between them is also highlighted by their chronological relationship. Finance precedes production, which generates income. If the act of investment creates savings in the same amount and finance precedes savings, finance is a condition to the generation of savings instead of the inverse causality usually assumed by classical economics.[3] In a corn economy, the inspiration for the village fair paradigm of neoclassical economics, the inverse causality may be valid. It is necessary to save corn to invest in additional corn production. In a monetary economy, in contrast, it is money that buys goods, including investment goods.

One should be careful, however, to realise that, if money creation is the effective condition to start the process of investment, it is not all that is required to sustain it. As Keynes once wrote:

The entrepreneur when he decides to invest has to be satisfied on two points: firstly, that he can obtain sufficient short-term finance during the period of producing the investment; and secondly, that he can eventually fund his short-term obligations by a long-term issue on satisfactory conditions. (*CWJMK*, XIV, p. 217)

When banks create finance, they are accepting becoming temporarily illiquid.[4] Banks typically issue short-term liabilities, such as demand deposits, or certificates of time deposits. Their assets have to be correspondingly short-lived in order to guarantee their safe operation. When a loan to an investing firm is made, the bank is assuming a speculative position by absorbing an asset, the loan, that is ultimately supported by an illiquid asset, the investment good bought by the firm.[5]

In addition, the firm itself also assumes a risky speculative position in this process, for the same reasons. It is financing the purchase of typically long-lived assets with the issuance of short-term liabilities, the only ones banks can accept. Thus both banks and investing firms find themselves in a vulnerable situation as a result of their operations. The ideal situation would, of course, be that in which the firm could find permanent holders of their liabilities that would allow it to pay back the bank loan. In this case the bank would have the liquidity of its balance sheet restored and the firm would have assets and liabilities of compatible maturities. The process of transformation of short-term into long-term liabilities is called funding. To be feasible, a funding operation requires the existence of wealth holders desiring permanent abodes of wealth, in contrast to banks which, when creating finance, are only searching for short-lived commitments.

The obvious candidates for the role of ultimate sustainers of investment are the new savers created by the very act of investment. We saw in the last chapter that, as a result of the investment and the operation of the consumption multiplier, we get to a situation in which new savings are being held (exactly equivalent to the new investment made) in the proportions that each individual desires to hold. It is voluntary savings that are being accumulated and for which vehicles are needed. If these new savers could be persuaded to hold their additional wealth in the form of titles to the new investment, using their inactive deposits (those representing their newly made savings) to buy long-term debts from the investing firm, both banks and firms, along with savers, would reach a stock equilibrium alongside the flow equilibrium reached through the multiplier.

Most neoclassical models of capital markets assume that the economy will converge to this equilibrium, but, as Davidson (1978a, chap. 12) has noted, it is also present in the Kaldor/Pasinetti models of steady-state growth. A Post Keynesian approach, however, should stress the difficulties in the way of such a solution since it totally ignores liquidity preference. As already argued above, to save is, of course, to demand assets but not necessarily (not even probably) the kind of assets that the investing firms are prepared to create. If savings are at least partially made because of uncertainties about the future, it is very unlikely that savers will agree to hold directly assets that may not be very liquid. It would not be a question of how high the propensity to save is but of how intense liquidity preference is.[6] The higher the preference for liquid assets, the higher will have to be the interest rates offered by firms to persuade savers to absorb their debts. As long as there is any positive degree of liquidity preference, any indebted firm will have to face some capital loss to obtain funding directly from savers.

The real alternative to reduce these losses lies not in persuading savers to save more but in creating institutions that allow savings to be used as funding at the same time in which they permit savers to remain relatively liquid. This is the role of financial institutions which, by pooling risks, are able to transform shorter- into longer-term assets.[7] They may be able to offer liquid assets to savers and at the same time supply longer-term funds to investors. The more sophisticated and diversified the financial system is, in terms of types of financial instruments and duration of commitments, the more efficient it will be to intermediate resources between savers and investors.

One cannot stress enough the point that for Post Keynesians the question is not the amount of savings (that is always equal to the amount of investments made) but its distribution (oriented by the multiplier) and its form (determined by the public's liquidity preference).[8] The efficient solution is the creation of a set of financial intermediaries that can satisfy both ends of the funds market, not increasing savings propensities (unless, of course, one is talking of investments greater than full-employment savings, a situation that is, in any case, supposed to be rare).

It is very unlikely that, even in the most developed modern economies, a perfect financial system will exist that will be capable of transforming all savings into funding for investment projects. Most probably, agents will have to adopt mixed strategies, combining funding operations with some degree of recurrent appeal to finance from banks. As Feijo (1991) has shown, we can understand Minsky's model of financial postures precisely as a modification of Keynes's original articulation of the concepts of finance and funding.

In fact, the point of Minsky's model is that agents may follow mixed strategies combining different kinds of commitments involving differentiated risks and degrees of vulnerability to changes in the operation of financial markets. Keynes's original sequential process, in which one starts from banks creating finance, the investment being made creating equivalent savings, the multiplier distributing these savings among voluntary savers and finally funding being promoted by financial intermediaries, does not have to take place in precisely that order.[9] The construction of the argument was, however, efficient in highlighting the essential elements of the problem, identifying the specific nature of each operation taking place and the agents participating in it. Minsky's model is also a stylized representation of the financial process, allowing explicitly, however, for the fact that finance and funding may not be just alternatives but may also act as complements.[10] From it, Minsky was able to derive a model of financial fragility that became a very important part of Post Keynesian macroeconomics.

FINANCIAL CHOICES AND MACROECONOMIC FRAGILITY

Minsky's model of fragility is based on the identification of 'postures' or balance sheet choices investors can adopt to sustain their plans. The essential insight offered by his model is to point out the possible implications of incompatibilities in the maturities of assets and liabilities chosen by investors for the stability of the overall economy. So, instead of Keynes's typical financial path connecting finance to funding, Minsky's approach will explicitly recognize the unlikeliness of obtaining funding in sufficient amounts to replace short-term finance and, thus, to allow all agents to operate with fully compatible balance sheets.

Minsky starts from the definition of three elementary financial postures; that is, choices as to the means of financial support to a given investment decision. The first posture, called 'hedge', refers to investors that only accept liabilities with maturities equivalent to those of the asset being acquired. Thus a hedger only invests if he already possesses the necessary resources beforehand or if loans can be found of the same maturity as the asset he desires. In terms of Keynes's language, a hedger does not accept the finance stage, being interested in investment only if funding can be obtained in advance. A hedger refrains from the risks of not being able to transform short-term into long-term liabilities after an investment plan has actually been implemented. It is a very conservative position that is defended against unpredictable developments in financial markets that could render inviable the conversion of finance into funding in the future.

Of course, the obtention of funding in advance of investment means that the hedger is able either to attract pre-existing savings that were being held in another form or to convince some agent to assume the conversion risks in his place. An investment bank, for instance, can provide funding for investors assuming for itself the risks of conversion of the debts (or stocks) it absorbed into the savings that will be available later. For the whole economy, funding cannot be increased in advance of savings having been created. Minsky's approach, however, highlights the fact that, for an investment process to begin, it may be sufficient that some other agent assumes its financial risks.

A hedger, then, if his expectations as to the yields of the assets being purchased are correct, is able to service his debts with the receipts of his portfolio. Being assured of long-term credit at the beginning of the period, he is sure that, no matter how financial markets change in the relevant future, he will be safe.

The second posture identified by Minsky is closer to Keynes's own picture of this process. Minsky calls it 'speculative'. It describes a situation in which the maturity of the investor's liabilities is shorter than that of his assets. In this case, the income generated by the assets will not be sufficient to liquidate contractual debts at the agreed dates and some rolling over of debts will be required. In a sense, this is the case in which a firm obtains finance for the purchase of an asset expecting that in the future it will be able either to roll over debt or to transform it into funding. It is a speculative choice since the firm cannot know in advance if banks will be willing to renew debts at acceptable terms or if the public will be willing to buy its debts or shares to fund its obligations. Adverse future changes in the state of financial markets may make these firms insolvent, even if the expectations about asset returns are confirmed.

Finally, Minsky defined as a Ponzi posture the case in which more than just rolling over of current debts is necessary. In the case of a speculative posture, the investor is able to pay the interest costs on the debt but has to roll over the Principal. The value of the debt remains constant. A Ponzi investor is not able even to service debts and thus has to appeal to banks to increase his debts by adding non-paid interest to the principal. For this kind of agent to remain solvent it is necessary for expected yields from assets to be sufficient to compensate for a rising debt. Of course this position is even riskier than the speculative posture, since unexpectedly intense rises in interest rates may lead the investor to insolvency.

To make these choices explicit allows us to see more clearly that, although financial uncertainties surrounding an investment decision cannot be eliminated, they can be shifted to other agents or socialized. Development banks are usually created to allow more hedgers to emerge, making feasible some investment that would only be implemented if the investors were animated by exceptionally high 'animal spirits'.

The degree and the efficiency with which this socialization of uncertainties is actually handled is an institutional question. The whole scheme also makes it clear that uncertainties are shifted but they are not eliminated. An efficient financial system, in this sense, may be one in which a maximum degree of socialization of financial risks is promoted, leaving to the entrepreneur mainly the uncertainties resulting from the investment itself.

An individual investor may be a combination of the three postures, adopting different financing strategies for different groups of assets in his portfolio. For the whole economy, in any case, the complexity of the process of capital accumulation becomes clear, since it will probably be containing all three types of choices at the same time. The proportions of hedge, speculative and Ponzi operations will determine the degree of macroeconomic financial fragility of an economy.[11] The higher the weight of speculative and Ponzi investors, the more vulnerable the economy is to changes in financial markets. Conversely, the higher the weight of hedgers, the safer the economy is, at least with respect to financial problems.

Minsky completes his argument by tracing the picture of a model of a business cycle based on changes in the degree of fragility of an economy. Beginning at the bottom of a recession, Minsky notes that a process of recovery is usually led by hedgers, since banks are unlikely to supply credit except to those very conservative agents that can demonstrate their solidity. To restrict credit to hedgers, however, means to forgo profit opportunities for banks, since speculative investors are not only more numerous but also are willing to pay higher interest rates (or to borrow for shorter periods). Thus, in the upswing, the proportion of speculative investors tends to increase. In the boom, Ponzi investors emerge, willing to accept any financial deal to allow the implementation of very risky investments. The increasing illiquidity of banks, however, may put a stop to the process of increasing indebtedness, even if the Central Banks do not. If credit is restrained, new plans may be choked off and aggregate demand may fall. In any case, a rise in interest rates is more than likely to ensue, strangling some investment plans. A fall in aggregate demand (or even its failure to grow at the same rates as before) may disappoint income expectations of not only speculative and Ponzi investors but even of hedgers. If this happens, a crisis will take place, leading to a wave of insolvencies and, eventually, if a debt deflation process is initiated and the government does not take active measures to stabilize the economy, to a depression which only hedgers are likely to survive, to begin the process anew.

Minsky's portrayal of the financial process is thus an advance on Keynes's original picture that is not, in any case, incompatible with it. The same elementary concepts are involved, and particularly the distinction between finance and funding, allowing, however, for the development that these relations have suffered since Keynes's time. More than that, it becomes possible to explore permanent or durable (rather than sequential) combinations of finance and funding operations, recognizing that investments are rarely sustained by pure finance or pure funding which allows the investigation of the ways and means by which they may be combined into a definite financial strategy by investors.

SUMMING UP

This chapter closes our presentation of the propagation mechanisms operating in a monetary production economy by showing the other face, the financial side, of the multiplier. We have thus described a process in which the creation of money conditions all behaviours and in which monetary variables are present at all of its points. This vision of the multiplier problem, and of the very notion of equilibrium that is proposed by Keynes and Post Keynesians, should be contrasted with the much more simplistic models offered by the neoclassical synthesis, in which the flow equilibrium in the goods market seems to be the end of the story of a mechanism that preserves the dichotomy between real and monetary variables against which Keynes formulated his strongest arguments.

In the post Keynesian approach, savings are not a precondition to investment. Money creation is. To invest is to buy investment goods and, to buy goods of any kind, an agent needs money. The amount of money an agent has access to does not depend directly on his income, since he may have access to credit, the creation of purchasing power by banks. Savings are created when an act of investment takes place. They are thus simultaneously created with investment, accompanying it as a shadow.

The financial sustaining of accumulation, however, is not just the creation of bank money. When a firm borrows from a bank to buy an investment good, both the bank and the firm become less liquid than they desire. The firm is financing the purchase of a long-lived asset with short-term loans. The bank is ultimately dependent on the success of the firm in funding its debt to have its loan repaid. It is therefore necessary that the firm be able to place long-term debt claims with the public, directly or through financial intermediaries, to balance its own position and that of the bank. The demand for the new assets should come from those who are saving out of the increased income caused by the original investment. In the aggregate, there are precisely enough savings to fund the new investment goods. The difficulty lies in the liquidity preference of savers that may prevent savings from being used to fund the firms' debts. To satisfy both savers and firms is the main role of financial intermediaries that will issue liquid assets to the public and provide funding for the firms.

Finance and funding, however clear the theoretical distinction between them may be, are not in reality completely incompatible. Agents may try to fund part of their investments and keep the rest sustained by shorter-term debts. Minsky's taxonomy of financial postures makes it possible to replace a more mechanistic sequential approach with the acknowledgement of mixed strategies by investors, depending on their perceptions and expectations about the future behaviour of financial markets.

The whole scheme, besides clearing up the relations between the notions of savings, finance and funding, allows us to perceive that the essentially speculative nature of investment, that is, the exchange of money now for an unknown amount of money later, does not disappear, no matter the kind of institutional relations that are established among the main agents in this process. An efficient financial system socializes uncertainty, reducing its burden on the entrepreneur and sharing it with savers and financial institutions: an act of investment implies the acceptance of illiquidity by somebody.

NOTES

1. 'The psychological time-preferences of an individual require two distinct sets of decisions to carry them out completely. The first is concerned with that aspect of time-preference which I have called the propensity to consume, which ...

determines for each individual how much of his income he will consume and how much he will reserve in some form of command over future consumption.

But this decision having been made, there is a further decision which awaits him, namely, in what form he will hold the command over future consumption which he has reserved, whether out of his current income or from previous savings' (Keynes, 1964, p. 166).

2. Alternative ways of telling this story that are, in any case, close to this are found in Davidson (1986) and Chick (1983b).

3. 'But "finance" has nothing to do with saving. At the "financial" stage of the proceedings no net saving has taken place on anyone's part, just as there has been no net investment' (*CWJMK*, xiv, p. 209. See also ibid., p. 217 and Davidson (1987b, p. 55). For a different perspective, see Terzi (1986/7).

4. For investment to take place somebody has to become illiquid, at least temporarily. See *CWJMK*, xiv, p. 218; also Kaldor (1980) and Asimakopulos (1983).

5. Actually, to reduce the risks supported by banks some collateral asset may be required from the borrower as a safety margin against non-compliance with the terms of the loan contract.

6. In this sense, the completion of the multiplier operation is not sufficient to reach full equilibrium, as Asimakopulos (1983) has suggested. The point is not how much the public is willing to save but how much wealth it is willing to hold in less than fully liquid forms. See *CWJMK*, v, chap. 10; Kahn (1984).

7. 'Financial institutions, when functioning properly permit entrepreneurs to increase the rate of installation of additional illiquid capacity and the attendant expansion of output while simultaneously caring for the liquidity desires and needs of the private sector by creating various liquid assets (time machines) and organizing ('making') continuous markets for the purchase and resale of these time machines' (Davidson, 1982, p. 38). See also *CWJMK*, v, chap. 10; xxi, chap. 6.

8. The intrinsic connection between the multiplier and liquidity preference has been stressed by Kregel. See Kregel (1984/5, 1985).

9. As a matter of fact, Keynes himself warned that that sequence would vary from case to case, depending on, among other things, the nature and functions of the actual institutions operating in each case. See *CWJMK*, xiv, pp. 208–11.

10. As Chick (1983b) and Feijo (1991) have insisted, Keynes's actual treatment of the concept of funding was very perfunctory, most of the time limited to the pointing out of the essential contrast between finance and funding, and dedicating much more attention to the former.

11. See Minsky (1982, p. 18).

APPENDIX: THE FINANCIAL SIDE OF THE MULTIPLIER – A NUMERICAL ILLUSTRATION

Let us take a situation with the following characteristics. There is one firm making investments and one bank creating money. The firm has no accumulated profits, depending entirely on bank credit to make purchases of investment goods. It is planning, given the state of long-term expectations and the current interest rate, to invest the amount of $10. The marginal propensity to consume is 0.5.

The process begins with the firm borrowing $10 from the bank. As a result, the balance sheet of the bank now shows $10 of assets represented by the loan to the firm and $10 of liabilities represented by the deposits created in the name of the firm. The firm, on the other hand, has $10 of assets represented by deposits and $10 of liabilities for the debt with the bank.

In the next stage, the firm spends the $10 to buy investment goods. In its balance sheet, capital goods replace deposits on the asset side, all the rest remaining the same.

Now there comes onto the scene the producer of capital goods which, receiving the order for production of goods worth $10, creates income to that value (paying for wages and other incomes, ignoring intermediate consumption of raw materials). In a first moment, these income earners see their income rise by $10, but all of it being held in the bank as deposits transferred from the account of the investing firm. Since no act of consumption has yet been made with the newly earned income, all of it is being saved. Clearly, there is an excess saving being made by agents who can resolve the situation by increasing their consumption to the value of $5, given their marginal propensity to consume. These agents are now consuming $5 and holding $5 as savings in the form of inactive deposits in the bank.

When the additional spending in consumption goods is made, income of production factors in these sectors increases by $5. Again, when receiving these revenues agents have new income equal to new saving to the value of $5, as inactive balances held in the bank. To balance their position, they will save $2.5 and spend $2.5. Now the proprietors of production factors in the two first stages of the process are in 'real' equilibrium, and the savings they are holding are voluntary. With the additional $2.5 spent in consumption goods, the process is renewed, and so successively until all excess savings have disappeared, being transformed into voluntary savings held as a proportion of an increased income.

When this is achieved, we still have three unsatisfied agents (or groups of agents). The firm is concerned with the incompatibility between the assets and liabilities in its balance sheet. The bank is dissatisfied with the possible illiquidity of its assets if the firm shows itself unable to liquidate its debt. Savers may be at least partially dissatisfied with holding savings entirely in the form of non-interest-earning deposits. The perfect equilibrium would be reached if savers used their aggregate savings of $10 to buy shares of the firm, to earn future dividends; the firm, with the receipts of $10, would liquidate its short-term liabilities with the bank; and the bank would be liquid again to supply loans for another borrower.

If, however, there is some degree of liquidity preference, this solution cannot be achieved. If liquidity preference is so strong that all savings will be held in money form, the firm will either have to rely on the will of the bank in rolling over the debt for the life of the asset or will try to sell securities at much undervalued prices, suffering heavy capital losses. This result follows no matter how thrifty savers may be: it is not a question of propensity to save – that is, how much saving consumers are willing to make – but of their liquidity preference; that is, of the form in which they want to hold their wealth. If a less extreme case is assumed, in which the public may absorb some shares but not the whole value of the new assets ($10), preferring to keep some proportion in liquid forms, financial institutions may bridge the gap, by accepting deposits from the public and lending them to firms.

10. Employment, Wages and Income Distribution

The elements presented up to this point were combined by Keynes into a theory of determination of employment levels. The theory of employment was to synthesize all the processes taking place in a monetary economy in a short-period framework. As we discussed in Chapter 2, the concentration on the study of short-period positions was due to the assumption that short-run economic processes would actually tend to short-period equilibrium positions, since there was a reasonable identity between the theoretical determinants of a short-period equilibrium position and the actual influences that affect the decisions of agents in the short run. No such realism was expected to attach to the study of long-period positions. It may be worthwhile to repeat a quotation already given in Chapter 2:

> Thus we are supposing, in accordance with the facts, that at any given time the productive processes set on foot, whether to produce consumption goods or investment goods, are decided in relation to the then existing capital equipment. But we are not assuming that the capital equipment remains in any sense constant from one accounting period to another.
>
> If we look at the productive process in this way, we are, it seems to me, in the closest possible contact with the facts and methods of the business world as they actually exist; and at the same time we have transcended the awkward distinction between the long and the short period. (*CWJMK*, XXIX, pp. 64–5)

The long-run, then, which is a calendar time concept, is a succession of short runs (cf., also, Kalecki, 1971, p. 165). Long-term historical processes do not follow a pre-determined path towards long-period gravitation centres. Rather, they result from the continuous re-creation of restrictions and constraints on agents' actions that follow from their own decisions and actions in the past. At any given time, entrepreneurs have to make decisions facing the constraints represented by their inherited structure of assets and liabilities, by existing institutions and practices, by legal dispositions, and so on. Some of these may be changed in consequence of the very decisions made. New short-period possibilities are open, to which the economy may tend. The succession of short-run positions, gravitating around short-period equilibria (which, one should remember, are defined by desired purchases of consumption goods and capital goods, thereby defining a path for capital accumulation) characterizes a long-term process.

Thus the concentration on short-period equilibria does not mean that long-term processes were considered irrelevant by Keynes or his followers. It does mean that long-term processes have no reality beyond their short-run manifestations and as durable restrictions (but not determinations) on actual development paths.[1] The focus on employment, on the other hand, is due to its role as an index of the global economic situation and, without a doubt, to the novelty represented by the notion of unemployment equilibrium. One should keep in mind, in any case, that not only is the level of employment related to a level of aggregate income but it is also related to a given level of investment and of consumption, as well as to a stock equilibrium in assets markets. The theory of employment is thus a synthesis of Keynes's and Post Keynesian macroeconomics. It does not refer to partial equilibrium characteristics of the labour market. Rather it synthesizes and measures the results of all the central processes that operate in a monetary economy. To put the same point in a different way, the quest in the short-period analysis is for an adequate characterization of the situation around which the actual short-run path of the economy is to be defined. Keynes described two possible ways to describe these short-period equilibria (Keynes, 1964, chap. 4): to present them in money values or in wage units. The latter's role is to show us the effective command on social wealth that an accumulation of specific forms of wealth confers. This power is measured by Keynes in the same way Adam Smith had done: through the capacity to mobilize labour, in what became known as the labour-commanded theory of value. Command over labour is the 'real' measure of value in a monetary economy. Smith had proposed this idea for long-term analysis. Keynes extended it to short-term analysis as well. That is why one confers such a crucial meaning upon the study of employment in Keynes's and Post Keynesian economics.

In Chapter 18 of *The General Theory*, Keynes gave us a highly stylized and simplified description of these processes and the causality sequences in which they are articulated. Using a language appropriate to formal modelling, Keynes defined three equations and three endogenous variables. The first equation was the liquidity preference schedule that, with a given money supply, would determine 'the' interest rate. Given the interest rate, from the schedule of the marginal efficiency of capital one could determine the level of investments. Given investments, one could read, from the propensity to consume, aggregate consumption and thus total income, which, in the short period, would imply a certain level of employment.

An alternative presentation could start from given stocks of the various existing assets and a given state of long-term expectations. Prices of assets and the money rate of interest would then be determined, from which one would know the demand for money, for other liquid assets and for investment goods. With the demand for investment goods identified, one would read from a flow-supply schedule for investment goods the amount of new production that would take place. Given the value of newly produced investment goods, one could read from the propensity to consume the amount of aggregate consumption and from here on both schemes would give the same information.

A short-run equilibrium would be reached when producers' short-term expectations proved to be correct. In other words, if producers of investment goods and of consumption goods could correctly predict the demands for their goods, production would be undertaken in the necessary amounts and the level of employment reached would be sustainable. In Chapter 3 of *The General Theory*, Keynes presented the aggregate demand curve as the producers' expectations as to the receipts that would accrue to them at the various levels of employment. An aggregate supply curve would show the minimum receipts that were required by entrepreneurs to induce them to offer a given level of employment. The level of employment for which aggregate demand and supply were the same was the point of effective demand and that would be, if expectations were correct, the short-period equilibrium level of employment of this economy.[2]

An important feature of Keynes's theory of employment is that it does not refer to a labour market but to the goods market. In

Keynes's view, adopted by Post Keynesians, neither employment nor real wages are determined by the interaction between workers and capitalists in a labour market. Employment, as we saw, is determined by the producers' expectations as to the level of demand they will find in the market. Real wages, on the other hand, are also taken as endogenous.

In *The General Theory*, real wages are endogenously determined, given the assumption of decreasing returns. Profit-maximizing firms will pay real wages that are equal to the marginal productivity of labour at the chosen level of employment. Other Post Keynesian approaches, based mainly on Kalecki's works, assume constant returns and mark-up pricing. In both cases, workers can bargain their money wages but once these money wages are set, they become part of the costs of production to be shifted to prices either because they determine marginal costs, as in the traditional models, or because firms mark up current costs, including labour costs, to determine prices.

Money wages are usually taken as given because of their dependence on complex bargaining patterns.[3] If technical laws of returns are known or mark-ups are fixed, money wages become the basis on which the price system is erected. Prices will be set at the levels that allow either competitive firms to maximize profits or oligopolies to reach their target returns. In sum, in this theory, we find the value of employment (and of real wages) in the goods market, while the price level (given the money wage) is read from the 'labour market'. This feature is not just an illustration of the interchangeability of markets as that which is characteristic of Walrasian models, where everything depends on everything else. It is based on the causation chains starting from entrepreneurial decisions that define a monetary economy.

Post Keynesian price theories actually recognize that one should conceive of two basic price levels in a monetary economy: currently produced goods, the prices of which are obtained by the application of some mark-up on production costs, and assets, whose prices are determined by the expectation of future returns.[4] The relation between the two sets of prices is of crucial importance to the determination of income and employment. This is so because there is an industry in which the two price levels cross each other's path: the investment goods sector. As we saw in Chapter 7, production of investment goods depends on the relation between their demand and supply prices (that determine their spot and forward prices). From this relation one determines the level of investment and thus consumption, total income and employment. Although current prices of goods are determined fundamentally by current costs and prices of assets by expected returns, only some ratios between them are compatible with some desired level of employment, such as, say, full employment.

FUNCTIONAL INCOME DISTRIBUTION

The examination of the behaviour of wages takes us to an important area of development of Post Keynesian thought, which is income distribution. In fact this is a topic to which Post Keynesians have been contributing for at least as long as they have to the theory of effective demand itself. On the other hand, it is also a field in which some deep discomfort is still felt with the incapacity of integrating all the important arguments raised by Keynes and his followers into a coherent whole.

Thinking about income distribution is as old as political economy itself. Perhaps only the debate about the virtues of foreign trade may be an older issue, going back to 'pre-scientific' times in the development of economic thought. Political economy was born of the attempt to identify development patterns or 'laws of motion' that could define the ways and means to expand the wealth of nations. According to classical political economists, such as Smith, Ricardo or Marx, a capitalist economy was constituted by three fundamental social classes: workers, manufacturers (whom we would nowadays call capitalists or entrepreneurs, depending on our theoretical affiliation with Marx or with other authors such as Schumpeter or Keynes) and landlords. These classes were defined by their role or function in the productive process: workers were those who created a product which, under modern conditions of production, was superior to their subsistence needs, generating a 'surplus' product or value; capitalists would appropriate this surplus to invest it in the enlargement of productive facilities, increasing thereby the capacity of nations to create wealth; landlords were just a survival of past times, having the purely negative function of destroying part of the surplus product through non-productive consumption. In this kind of economic society, the increase of the wealth of nations naturally depended on the functional income distribution profile: workers had to be allotted the wherewithal for their survival; of the remaining surplus, the larger the share assigned to capitalists instead of landlords, the quicker could wealth be accumulated.

This was certainly the core concern of classical political economy. As Ricardo, perhaps the greatest of classical political economists, put it,

The produce of the earth – all that is derived from its surface by the united application of labour, machinery, and capital – is divided among three classes of the community; namely, the proprietor of the land, the owner of the stock or capital necessary for its cultivation, and the labourers by whose industry it is cultivated ... To determine the laws which regulate this distribution is the principal problem in Political Economy. (Ricardo, 1971, p. 49)

Neoclassical economics changed the question to be asked (features of static equilibria instead of laws of motion), as well as the social framework in which distribution was to be considered (individual consumers and sellers of specific productive factor services were substituted for social classes). This school is still concerned with functional income distribution but this is now connected with the performance of productive services. The compensation received by owners of factors of production has to conciliate the intensity with which each factor is used with their physical availability. Factor services prices have the role of rationing scarce resources among their potential uses, leading rational agents to select those ends for which some combinations of existing factors constitute the most efficient means. In other words, the compensation earned by owners of productive factors serves to orient the allocation of resources among their alternative uses.

The difficulties that plague neoclassical theories of income distribution are well known by now.[5] These models face great difficulties in taking into consideration capital and profits. Capital cannot be 'scarce' in equilibrium, since it is constituted by reproducible commodities. It is not a physical datum. Profits, then, cannot exist in equilibrium (see Schumpeter, 1934). Neoclassical distribution theory can only be conceived for capitalist economies where capitalists only exist ephemerously and profits keep vanishing.

Despite some important differences in many respects, classical and neoclassical theories of income distribution share some features that make it difficult to insert them into a macroeconomics of a monetary economy, in the sense given to this expression in this book. In particular, one should note that both approaches are developed for long-period equilibrium conditions (see Garegnani, 1983). We have already examined in detail the limitations of this notion in a Post Keynesian view. Secondly, both schools ignore the mechanisms through which a profile of income distribution is established in a monetary economy. They are 'real' theories of income distribution, directly relating real influences to real results. Variables such as money wages or interest rates are either ignored or analysed in ways independent of monetary forces.

Functional distribution was not a primary concern of Keynes in *The General Theory*. The debate around the determination of real wages in that work is developed mainly as a criticism of the notion that it was a determining force behind employment changes rather than as a positive theory of income distribution. Most remarks on this subject are incidental and Keynes never tried to integrate all his propositions about wages, the revenue of entrepreneurs, interest rates and so on into a coherent model of functional income distribution.

Many reasons may have contributed to this neglect. Firstly, to a large extent, the examination of distribution profiles was strategic to approaches that took aggregate income as given. The only way for a given class to improve their position was by reducing some other class's share. The study of conflict, the limits to it and its implications, were naturally the central concern of these approaches which located in the appropriation of income by some specific social group the key to the knowledge of 'laws of motion'. From the time of *The General Theory* on, conflict over income shares became obfuscated because it was important only in the rather extreme conditions of full employment. With variable aggregate income, one group may increase its access to goods and services without necessarily conflicting with other social groups. The central concern then became how to achieve the greatest income level possible, to accommodate the various claims to it without having to create conflicts. Accordingly, the formation of functional income claims became a secondary issue, treated in isolation by Keynes, reserving the global analysis for the determination of aggregate income. This was strengthened by the rather surprisingly scant attention given by Keynes in *The General Theory* to questions such as how to fund long-term investments. This seems to have led him to underestimate the importance of functional distribution in approaching financial problems, in particular the formation of prices and the decision by firms to retain profits, a point that attracted the attention of Kalecki, among others.

One can certainly identify, nevertheless, in *The General Theory* and in the debates that followed its publication, some important elements for a model of functional income distribution. Firstly, we have Keynes's theory of real wages, already mentioned above. In *The General Theory*, he does not try to go beyond orthodoxy in proposing real wages to be determined by profit-maximizing firms operating under decreasing returns of the intensity of factors. In this case, real wages are determined by the marginal productivity of labour, which means that they are technically determined, at least for a given structure of production (which is assumed fixed for the purpose of developing aggregate models). In debates after publication of *The General Theory*, Keynes came to accept the hypothesis of constant returns (constant marginal productivity of labour) but did not elaborate on its implications except in what relates to employment-expanding policies.

Keynes also gave much attention to the determinants of interest rates in developing his liquidity preference theory, but, again, the implications of this theory for a theory of income distribution were not drawn. Less well noticed are his remarks on the remuneration of capital. In this aspect Keynes seemed to lean towards a Smithian notion of surplus value accruing to capital because of its scarcity. The latter notion, however, has a very different meaning as compared to the neoclassical view of scarcity. Capital is scarce not for natural or physical reasons but because of institutional forces that operate to preserve its rarity when compared to labour. In particular, capital is scarce because of the alternative ways of accumulating wealth that set a floor for the returns on capital assets, preventing them from becoming abundant as they technically could. This, as a matter of fact, was the foundation on which Keynes's famous remarks on the 'euthanasia' of rentiers was based.

In addition to these rather scattered remarks, Keynes was also concerned with a different analytical framework from that used by classicals and neoclassicals alike. His theory was a theory of a monetary economy in which important results like the income distribution profile could not be defined ignoring monetary variables and mechanisms. In fact, in a draft of *The General Theory*, Keynes defined a cooperative economy as being one in which

the factors [of production] are hired by entrepreneurs for money but where there is a mechanism of some kind to ensure that the exchange value of the money incomes of the factors is always equal in the aggregate to the proportion of current output which would have been the factor's share in a cooperative economy ... (*CWJMK*, XXIX, p. 78)

In contrast, in a monetary economy, 'entrepreneurs hire the factors for money but without such a mechanism as the above' characteristic of neutral economies (ibid.). According to Keynes, 'it is obvious ... that it is in an entrepreneurial economy that we actually live today' (ibid.). In such an economy, 'the volume of output which yields the maximum value of product in excess of real cost may be "unprofitable"' (ibid., p. 67). This may happen because in monetary economies effective demand may be deficient (see ibid., pp. 80–1, 86).

The implications of these principles for the theory of employment have already been discussed. But even a quick glance at the way Keynes presented his notion of a monetary economy is sufficient also to identify the lines along which the discussion of the determinants of the profile of income distribution should proceed.

Two main features defined the way a monetary economy works. On the one hand, purchases and sales are contracted in terms of money instead of goods. Sellers and buyers enter into forward money contracts on the basis of their expectations of the evolution of the purchasing power of money in terms of their relevant baskets of goods. When the time comes, agents receive money, not goods, which they can spend whenever they want to, on whatever goods they may desire. On the other hand, these economies lack mechanisms of pre-coordination of decisions. There are no means by which would-be spenders can (or have to) specify the nature and the timing of their demands to orient sellers with certainty.

From these features two main implications can be derived. First, as Davidson (1982, p. 68) has put it in his criticism of Clower's *Say's Principle*, it is liquidity, not real income, that constrains purchases. In a monetary economy, money buys goods; but money can be earned as income or obtained by issuing debt. Secondly, the level of income (and of employment) to be generated depends on the expectations of firms as to how much they will be able to gain when the period of production is over and sales are completed.

A model of income distribution for a monetary economy has to be compatible with these features. It has to deal with money forward contracts, liquidity, financial transactions, expectations of money profits and changes in money prices and wages. However, none of the available models of income distribution, which in some sense are connected to Keynes, complies fully with these requirements.

ALTERNATIVE POST KEYNESIAN APPROACHES TO INCOME DISTRIBUTION

Most modern Keynesian models of income distribution derive their foundations from two main sources: (1) Kalecki's work on the determination of profits,[6] relating the structure of aggregate demand to income distribution; and (2) Harrod's extension of the General Theory to long-period growth conditions, in which the equilibrium path of the economy was related to its propensity to save.

Kaldor was the pioneer among the authors of Post (or neo-) Keynesian models combining these features. To put it very succinctly, the central proposition of these models is that an economy can adjust to an (externally) given equilibrium growth path through changes in income distribution. If a given growth rate requires an amount of investment that exceeds full-employment savings, inflation redistributes income in favour of profits. The propensity to save out of profits is assumed to be higher than that out of wages, so that redistribution ensures that the growth path can then be sustained.[7]

The solution to Harrod's 'knife-edge' problem was thus proposed as residing in changes in distribution. Investment expenditures had a priority claim on income. As Kaldor assumed full employment, this meant that consumption was determined as a residual. Given the assumption that most (or all) of investment was financed out of profits, while most (or all) of the consumption was financed out of wages, the distribution of full-employment income between profits and wages was then determined.[8]

Compared to Kaldor's neo-Keynesian model of distribution, Kalecki's approach is less definite in its results. Kalecki proposes a theory of profits in which only capitalists' expenditures may be independent of current income. Workers neither save nor dis-save, having their expenditures constrained by wage income. As capitalists' expenditures are not constrained by earned profits, the necessary equality, under conditions specified by Kalecki, between aggregate profits and the aggregate value of investment and capitalist consumption led him to propose that causality runs from the latter to the former.[9]

Kalecki's theory is much less definite about the profit share, that is the relation between profits and total income, which, in the simplified conditions of most models, means between profits and wages. The model is generally closed by assuming a definite relationship between profits and wages based on microeconomic relations, such as the degree of monopoly. Kalecki, however, never offered a satisfactory theory of the degree of monopoly. In his *Theory of Economic Dynamics* he presented a measure of it and some brief remarks about what may influence its size. A measure, however, is not a theory.[10] In addition, the degree of monopoly is a microeconomic restriction that cannot be unambiguously transformed into a macroeconomic parameter.[11]

In some of his works Kalecki introduced an instrument borrowed from Rosa Luxemburg and, more distantly, from Marx (Kalecki, 1971, chap. 14). He assumed that all productive sectors could be aggregated in three 'departments': department I producing investment goods; department II producing luxuries for capitalists' consumption; and department III producing wage goods. According to Kalecki, the departments should be taken to include the production of their inputs, being completely vertically integrated.[12] In this model, if the difference between wage goods and luxuries is well defined so that workers cannot consume goods from department II, once capitalists decide how much to invest and to consume, the amount of employment in sectors I and II is determined. The amount of employment in department III then has to be sufficient to supply wage goods to workers in departments I and II as well as to its own workers. Thus, for a given wage, the aggregate shares are determined. Possibilities of income redistribution in such an economy are limited by the size (or growth rate) of department III.[13]

The central difficulty of the model resides in its necessity of sharply differentiating wage goods from goods consumed by capitalists. More general versions of this kind of model, such as Marx's own (Marx, 1978), rely only on the difference between consumption

172 *The Operation of a Monetary Economy*

and investment goods. In modern capitalist economies, mass production probably falsifies Kalecki's hypothesis in determining the results again.[14]

If Kalecki's premisses are insufficient to close a model of income distribution, one should recognize that Kaldor's model does it only at the cost of having to introduce some heroic assumptions. First, the model is built for full employment conditions, making it possible to treat income as given. Changes in aggregate profits then become changes in profit shares. The second assumption is that investment is externally given. Again, in a steady-state model with an accelerator type of investment function at full employment, one is prevented from investigating other possible feedbacks on investment or investigating the possibility of changing demand patterns. Technology is introduced in the model through a technical progress function that gives the equilibrium rate of investment to which income distribution has to be adjusted.

Both Kaldor's and Kalecki's models are insufficient as explanations of income distribution in a monetary economy. They are basically 'real' models in which demands in real terms determine income shares. Kaldor does introduce price variations but as an ad hoc mechanism of adjustment requiring a full employment assumption. Kalecki does not deal with money prices and his treatment of financial variables is rather perfunctory. He assumes that the supply of finance is infinitely elastic to capitalists but completely inelastic to workers. As a consequence, once an expenditure plan is adopted by capitalists nothing can prevent it from being implemented and, therefore, the profits from materializing.[15] The whole discussion is actually conducted in real terms, so there is no space for monetary or financial variables in the model.[16] Both models actually try to determine the behaviour of profits, introducing strong arbitrary assumptions to obtain also the behaviour of income shares.[17]

The perplexities of the question are not eased by appealing to other non-orthodox models, such as the neo-Ricardian production prices model. This approach does not deal with money prices or remunerations, but with the distribution of surpluses of goods an economy may generate, given technology, above its physical reproduction. In reality, neo-Ricardian models are concerned with the effects of distribution of relative prices rather than distribution itself. The model is open with respect to shares as long as some minimum requirements are respected, such as the real wages being sufficient to ensure the survival of workers.

In conclusion, the principles that define the working of a monetary economy, although obviously related to the question of income distribution, are not yet adequately integrated even into Post Keynesian models. These models can be used to describe, under certain assumptions, a given distribution profile but they do not allow us to understand how it was actually achieved nor how it could be modified. This is so because they do not show how real-world variables, such as money wages and prices, are set or finance is obtained. One still largely relies on treatments that may even be incompatible with the fundamentals of a monetary economy.

DISTRIBUTION IN A MONETARY ECONOMY

The core of Keynes's *General Theory* could be seen as consisting in the rejection of the orthodox view that a decentralized market economy had a unique equilibrium position determined by objective factors such as technology and availability of materials and/or labour force. A monetary economy, in contrast, may find itself in any number of 'unemployment equilibrium' positions, depending on the state of expectations and the policy of the authorities. As Keynes noted in a fragment dated November 1932, the point was not just a difference between the variety of possibilities open in the short period against the uniqueness of long-period results. He stated that 'there is no unique long-period position of equilibrium equally valid regardless of the character of the policy of the monetary authority' (*CWJMK*, XXIX, p. 55).

That Keynes did not think this 'indeterminacy' to be restricted to the level of income but also to attach to income distribution is witnessed by the opening pages of Chapter 24 of *The General Theory* (Keynes, 1964, pp. 372–4). The profile of income distribution is not solely the result of the operation of purely economic mechanisms. It is the result of a conflict that is ultimately decided by power. These power relations are reflected in the institutions and rules that limit and organize the distributive conflict. Being part of a larger social process, there is no a priori reason to suppose a unique distribution profile to be compatible with the operation of a given economy.

One important innovation present in Keynes's works, to be

further developed by Post Keynesians, is the development, in parallel to functional distribution models, of the concern with personal income distribution. The classical focus on capital accumulation led to special attention being given to the profit share. Keynes and Post Keynesians, on the other hand, are also concerned with supporting adequate levels of effective demand and with fairness. The focus on effective demand leads us to consider how different groups spend their incomes. The focus on fairness requires that we consider the possibilities of giving access to consumer goods in adequate amounts to the largest possible portion of the population.

As regards effective demand, starting from the assumption that investment is done by firms, not by households, there is no theoretical reason to suppose that the quantitatively most important element of aggregate demand, that is consumption, is differentiable in terms of 'social classes'. Rather, the Keynesian approach to the propensity to consume is to consider that it is the size distribution of income that counts. In other words, it is not whether the agent is a 'capitalist' or a 'worker' that matters, but whether he is a member of a high-income class or any other. In fact, Kaldor/Kaleckian models of income distribution propose the use of labels such as 'capitalists' or 'workers' to distinguish between values of the marginal or the average propensity to consume.[18] These models appeal to an intuitive, but not always theoretically solid, association of capital ownership and 'richness', as well as the activity of working and poverty. These relationships are less and less valid for modern societies, where the largest segment is constituted by middle classes. The association between the images of the rich, fat bourgeois and a low propensity to consume (because of their large incomes or because of their austere habits, depending on the ideology of the observer) and the poor, squalid worker who would consume all his income (again, either because he is poor or because he is a spendthrift) comes from nineteenth-century literature, not necessarily from modern sociology.

If one considers that different compositions of aggregate supply may be compatible with different profiles of income distribution that depend on the share of each income-size group in the overall distribution profile, it is then realized that there is no reason, at least from the point of view of effective demand, to suppose the existence of unique global equilibria in monetary economies.

The concern with fairness leads Post Keynesians, as it led Keynes, to the study of the forms through which it is possible to change the access agents have to goods in relation to the income they originally earned. This leads directly to the study of fiscal means of personal income redistribution, which is the main instrument of social reform envisioned by Post Keynesians. We will return to this point in Chapter 12.

As regards functional distribution, modern Post Keynesian analysis has also moved towards the proposition of multiple equilibria. The abandonment of the assumption of decreasing returns has opened the way to analysis of oligopolistic pricing and to the study of different, more complex, relationships between wages and profits along basically Kaleckian lines. The knowledge of functional distribution remains important, especially from the point of view of determining the financial relations that support capital accumulation, either through the internal (to the firms) generation of investable funds (Eichner, 1979; 1980; Harcourt and Kenyon, 1982; Sawyer, 1982; Reynolds, 1987) or through the financial relations that are established through financial markets, both at the micro- and at the macroeconomic level of analysis (cf. Minsky, 1986).

Joan Robinson has noted that 'the capitalist rules of the game are favourable to establishing property in debts' (Robinson, 1969, p. 7). More generally, however, one could say that the rules of the game in a monetary economy are favourable to profits as against labour incomes. This has been known at least since Adam Smith pointed out the greater ease with which capitalists can organize themselves when contrasted to the association of workers (Smith, 1974). Smith's argument, however, and all of its modern variants, refer to a power balance that can change and has changed. The rise of large and powerful unions in the twentieth century has shown that large numbers need not be an impediment to organization. There is a deeper sense, however, in which we may say that the rules still favour profits and it has to do with the way prices are set.

Atemporal neoclassical theory tends to make us forget the sequential nature of capitalist production. In contrast to general equilibrium models, exchanges in real-world capitalist economies are not all simultaneous. Goods and factor services are not traded directly for each other, with all prices being determined at the same instant. In the real world, production (and investment) takes time and has to be organized before the sale of final goods can take place. Pricing of factors of production and of final goods faces different constraints.

Firms operating in a monetary production economy have to develop strategies to cope with an uncertain future. They do not limit
themselves to reacting to the environment, but try to shape it in their
favour. Controlling financial resources and physical means of production, their expectations and decisions largely determine important elements of the environment in which they operate, such as the
income of buyers. Nevertheless, no isolated firm or even group of
firms can guarantee individual success. As Keynes has proposed, in a
monetary economy every enterprise is speculative and firms have to
deal with uncertainty (*CWJMK*, XIX, p. 114).

Firms, like workers, make their calculations and set their income
expectations in terms of money.[19] Firms invest money to obtain
more money (*CWJMK*, XXIX, p. 89). In this context, the existence of
forward contracts in terms of money becomes essential to organize
productive activity in a complex interrelated system (Davidson,
1978a, pp. 57, 60). This is the foundation of the liquidity premium of
money (Keynes, 1964, chap. 17).

Hence the concentration upon money does not result from any
kind of money illusion. It relies on the assumption that money is a
good 'liquidity time-machine', transporting purchasing power
through time, in the wings of forward money contracts (Davidson,
1978a and b). Agents, then, make their bids for income shares in
terms of money, based on their expectations of what it will mean in
terms of real incomes when the process is completed.

The process of price formation, for labour and goods, is the arena
where the bids are made. It is here that the rules favour profits. In an
uncertain world, to be able to wait and give the final word is a bonus.
In a Walrasian world of simultaneous transactions in all markets,
including those of factors, this makes no difference. In a Keynesian
monetary economy, the price of labour is a cost that must be known
to the firm in order to set the prices of goods. Labour is sold, then,
through forward contracts, pre-determining money wages for the
period covered by the contract. No such need to sign forward
contracts exists for final goods. As a matter of fact, a system of
complete future markets for final goods is incompatible with a
monetary economy. Therefore prices of final goods do not have to
be set in advance as the price of labour does. This means that, when
firms set their prices, making their bids for income-to-be-generated,
money wages are already determined. Workers have to make

decisions based on expectations of prices of goods. Firms make decisions on the knowledge of wages. If firms have target rates of return, they can scale up money wage costs when the latter are established to defend their goals.

Under uncertainty mark-up pricing is the most rational strategy open to firms (Davidson, 1978a; Sylos-Labini, 1984). Firms can adjust their mark-up and prices in order to maintain the financial feasibility of their plans when there is a change in the environment, these including changes in money wages (Eichner, 1980).

These principles underlie Keynes's statement that workers can bargain their money wage but not their real wage, which does not thus depend on any special assumption, such as money illusion by workers. It is just a result of the way prices are formed in a monetary economy that allows firms to set their own strategy after the workers have made their bid. In this sense, even the introduction of escalator clauses does not change the situation because all it does is to set a rule to change money wages. In any case, firms can and will change their prices after workers have set theirs. Escalators then probably become no more than sources of price instability, being unable to change the situation of workers. In a monetary production economy, the rules will favour firms against workers.[20]

The above discussion does not mean that any action by workers is doomed, but that functional income redistribution strategies that do not interfere with this mechanism in some way are destined to fail.[21] This discussion, so far, has concentrated mainly on microeconomic mechanisms, since we could say that it is at this level that the bids for expected income are made. Furthermore, income expectations by firms determine the point of effective demand and therefore the amount of income to be distributed.

In *The General Theory*, Keynes assumed that entrepreneurs always entertained 'correct' short-term expectations (*CWJMK*, XIV, p. 182). This assumption allowed him to concentrate on more important subjects than 'deficient foresight' and was supported by Keynes's views on probability (Carvalho, 1988). Be that as it may, it is assumed that entrepreneurs are able to estimate incoming demand for consumption goods, which is induced by income changes, but also the demand for investment goods, which is not. This means that individual expectations are assumed not to be disappointed, making the macro result that which is expected by each and every agent.

FINANCE

The existence of credit makes demand at least partially independent of income. At this point, again, the rules are favourable to capitalists. Credit is supplied by financial institutions on the basis of security margins; that is, depending on the possession of some kind of asset that can be used to liquidate the debt in case of insolvency (Minsky, 1982). Both the amount of credit to be supplied and its terms are related to the size of the margin (cf. Kalecki, 1971, chap. 9).

Workers may have access to external finance but on a more limited scale because of the more uncertain nature of their main 'asset': human capital. A labour asset is illiquid and cannot be taken over by a bank to cover a debt. Moreover, its returns are also uncertain, given the possibility of unemployment. Capitalists have tangible assets. Besides they may and do use credit to buy assets rather than consumption goods, which means that at least part of the debt issued by capitalists is potentially self-liquidating. Easier access to credit allows capitalists to exercise demand over goods beyond or in advance of their income to an extent that is not permitted to workers. As Kalecki argued, this is what gives capitalists the power to 'determine' their profits. In sum, the rules of the game are favourable to profits because of the way prices are formed in a monetary economy and external finance is supplied. All this means that redistribution of income in favour of wages can only be achieved through some kind of intervention in the pricing mechanism.

As Pasinetti (1962) has noted, if workers were allowed to save, and supposing these savings to be borrowed by capitalists to finance investment, the distribution of real income would no longer correspond to the distribution of claims on income. Capitalists would be exercising a real demand with workers' resources. Financial relations would then have to be introduced to allow us to understand the sequence of events leading to the final profile. On the other hand, if workers could borrow from capitalists or from some other external source, the demand for wage goods would increase and the share of profit earners in the appropriation of real income would fall. This would be equivalent to a reduction in the average profit/wage ratio in terms of real income, even if not in terms of earned income.

If workers can actually reduce the average profit/wage ratio of the economy, the same amount of expenditure on investment goods will induce a higher aggregate expenditure in consumption goods. The aggregate profit share falls but not the aggregate amount of profits. A monetary theory of income distribution cannot evade the issue of how money wages and prices are formed and how purchases are financed. In both issues the rules are biased in favour of profits. As the historical record shows, however, the rules tend to conserve rather than to determine a profile. Profit shares are found to be widely different in a comparison between countries although their stability through time seems to be common to a large number of experiences. The differences may be due to practices or institutions that are particular to each country and show that income may be redistributed if those circumstances are changed.

SUMMING UP

In this chapter we have shown that, in a monetary economy, the level of income and of employment at any given moment depends on the decisions of wealth holders, particularly capitalist firms, as to the forms in which wealth is to be held. In a monetary economy, current purchases of assets depend on the expectations of agents as to future yields. If the state of long-term expectations is favourable to the acquisition of investment goods, investment expenditures will be made, increasing income and stimulating consumption.

It is argued that workers do not have the power to determine the level of employment or the real wage rate. Employment depends on the state of short-term expectations by firms, and the real wage depends on the pricing policies of the firms. Workers do bargain money wages but these are not representative of the actual purchasing power they will be able to achieve. Money wages in Post Keynesian models serve instead as the basis for the determination of price levels.

Income distribution in a capitalist economy reflects its power structure. The distribution of power, however, is not just a question of organization and of numbers but also a question of institutional structures and practices. The question is made even more complex in Post Keynesian theory because total income to be distributed is not given. Patterns of interaction between social groups can lead to an increase in total income rather than a conflict for a fixed prize. As seen in the contrast made between Kalecki's and Kaldor's approaches, when total income is variable, the model becomes much more uncertain in its results. Firms (or 'capitalists' if one wishes) have the power to set prices after money wages are fixed and have preferential access to finance, thus having their possibilities of absorbing goods and services only loosely restrained by their current income. Redistributive attempts that only deal with money wages are likely to be inflationary to the extent that they do not change the fundamental factors that guarantee the privileged hierarchical position of firms in a monetary economy.

Functional income distribution, that describes income appropriation by social classes, is not the only aspect to be considered, either as a subject of study or as a field of political intervention. Post Keynesian analysis relates functional distribution to the need to finance capital accumulation, but it also encompasses the study of personal income distribution to analyse patterns of aggregate demand as well as to develop propositions of social reform through fiscal means of income and wealth redistribution.

As a result of the attempt to combine all these characteristics, models of income distribution for monetary economies tend to be very complex and none has been satisfactorily completed to this date, although many have been developed contemplating partial aspects of the question. The way ahead must consist in Post Keynesian studies of personal income distribution and effective demand, combined with a Post Kaleckian perspective on functional income distribution and the financing of aggregate demand.

NOTES

1. 'Everything that happens in an economy happens in a short-period situation, and every decision that is taken is taken in a short-period situation, for an event occurs or a decision is taken at a particular time, and at any moment the physical stock of capital is what it is; but what happens has a long-period as well as a short-period aspect. Long-period changes are going on in short-period situations. Changes in output, employment and prices, taking place with a given stock of capital, are short-period changes; while changes in the stock of capital, the labour force and the techniques of production are long-period changes (Robinson, 1969, p. 180).

2. It is not clear from *The General Theory* what would happen if short-term expectations were disappointed. Hicks (1974) suggests a quantity adjustment process based on changes in the level of inventories. Amadeo (1986) suggests that, given Keynes's assumption of perfect competition, prices would change to adjust actual demand to supply. Keynes himself discarded this question, saying

that 'the theory of effective demand is substantially the same if we assume that short-period expectations are always fulfilled' (*CWJMK*, xiv, p. 181). Keynes stated also that 'the main point is to distinguish the forces determining the position of equilibrium from the technique of trial and error by means of which the entrepreneur discovers where the position is' (ibid., p. 182). It is with the former that Keynes is concerned in *The General Theory*. For a discussion of the behaviour of the 'labour market', see Davidson (1983). A criticism of Post Keynesian propositions is presented in Dutt and Amadeo (1990), pp. 122–39).

3. Some Post Keynesians seemed to feel uncomfortable with the exogeneity of money wages, adhering to some form of Phillips curve or, more recently, to 'competing claims equilibrium models', defined in NAIRU approaches. For a simple definition of a NAIRU (non-accelerating inflation rate unemployment) model see Soskice and Carlin (1989). We will return to this point in Chapter 11.

4. Townshend, in a paper that did not have the influence it deserved, has proposed the foundations for a Keynesian theory of value, based on the notions of uncertainty and liquidity, that would unify both price levels. Unfortunately, his proposal is yet to receive the attention it merits in a field that has been neglected even by Post Keynesian researchers, with practically the sole exception of Shackle. See Townsend (1937).

5. The most important of these difficulties were debated in what became known as the Cambridge Controversies. The most authoritative exposition of these controversies is found in Harcourt (1972). Shorter versions of it can be found in Harcourt (1982), part 5 and Harcourt (1986), part 3. See also Kregel (1975).

6. Kalecki's famous aphorism that 'capitalists earn what they spend' had also been proposed by Keynes in *A Treatise on Money*, with the image of the widow's cruse. Kalecki, however, has had in this particular point much more influence than Keynes. The widow's cruse metaphor seemed to have left a bad impression, even on Keynes's closest collaborators. See *CWJMK*, xiii, pp. 339–42.

7. See Asimakopulos (1980/1) and Kregel (1971) for a more detailed discussion of Kaldor's growth model.

8. Although not the distribution between workers and capitalists. Pasinetti offered a model where this distinction is developed. See Pasinetti (1962) and Kregel (1971). However, the reliance of Kaldor on full employment conditions and of Pasinetti on long-run full equilibrium was also a cause of discomfort for many Post Keynesians. See, for instance, Asimakopulos (1988, pp. 134 and 152–3).

9. For a closed economy without government.

10. Many Post Keynesians would dissent from this proposition. See, for instance, Sawyer (1982); Reynolds (1983 and 1987); Skott (1988).

11. 'the aggregate degree of monopoly depends on the industrial composition of production. Industries differ in terms of the degree of monopoly and of the response of costs to changes in output, and the relative weights of different types of industries will affect the overall picture' (Sawyer, 1982, pp. 94–5).

12. Marx's departments were not vertically integrated. The premises underlying Kalecki's treatment were criticized by Keynes. See *CWJMK*, xii, pp. 837 ff.

13. Which strengthens the point raised in note 11 above, since the profit share could be seen as the ratio between the value of investment and capitalist consumption to total income, or, using the 'departments', the ratio (DI + DII)/(DI + DII + DIII), which obviously depends on the composition of aggregate production.

14. On the other hand, in developing countries, where markets are smaller and income is highly concentrated for historical reasons, demand patterns are sharply discontinuous and Kalecki's model may fit better.

15. Again, see *CWJMK*, xii, pp. 838–9, for a discussion of the point with Kalecki.

16. In the first versions of his business cycle model the rate of interest was present

but Kalecki eliminated it on the grounds that 'the rate of interest is an increasing function of gross profitability', a variable already included in the model (Kalecki (1943), 1971, p. 7).

17. Some authors defend the view that Kalecki's distribution model is more flexible than it looks. Asimakopulos (1988) states that Kalecki admits that workers' pressures can actually reduce mark-ups, increasing thereby labour's share of income. Sawyer (1982) seems to present a similar view, suggesting, like Asimakopulos, that not only can the mark-up be reduced but that it would actually increase employment. It is hard to see how this statement can be sustained, however, beyond the rather vague remarks by Kalecki that firms may refrain from overexploiting their market power in order not to excite workers' demands. Sawyer states that, in Kaleckian approaches, 'labour is not a passive economic agent, but bargains with firms over real wages' (1982, p. 11). However, what the author establishes is that workers have real 'targets', which they have to translate into money targets since the latter is what is really bargained anyway (ibid., p. 105). Keynes insisted on the fact of wage bargaining being conducted in money terms. This is not to say that workers have money illusion, but that workers cannot control the prices of wage goods that ultimately determine the real meaning of agreed money wages. It is not clear what, in the statement that workers have real wage targets, can modify this. For a criticism that forced decreases in mark-up can stimulate employment, see Skott (1988, p. 25).

18. As put by Sawyer (1982, p. 105), the 'belief that the propensity to save is larger for higher income households than for lower income households, and that the share of household income derived from non-labour income rises with income . . .'. This author is certainly much more rigorous than one can ordinarily find, postulating a testable empirical proposition to justify what is, in fact, an empirical relation.

19. As Joan Robinson put it:

The reason why the plain man concentrates upon money is that he can hope (according to his personal circumstances) by working, saving, speculating, employing labour, demanding a rise in pay, to increase his command over money, whereas the purchasing power over goods and services that a unit of money represents is something arising out of the total operation of the economy, which he can do nothing about. (Robinson, 1969, p. 25)

20. Repressive policies on the power of firms to determine prices may not be effective to alter these results, at least in the short to medium term. As Weintraub (1978) has argued, restrictive monetary policies, for instance, may cause unemployment rather than price restraint if mark-ups are resilient. As Sylos-Labini (1984) has suggested, restrictive policies may work to hold prices stable if they restrain prices of factor services (through unemployment of labour and resources), which is the opposite situation to the one to which the redistributive initiative refers.

21. We may consider that workers have, in some cases, a veto power on decisions of capitalists, but not a power of initiative. Under full employment, workers may paralyse the economy but their demands will generate inflation, not redistribution, unless other restrictions are assumed to operate on the freedom of firms to set prices. See Kahn (1972, p. 103). Kalecki suggests that workers can create political rather than economic problems. See Kalecki (1943).

PART III
NEW PERSPECTIVES

11. Inflation, High Inflation and Hyperinflation

Modern market economies are built on the assumption of stable prices. Time-related production and accumulation activities in a complex system of input/output interactions demand the development of forward contractual relations. The possibility of calculation which underlies decisions of firms to produce and to invest demands a unit of value that is recognized by all participants and that is expected to remain stable over time to serve efficiently as money of account to the acceptance of contractual obligations. Contracts denominated in a common unit are, then, a vital institution to connect agents in a market economy in a point in time and over time (*CWJMK*, XXVIII, pp. 252, 255; Davidson, 1978a and b).

Agents may have 'real' goals but money is their common language and the contract system serves to establish the grammar rules of this language. Price stability then means that the 'meaning' of a given money sum may be intelligible to the agents entering into a contract, allowing them to judge whether or not to accept its terms.

Obviously, it is not thought to be required that prices should be absolutely stable. One could even doubt whether the notion of an absolute value of money makes any sense (*CWJMK*, V, book II). What is important is the 'convention' of stable prices, the general belief that no systematic or irreversible general price level changes can take place that could invalidate monetary calculations. This convention sustained the inelasticity of price expectations that characterized much of the history of modern capitalism, at least until relatively recent times.[1]

In the post-Second World War period, the situation changed. In contrast with cyclical movements around a zero (or quasi-zero) trend, one began to observe price movements around clearly ascending trend lines. Periods of deflation became rare or non-existent. After a timid appearance in the 1950s, inflation grew steadily in the 1960s and early 1970s and was brought under relative control afterwards through policies that did not hesitate to sacrifice employment and income to obtain some measure of stability. In South America the changing environment was, if anything, much more visible. Much higher inflation rates were reached as early as the late 1950s and the evolution of prices was generally even worse in the following three decades.

Despite this worsened state of affairs, the performance of most of these economies was very satisfactory, at least until the early 1970s, when stagnation ensued. This raises one important question: how much inflation can a country endure while still sustaining adequately its production activities? A Post Keynesian answer must focus on how and how far institutions are changed to deal with inflation. History has presented us with three kinds of experiences in relation to prices: (1) stable prices and transient moderate inflation, where no institutional change was introduced; (2) moderate to high long-term inflation, where institutional innovations are introduced, notably indexation of contracts; and (3) extremely high rates of inflation in explosive processes, called hyperinflations, where no institutional change is introduced in time to avoid disintegratory pressures on the economy. Despite their being definable as different processes, with their own roots and dynamics, under some conditions an economy may transit from one type of inflation to another. In what follows we will be concerned to study the features of each of the three types of inflationary processes listed and the critical points of transition between them.

INFLATION AMIDST STABILITY

According to Keynes (1923), the nineteenth century was the period in which the convention of stability was formed, since the long-term behaviour of prices did not show any identifiable trend. Of course, price stability could be broken and was broken many times. Nevertheless, the convention of stability meant that these interruptions were transitory or connected to some legitimately unpredictable event against which, precisely because of its unpredictability, no precaution of any kind could have been taken.

In general, inflationary episodes could have their roots known and attacked without causing any permanent damage, since they would be alien to the normally operative forces in the economy. Moderate rises in prices were believed to be reversed by similar random events in the opposite direction. 'Normality', thus, was defined as a situation of overall price stability. Being 'normal', stability was the situation to which agents always expected the economy to return. No major changes were necessary to cope with these pressures. Institutions developed on the assumption of stability were efficient in the long term. Innovations were not worth their cost. As Keynes remarked after the First World War: 'A sentiment of trust in the legal money of the State is so deeply implanted in the citizens of all countries that they cannot but believe that some day this money must recover a part at least of its former value' (Keynes, 1920, p. 224).

Sometimes, however, fundamental stability could be broken in violent, explosive ways, generating hyperinflations. In these times, to recover past normality patterns could prove to be impossible. Reconstruction of new foundations for price stability could then require deeper measures of intervention than mere manipulation of fiscal or monetary policies.

In a hyperinflation, pressures on the level of prices would accumulate, while most agents would still persist in the convention of stability. In these processes, however, sooner or later some fact would end up triggering a sudden realization on the part of the public that the patterns of the past were gone forever. Accustomed to stability, agents would panic, intensifying disequilibria and leading to the final disintegration of the monetary system, preventing any form of going back to the status quo ante. Post-hyperinflationary stabilization would require new starting points for the definition of money and relative prices. Monetary reforms could introduce new monies of account to ease the transition to a new system of contracts.

The trust in the legal tender as a stable representation of purchasing power depended, naturally, less on psychological characteristics of people (although this factor should not be neglected) than on institutional factors and practices that served to anchor the formation of prices. The general acknowledgement of these anchors served to sustain inelastic expectations as to the behaviour of prices in the future.

Perhaps the most important of these anchors has been represented by gold in the several forms of the gold standard adopted in the nineteenth century. It is well known that the efficient operation of the gold standard was achieved in those times more by demand controls than by supply factors or the effective availability of gold reserves. Keynes himself, while a lifelong critic of a strict adhesion to gold standard rules, always recognized the standard's strength as a generally accepted symbol and measure of value (see, for instance, *CWJMK*, XXV). In any case, the main stabilizing role of the gold standard was to signal to agents that general price movements in any direction could not be indefinitely sustained. Either because of the actual exhaustion of reserves (in the 'automatic' gold standard) or because the monetary authorities would take steps to avoid a reduction of reserves, agents knew that inflation would be repressed and normal conditions restored. Inflationary pressures would cause an increase in the transactionary demand for money that could not be satisfied, given the limits represented by the gold reserves on the issue of money. Interest rates would go up, demand would diminish and prices would, thus, go down again. The gold standard did not work with such efficiency, but it was sufficient to ensure the confidence of the general public.[2]

It is interesting to note that, in exceptional periods, such as wars, the gold standard could not be maintained. Its suspension, however, strengthened the idea that the stability of gold prices was part of 'normality', to be restored when the extraordinary times were over. Persistent inflation was thus a sign of crisis or national emergencies that would disappear when normality could be achieved again. Economic agents therefore had no reason to prepare against permanent inflation since permanent inflation would be equivalent to permanent emergencies, which was a contradiction in terms. Inflationary losses (or gains) could be seen as equivalent to losses or gains from earthquakes or wars or any other such 'extra-economic' causes.

SYSTEMIC INFLATION

After the Second World War, inflation gradually became part of 'normality' itself. In the 1950s slow but persistent rises in prices only intensified in exceptional times, such as the Korean War. However, at the end of the decade and the beginning of the 1960s the existence of a rising trend in prices, as well as the increasing unlikelihood of deflationary movements, became clear to economists, if not yet to the general public.

Many reasons have been pointed out to explain the emergence of an inflationary 'bias' in capitalist economies. One may refer to the radical change operated in the definition of the role of the state. As a consequence of Keynesian 'ideologies' there became part of the culture the idea that the state is responsible for maintaining full employment and for preventing even minor fluctuations of economic activity. In parallel, large-scale unionization and the growth of monopolies may have made wage-bargaining processes obsolete (Weintraub, 1978).

Labour 'discipline' based on the existence of an industrial reserve army of unemployed labour disappeared. On the side of capital, oligopolies also became more powerful to shift any increase in costs to prices, reducing the stimuli to drive 'hard bargains' that could make them unpopular with unions. Distributive conflicts are not a novelty in a capitalist system, but the strengthening of bargaining positions was. The solution for the conflict between powerful warriors such as modern labour and modern capital was inflation. An 'inflationary pact' developed, through which it became a least-resistance solution for large firms to accept any money wage demands (as long as it did not weaken its competitive position relative to other firms in the industry) since it could simply shift them on to customers. For labour leaders these shifts to prices would hardly be recognized by workers as resulting from their own pressures, since in most cases wage bargaining takes place on an individual industry basis, concealing from agents the aggregate effect of each bargain. The inflationary pact thus satisfies both large firms, which obtain industrial peace, and labour leaders, who are seen as successful negotiators by the rank and file.

This new situation was made possible by the weakening of monetary discipline as well. Pure paper-money systems have no endogenous limits or stimuli to discipline. Unless politically motivated monetary authorities decide to control the process (risking the generation of problems such as unemployment, bankruptcy and so on), there is no reason why increases in nominal demand for money caused by inflation could not be accommodated. Pure paper-money systems have no intrinsic power against inflationary processes.[3]

As a consequence of all these changes, modern inflation assumed a systemic nature instead of its episodic character in the past. Perceptions of these changes, however, were delayed by the deepness with which confidence in money was rooted in human practices and beliefs. These beliefs were only shaken after repeated losses caused by permanent inflation in an institutional system designed for stability.

The disequilibria that emerged were specific forms of the disturbances in relative prices caused by the differences in speed of adjustment to inflationary pressures of the various sectors (Moore, 1983, p. 176). The difficulty is to distinguish changes in relative prices that are 'legitimate' from those that are caused by inflation spreading at different speeds throughout the economy. Productive sectors that operate on the basis of long-term contracts are immediately penalized by inflation. Differences in competitivity, market power or just plain agility in perceiving nominal changes are enough to generate real effects upon inflation. Utilities that usually have their prices controlled – taxes, rents, wages – all suffer losses in greater or lesser degree because of being restrained by contracts or other practices that assume stability.

The list of evils created by inflation is well known. Weintraub (1978, pp. 29–33) gave an almost exhaustive list of them: (1) it redistributes income blindly but not randomly, often favouring the rich against the poor, the capitalist against the worker; (2) it 'clouds rational long-range economic planning'; (3) it favours financial capital as against productive capital; (4) it misleads entrepreneurs into consuming their capital as if it was income; (5) it induces the development of defensive speculative practices; (6) it detracts public attention from more fundamental problems; (7) it distorts the fiscal structure of the state; (8) it affects exchange-rate behaviour; (9) it reduces the efficiency of money-payment mechanisms; and (10) it stimulates the appeal to policies that may be damaging to market economies, such as price controls.

As Feijo (1991) added, following the work of A.D. Bain, inflation also affects interest rates and the profile of long-term finance to the detriment of long-lived investments. All these effects may perhaps be condensed into three groups of problems: (1) the destruction of the contractual money of account that ceases to inform about the real nature of obligations being accepted for future liquidation; (2) prices ceasing to be informative about even current conditions of profitability, competitivity and so on; and (3) the increase of uncertainties about the future caused by the incapacity to map sequels from the present since they depend on changes in attitudes and practices the timing and extension of which cannot be anticipated by agents. No less important than these economic effects, continuing inflation causes serious political problems as well. The perception, justifiable or not, that inflation results from 'abuse of power' (both on the part of firms and on the part of large unions, as became clear in recent years) erodes the sense of common objectives on which the idea of nation is based. In addition, the realization that large speculative gains can be made by those who know how 'to play the inflation right' erodes both the ethics of work and the notion that calculated effort is the means to improve one's situation, fundamental features of the capitalist order (see Weber, 1968). Political conflicts and shortened horizons can make the economic situation of a country unmanageable, at least until the crisis becomes so deep that survival is accepted as a new unifying goal for society.

The main point raised so far is that inflation heightens uncertainty. Because inflation increases uncertainty, making it more difficult to formulate hypotheses and probability relations to orient the formation of expectations and the choice of strategies, it causes more damage to those activities for which distant temporal horizons are more important. Investments in capital goods and long-term finance tend to disappear, replaced by shorter and more flexible kinds of commitments that allow rerouting if some unpredicted development ensues. Private agents begin to include explicit estimates of inflation in their plans and contracts, something which intensifies current disequilibria since there is no reason to suppose convergent expectations if we live outside the peculiar world of new classical economists, who suppose that agents share the same beliefs about economic processes when not even economists are able to do so. Under these conditions, the intervention of the state in the economy as an entrepreneur becomes unavoidable, for it is the only agent that can risk those long-term initiatives from which private agents refrain. As Keynes observed in the 1920s, an increasing degree of 'socialistic control', by which he understood the direct intervention of the state, is a necessary result of inflation (*CWJMK*, XVII, pp. 183–4). If inflation accelerates beyond what can be absorbed by an institutional system built on the assumption of stability, the need for change will become overwhelming. Agents cling to the existing contractual system because it is an efficient way to organize production, since it allows the entrepreneur to perform a reasonably safe forecasting of his future costs and, sometimes, also his receipts. When this capacity to forecast is reduced, agents may wonder whether the system is worth holding. When the uncertainties caused by inflation as to the future real value of the money in terms of which contracts are made are greater than the perceived gains of having pre-determined claims and obligations in terms of money, agents will look for alternatives. These may be either the breakdown of the contractual system, as happens during hyperinflations, or the development of institutional innovations. Systemic inflation, then, may lead to a change in the monetary regime itself, changing rules and practices, particularly of contracts. When this happens, the economy may move into the high inflation regime.

THE HIGH INFLATION REGIME

The concept of high inflation was developed in the late 1970s by Latin American economists, notably from Argentina,[4] to deal with situations in which inflation is too high to allow the maintenance of forward contracting in terms of money but is not high enough to disintegrate the economy, as is the case with hyperinflation.

The properties of such a system were relatively unknown. Perceptive analysts, such as Jackson, Turner and Wilkinson (1975), who modelled intense inflationary processes under the label 'strato-inflation', could not explain how a 'disequilibrium' configuration could be sustained for so long as has been the case in some countries. The Brazilian economy, for instance, has lived with high inflation for more than 30 years, most of which were years also of intense growth, uninterrupted even by the first oil shock of the early 1970s, chaotic developments emerging only after 1985 (Feijo, 1991).

The key to understanding the relative stability found in countries living under high inflation is the perception of the way institutions and behaviours can adapt to high and persistent inflation rates. New institutions serve as the basis for the definition of 'normality' patterns that allow economic relationships between agents to be developed and growth to be resumed. Distributive conflicts are much reduced in drama and intensity if growth takes place, since relative gains and losses can then refer to additions to income rather than to absolute levels, which is the stability condition identified by Jackson, Turner and Wilkinson (1975). A high inflation regime is much more vulnerable to shocks than the regime of stable prices or of equilibrium inflation (those inflationary processes that are not thought to be dangerous enough to threaten the continuity of economic life or to require institutional innovations as defences against inflation), creating a very unstable kind of equilibrium. If shocks disorganize the operations of the economy, production and investment may be affected, growth rates reduced and the system may then collapse.

In an almost tautological sense, inflation should be seen as a process of conflict over income shares. The conflict, however, unfolds according to some 'rules of the game' that regulate the ways through which prices and money incomes are set. These rules determine the efficacy of each group's strategy in reaching their target. Thus with generally stable prices, for instance, workers expect rises in contractual money wages to be converted into rises in real wages. A high inflation regime emerges when the continuous disappointment of expectations leads agents to question the rules of the game themselves. Contractual claims denominated in money cease to be acceptable predictors of real income. The transition to high inflation regimes takes place when inflation is so intense that the risks surrounding prediction of the future value of money make it impossible to accept future obligations denominated in it. Differences in expectations as to the future path of inflation and in the capacity to react to its accelerations or decelerations when inflation rates are very high prevent agents from entering into forward contractual obligations, the real value of which can suffer variations large enough to offset any expected advantage from accepting the contract itself.

Money forward contracting thus becomes impossible when inflation is believed to be permanent and high enough to systematically supplant any other random influence on the value of contracted obligations. A high inflation regime emerges when new rules of contracting are developed. This regime is defined by the development of new contractual rules, designed to adapt the system to the perception that inflation ceased to be just a contingency and became a systematic and important trend in the economy. Since contracts are an institution created to reduce the uncertainties of the future, they now have to deal with the influence of persistent inflation that is to change the actual real value of money when compared to the expected value of money when the contract was accepted. The actual real value of indexed contractual obligations will depend on the index chosen for value adjustment and on the period after which the adjusted value will be paid. The contracting parties know that the purchasing power of a monetary unit will be reduced although only in rare instances will they know by how much.

It is to deal with this difficulty that indexation is introduced. Indexation means that agents will be allowed to contract in a money of account that is convenient to them; that is, the unit that represents that basket of goods they ultimately have in mind when accepting claims and obligations in money in a stable-prices regime. A common money of account that is characteristic of a monetary economy is abandoned in the attempt by each group to defend itself against the changes in the 'real content' of this unit that could generate unpredictable changes in the real value of obligations and claims they judge acceptable. In its purest terms, indexation means the proliferation of monies of account with the effect of legitimizing demands for the social product that, being denominated in independent units of account, may be inconsistent with each other. Sharing a common unit of measurement makes the redistributive nature of inflation explicit, showing that somebody's gain may be somebody else's loss. However, with indexation, nobody recognizes any loss, since they are allowed to place their claims directly in the unit that measures their real income targets. If inflation results from inconsistent claims on the social product, indexation only masks this inconsistency. What is worse is that, if the right of definition of monies of account specific to persons or groups is legitimized, distributive conflicts become institutionalized and insoluble.

As Leijonhufvud (1981) has correctly pointed out, there is nothing trivial in the choice of an index. Different agents have different goods, or the same goods in different proportions, in their relevant baskets. Moreover, agents entering into contractual obligations with different partners will find themselves involved with different units of account for their inflows and outflows of resources, living under uncertainty about the future exchange rates between the different units of their claims and liabilities. In fact the excessive degree of uncertainty that such a system would create leads the state to impose a restricted set of indices that agents have to accept in their private contracts. Even though common fixed baskets for agents with different needs would seem 'suboptimal', it may be an efficient solution when one considers the uncertainties mentioned above. Thus, under

Figure 11.1

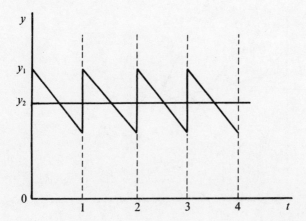

high inflation, agents tend to accept adjustment indices that reflect only approximately their own real expectations of income but that seem to be, in any case, better than having to enter into contracts in terms of money.

The second element of an indexed contract is the period of adjustment and settlement of obligations. Most of the orthodox students of indexation suppose it to be instantaneous, which gives it the property of making indexed incomes 'rigid'.[5] Lags of two kinds may affect the real income that is actually received (or paid) from an indexed contract: (1) there is an interval of time necessary to collect and process price information; (2) payments are not made continuously but at discrete points in time at the end of an agreed period. The first kind of lag means that a given loss of real income caused by rising prices will only be paid after some time has elapsed, causing losses between the two dates. The second kind causes an additional loss to appear if the payment of compensation is scheduled at some date later than that of calculation of the index itself. If inflation rates are constant, the agent will not be able to maintain his 'peak' income, but will maintain his average income constant. If inflation is accelerating, the lags will cause, *ceteris paribus*, losses in average income as well. This is shown in Figures 11.1 and 11.2. In both figures we assume that the agent's income is adjusted at the end of a given period, during which prices have been rising. Figure 11.1

Figure 11.2

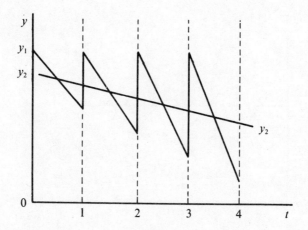

shows a situation in which prices rise at a constant rate. 'Peak' income is y_1, reached only at the moment payments are made. Average real income is y_2. In Figure 11.2, inflation accelerates from one period to the other, which means that money income will have less and less real value. Perfect indexation reconstitutes 'peak' incomes but is powerless to sustain average incomes.

Widespread indexation is not the only feature of a high inflation regime. A second characteristic refers to the determination of flow-supply prices. Indexation cannot be universal because its role is periodically to restore a given structure of relative prices and incomes. If the problem of inflation is to induce 'false' relative price changes, the problem of indexation is not being able to sort out 'legitimate' relative price changes. Indexation of flow-supply prices would prevent the kind of adjustments that an efficient market system requires, those rooted in real causes such as technological changes, changes in tastes and so on. Firms adapt to high inflation by changing the way costs and mark-ups are calculated (Frenkel, 1979). Instead of taking historical costs as the basis for price determination, firms know that future costs will be necessarily higher than current or past costs. For this reason, current mark-ups on current observed costs have to be higher to cover the necessary increase in prime costs in the next period.

Thus a high inflation regime changes the way prices and incomes are set. The new institutional (contractual) rules and the behaviour of price makers define a regime that may be seen as a new kind of equilibrium. Indexation does not allow agents to maintain their income targets but it is seen as a way of organizing the distributive conflict. The alternative to it would be some kind of continuous bargaining process that would take time and resources and would probably be seen as unfair to those agents that were less organized. Agents accept longer indexed contracts because, *ceteris paribus*, they minimize losses between negotiating periods. As long as the income losses between negotiations are balanced by the benefits of avoiding conflicts or by the overall gains that an organized economy offers, by being able to grow, a high inflation regime will define an equilibrium. Nobody is really getting what they want but what they avoid is good enough to compensate for this, especially if they do get to grow so that income from other sources increases to offset inflationary losses.

Such an equilibrium is, however, unstable. The root of instability lies in the fact that contractual incomes are adjusted for past inflation but flow-supply prices are formed according to expectations of future inflation. If reasons emerge to expect a future acceleration of inflation, the regime may crumble, as will be seen below.

FRAGILITY AND INSTABILITY OF THE HIGH INFLATION REGIME

A high inflation regime is a fragile arrangement. It constitutes a kind of knife-edge equilibrium in which agents compare their income losses (caused by lagged adjustment) with the saving in costs of conflict. Nobody can maintair their desired position, because peaks of real income reached when 'corrected' payments are made begin immediately to be eroded by continuing inflation. On the other hand, firms have always to face the uncertainties of a dual system where production costs are at least partially indexed (labour costs, financial costs, taxes and so on) but their receipts are not. They have to engage in production processes without always knowing how high some of their costs are really going to be. Firms that lose relative position, because they do not react as quickly as others to inflation, will see their costs increase with the average price level.

The root of fragility lies in the fact that contracts are indexed to the past while flow-supply prices are 'indexed' to the (expectations of the) future. As long as the future repeats the past, the system works. However, shocks can sever the past from the future, causing prices and contractual incomes to move in incoherent ways. With constant inflation rates, income losses relative to their peak will also be constant and, if they are lower than the estimated costs of conflicting, the system will last. Predictability will increase and production may then proceed as if prices were stable. If, on the other hand, the system suffers a shock, which may be a supply shock such as the oil price rises of the 1970s or an expectational shock (when agents for some reason expect some acceleration of inflation), it can degenerate into a hyperinflation.

The fragility of the context is further aggravated by two additional characteristics of a high inflation situation. On the one hand, given the shortening of contracts resulting from inflationary uncertainties, no hedgers, in the sense of Minsky – that is, those investors who only accept financial obligations with the same temporal profile as their assets – can exist since long-term finance is not supplied (see Feijo, 1991). In addition, the field of action of economic policy is drastically reduced as a result of institutional change. Monetary policy is doubly affected. To the extent that financial contracts are indexed, the supply of legal tender has to increase as the value of debts in terms of it increases. Indexed contracts are enforced by the state so the state has no choice but to provide as much legal tender as may be necessary to enforce them. In addition, interest rate policies are also made rigid. Money rates have to follow inflation to be competitive with indexed financial instruments (Carvalho, 1986). With high inflation, to do otherwise would be to cause a 'flight from money' to goods or to foreign assets that would intensify the disorganizing pressures already operating in the system.

Fiscal policy will also meet some important difficulties. Many government expenditures will be indexed. Certainly public debt will be subject to indexation. Government incomes, on the other hand, will suffer what is called the Tanzi effect: the lag between the tax-generating operation and the moment the government actually receives the tax revenues erodes the real value of the revenues, causing deficits to emerge even in a budget that would, under price stability, be balanced. This imbalance will emerge even if taxes are indexed and will be worse the higher is the rate of inflation.[6]

In conclusion, a high inflation regime is an unstable system in which the possibility of coordination failures is institutionalized. Agents are always striving to recover their 'losses', only to see new ones appear. As long as these losses are contained in an acceptable interval, the system can work and, with a favourable environment, even prosper, as the Brazilian economy did in the late 1960s and early 1970s. However, the system could not resist the crisis that came later. In countries like Argentina, which did not quite share the prosperity of those years, the crisis was permanent (de Pablo and Dornbusch, 1988).

HYPERINFLATION

Hyperinflation is defined as a situation in which money contractual institutions can no longer be maintained or reformed. It takes place when inflation rates are so high and its acceleration rate so intense that no sufficient time is given for a process of institutional innovation, such as indexation, to develop. The national monetary system is then destroyed and replaced, firstly, by a direct exchange system and, later, by another monetary system, usually based on a foreign monetary unit, such as the US dollar. A hyperinflation is, thus, different from a high inflation because the latter refers to a new monetary arrangement, no matter how fragile it may be, while the former defines an explosive form of disequilibrium that cannot last for long.

A hyperinflation can also take place when excessive pressure is put on the institutions defining a high inflation regime. When current prices grow at rates higher than the ones in the past, indexation becomes less and less efficient as a protective device. There may come a point at which the loss of income caused by sticking to indexation becomes greater than the perceived benefits of having an automatic rule of nominal income increase. If this happens, the institutions of high inflation will crumble and a hyperinflation may ensue as agents try to defend themselves by other means. In particular, agents will try to escape from money, that is a social relation in a society that is falling apart, towards commodities that look like efficient individual life-savers.

We cannot say a priori how much acceleration inflation may suffer before indexation itself ceases to be seen as an efficient contractual instrument, leading agents to search for other strategies to orient their behaviour that could eventually lead to a hyperinflation. Hyperinflations seem still to be too rare to allow stylization into a general model. The European hyperinflations took place in economies that were not used to inflation and that were also going through some special kind of difficulties, such as, for instance, Germany's need to pay for war reparations in the 1920s. In modern times, hyperinflations have been a threat to countries long used to inflation, like Argentina, Brazil or Israel.

A hyperinflation is taken to be a mode of forming prices where expectations of future inflation and defensive strategies against it are the main (and practically the sole) determinants of current decisions by all agents. At a first stage, the breakdown of rules leads to wildly divergent expectations and to entirely inconsistent pricing policies. At a second stage, agents search for new units in terms of which they may recover the possibility of calculation. Some coordination is recovered and price stabilization can be successfully attained.

The existence of these two stages is clearly suggested by Bresciani-Turroni's classic 1937 study of the German hyperinflation. In it we can see that the period until August 1923 was characterized by a markedly divergent behaviour of prices (Chapter 1, graphs 5 and 6), followed by a strictly coincident path of relevant prices, pegged to the US dollar, revealing that the economy had found in the exchange rate a new source of information around which agents could form consistent strategies and some degree of coordination could be recovered (ibid., graph 7).

The passage to a hyperinflation can occur, in modern conditions, if excessive pressure is put on the institutions that define high inflation. External shocks, external debt servicing, sharpening of public-sector disequilibria, attempts to anticipate restrictive stabilization policies – all these factors or expectations can influence current pricing rules because, as we have seen, flow-supply prices are not subject to indexation. They are the open valve through which these pressures can be introduced into the contractual system, ultimately to destroy it.

Expectations of future acceleration of inflation lead firms to anticipate it by increasing their current mark-ups to cover for future cost increases (and avoid being left behind in relative terms). As Frenkel (1979) has shown, with changing inflation rates the uncertainty of the pricing decisions increases. Now the firm has to choose between two risks. On the one hand, there is the income risk, which is the possibility of marking up prices too high and facing a lower than expected demand. On the other hand, there is a capital risk, which is the risk of fixing too low prices and being unable to buy inputs and labour at their increased nominal values in the next period. The experience of countries like Brazil suggests that, with accelerating inflation, capital risk becomes more important than income risk. If the firm overshoots the 'equilibrium' price it accumulates liquid capital which will not only surely increase in value with the continuance of inflation but also serve as collateral for short-term credit. Capital losses, in contrast, have nothing to attenuate their effect: they constitute a net wealth loss for the firm. In sum, facing the choice between too low or too high prices, the safest policy is to overshoot. It is interesting to note that this may then become a self-fulfilling prophecy: if most firms overshoot, the price level will be higher and the strategy will be vindicated.

If pricing rules are altered in this manner, the contractual institutions that define a high inflation regime may collapse. The acceleration of price increases will depress real income between adjustments beyond what was expected and accepted by agents that saw indexation as a useful device. If the loss is meaningful, agents will try to contain damages by reducing the duration of the period between adjustments. The shorter this period, *ceteris paribus*, the lower is the loss. At the limit, if money incomes could be instantaneously adjusted to any price increase, no real loss would ever take place. Of course, the combination of this feature and mark-up pricing would lead to an explosion of prices. Long before this limit could be approached, however, the contractual institutions would already have been radically altered. On the one hand, shorter adjustment periods demand other kinds of indices than price indices. In most cases, the new adjustment index has been the exchange rate to the dollar. Contracts cannot, however, in general, be enforced in dollars in countries with their own legal tender. This means that the uncertainties surrounding deals in dollars can only be accepted in the very short term. Besides, in countries where exchange markets are controlled, the dollar may not adequately reflect price trends, inducing additional distortions in the pricing rules.

The abandonment of accepted indexation practices feeds back into the pricing rules of firms that try to develop quicker means of reaction to the new pressures. The acceleration of the whole process makes it increasingly difficult to keep order. Firms have to develop their own system of information and can no longer wait to see what others are doing. The disappearance of a common information source leads to widely divergent decisions. Drastic changes of pace take place and expectations become very elastic to current disappointments. Lagging behind competitors may be fatal: it is necessary to move all the time to try to stay put.

In this sense, a hyperinflation is not just a system where inflation rates are higher than before. Actually rates are higher because accepted coordination devices and sources of information collapse. The breakdown of the indexation system destroys the last remnants of liquidity that the legal tender could still possess and the most visible hyperinflationary phenomenon, the flight from money, then takes place. Uncertainty overcomes all. Nothing but the shortest-term plans are actually implemented. Conflicts are intensified. This is the critical stage of a hyperinflation.

This critical stage reflects the workings of an economy where firms and other agents lose every notion of normality. Heterogeneous expectations lead them to paths that are so entirely inconsistent that one cannot know with any degree of confidence what lessons to extract from disappointments. The only general rule is to avoid lagging behind others at any cost. The inflation rate jumps from one month to the next but the average price level conceals a high degree of dispersion, causing heavy windfall gains and losses to be distributed in an unpredictable fashion.

Keynes observed that paralysis in the face of uncertainty is not an acceptable choice for practical men. They try to 'behave exactly as we should if we had behind us a Benthamite calculation of a series of prospective advantages and disadvantages, each multiplied by its appropriate probability wanting to be summed' (*CWJMK*, XIV, p. 114). Calculation demands a unit of account. With the collapse of local alternatives agents sooner or later find in foreign monies a more efficient alternative unit. Historically, this foreign money has been the American dollar. Dollar prices of internationally tradable goods may serve as the anchor to the price system. The hierarchy of relative prices can be restored and a measure of normality reintroduced. When these relativities are recovered, conditions are ripe for the re-creation of a local money of account (Kaldor, 1982). Writing from Germany in 1923, Keynes observed:

The fresh collapse of the mark is a symptom of the progressive deterioration of Germany's economic position. Nevertheless, the adjustment between internal prices and external exchanges is now so rapid that the practical importance of the movement may be overestimated ... Debts expressed in marks have long ceased to be of any importance; wages and prices are adjusted rapidly; and people in Germany now hold such small quantities of cash in the form of marks that the injury inflicted on individuals, even by a big collapse, is not so considerable as might be supposed. (*CWJMK*, XVIII, pp. 161–2)

The recuperation of a money of account is, then, the strategic factor in ending a hyperinflation. Hyperinflation creates an acute consciousness of the need for a stable money and induces agents to search for that stable money themselves. In a high inflation regime, in contrast, the apparent normality of things sustained by indexation works as a powerful impediment to the adoption of more efficient stabilization policies. The discomfort and uncertainty of walking on a tightrope are concealed from agents as long as they do not move too much or too quickly. The risk of falling into the abyss of a hyperinflation is, however, ever-present.

SUMMING UP

In this chapter we have presented a Post Keynesian approach to inflation, arguing that one should distinguish between those inflationary processes that are realized to be persistent and those that are just transient. Even among persistent inflationary processes, their impact on the overall economy will depend on whether the rates are high enough to impose unexpected gains or losses higher than the benefits expected to accrue from the acceptance of a contract itself.

A Post Keynesian theory of inflation emphasizes changes in the nature of distributive conflicts, especially between labour and capital. Strong unions and strong oligopolies solve their conflicts with the generation of inflationary impulses. Demands for higher money wages are accepted by modern firms and shifted into prices, thus generating inflationary pressures.

Inflation causes windfall gains and losses for those who are quick or slow to perceive its operations. When these losses become too large, agents will refuse to accept obligations in money, since their 'real' content will be very uncertain. A high inflation regime is implanted when contractual rules are changed to include units of account other than the legal tender of the economy. Indexation, however, is not extended to flow-supply prices. The formation of the latter is based on the expectations of inflation by entrepreneurs. A high inflation regime is then shown to be a fragile kind of equilibrium between agents that have their income determined by the past behaviour of inflation and agents that look towards the future behaviour of inflation.

Finally, an examination of hyperinflationary processes is presented in which they are seen as a pathological state of coordination breakdown.

NOTES

1. According to Keynes, the history of the nineteenth century confirmed these expectations: 'the remarkable feature of this long period was the relative stability of the price level. Approximately the same level of price ruled in or about the years 1826, 1841, 1855, 1862, 1867, 1871 and 1915. Prices were also level in the years 1844, 1881, and 1914' (*CWJMK*, IV, p. 10).
2. A detailed analysis of the workings of the gold standard is provided by Keynes in his evidence to the MacMillan Committee on the monetary system, made in 1931. Keynes's part in the proceedings is reproduced in *CWJMK*, xx, pp. 38–311.
3. Both Fisher and Keynes argued that the lack of endogenous limits in fiat money standards made them entirely dependent on 'confidence'. See Fisher (1926, pp. 149–51, 293). The increased elasticity of modern monetary systems, according to Chick (1983a), is the main environmental difference to emerge between modern and Keynes's times.
4. The classic reference is Frenkel (1979). Frenkel has often pointed out the proximity of his models to the Post Keynesian approach of Sidney Weintraub.
5. See, for instance, Gordon (1983) and Benassy (1983). For a contrasting and far superior perception of the importance of adjustment lags, see Jackson, Turner and Wilkinson (1975).
6. In fact, other factors operate to reduce even further the efficiency of fiscal policies under high inflation. As Heymann and others (1988) have shown, budget calculations become very uncertain and programmed expenditures often exhaust assigned resources very early in the fiscal year. As a result, the decision on additional provision of funds is taken outside the process of budget fixation, favouring special-interest political deals and reducing the macroeconomic efficiency of state intervention. For a detailed theoretical and empirical examination of the difficulties surrounding stabilization policies in high inflation economies, see Feijo and Carvalho (1991).

12. Post Keynesian Perspectives on Economic Policy

A monetary production economy, as we have seen, is an economy in which the uncertainties of the future, through the influences they have on current prices of goods and assets, may cause unemployment, inflation, or both. Perfect coordination among agents and sectors may not be obtained since a monetary economy is a market economy, where there is no auctioneer or Gosplan-like institution that could, in principle, ensure that mistakes will not be made and imbalances will not take place (although the experiences with Ministries of Production in socialist countries have not been unqualified successes). Agents follow the signals they receive from markets and interpret them according to the theories they form about how the world works. These signals are not only necessarily incomplete, which means that the agent will have to rely in greater or lesser degrees on 'figments of imagination', but they may also be definitely wrong, misleading decision makers into choosing unsustainable strategies. For these reasons, Post Keynesians, as did Keynes in his time, propose that there is room for the intervention of the state in the economy.

The state has powers to influence or even to determine future paths that no private agent has. Its weight, its capacity to create money, the size of its administrative apparatus, all these factors allow the state to lead the process of development of a monetary economy. For Keynes and Post Keynesians it is not a question of replacing private property or the market as a distributive and allocative device but of allowing the state to issue the signals that markets are not able to and of pointing out the directions of development that the community may desire.

Keynes has noted, in *The General Theory*, that the policy implications of his model were half conservative, half revolutionary. Keynesian economic policies are surely not socialist policies, even though they have been generally embraced by social-democrats around the world. They are conservative in that they preserve private property, the market and individual decision making. They are revolutionary in that they intend to substitute conscious macroeconomic management for the blind acceptance of unregulated market movements.

CAPITALISM'S FAILURES

In the last chapter of *The General Theory*, Keynes stated that capitalist economies have failed in two regards: (1) they have not achieved an acceptable profile of income distribution, with the survival of deep inequalities; (2) they have not been capable of sustaining the full employment of labour and other productive resources. It is in these two areas that Post Keynesians define the greater possibilities for state intervention in the economy.

Inequalities in income distribution can originate in two ways. On the one hand, differences in individual capabilities, disposition to work or to accept risks, in preferences between consumption and accumulation of wealth, or even just plain luck, can lead to differentiated distribution profiles among individuals. On the other hand, inherited wealth may also be a cause of inequality. Keynes's view was that the first cause of inequality is inevitable and even healthy. It is to the second that there is reason to object. While it may be fair that exceptional effort or circumstance may be rewarded, there would be no reason why some groups of people should face privileged conditions from the start, since these would not be the reward for any special ability or skill. If the right of inheritance was restricted to some extent, through the imposition of transmission taxes, for instance, unfair inequalities could be attenuated, while socially acceptable inequalities, especially those due to the possession of special skills, would be preserved. It was a lifelong held view of Keynes that property rights to assets should be restrained through a more or less extensive appeal to capital levies. In particular, the majority of his most important proposals for social reform, such as his debates about the Beveridge Plan or the compulsory loan at the beginning of the Second World War, usually involved redistributing assets in favour of lower-income groups financed by capital levies. (See *CWJMK*, XXII and XXVII.)

The incapacity of a monetary economy to sustain full employment of labour and resources was a failure of a different nature, requiring more active intervention. A monetary economy requires the generation of adequate amounts of demand for goods for present consumption as well as for future provision. However, agents provide for present consumption by demanding goods, but for future consumption by holding money and other liquid assets. Thus consumers' decisions to provide for the future issue no signal to those who have to prepare themselves to supply goods in the future – those who have, in other words, to create at present the means that will allow them to meet future demands, whenever they come. Investors have, then, to decide subject to 'the dark forces of ignorance' and the uncertainties they feel may lead them to search for safety rather than running the risks of accumulating illiquid, and potentially unprofitable, assets. But the effects of possible mistakes are not confined to individual entrepreneurs, since in monetary economies agents are connected through the sale of goods and services as well as by financial ties. Under these circumstances, anybody's failures are, potentially, a threat to others. These uncertainties are rooted in the organization of the economy itself, requiring structural changes to be overcome.

Generally, the allocation of resources among their possible uses is not seen as a major problem requiring state action. Supply and demand are believed to direct resources towards the sectors that can best satisfy demands. The price mechanism is not without flaws but the alternatives do not seem any better. The recent collapse of central command economies seemed to give reason to Keynes. The profit motive, for Keynes, as for the classical political economists, is enough to obtain an adequate allocation.[1] It is the amount of resources put into operation, not the mode of using them, that was the problem. A subsystem of relative prices was failing, the price of non-liquid assets, when unemployment was generated, not the whole relative price system, and, in particular, not the subsystem of consumption goods prices.

THE ROLE OF THE STATE

To meet all the problems mentioned in the last section, we can think of three main forms of state intervention that could be considered: (1) to issue clearer signals to private agents in order to stimulate them to act, by increasing their safety and confidence in the future, providing the kind of information a private market cannot generate; (2) to create safety nets to contain damages when market failures take place; and (3) to transform the environment to increase the transparency of the structural constraints acting on the economy and the relationships among agents. In the first case, one is talking mainly of management and of increasing the efficiency of existing structures; in the second and third, of reforms, of changing the existing structures towards more socially rational procedures that can solve the evils of the unregulated operation of capitalism.

Post Keynesians follow Keynes's steps to conceive three lines of state intervention in the economy to remove or attenuate the failures of modern monetary economies. Firstly, institutional reforms should be promoted to improve the efficiency of coordination channels that connect agents, to generate better information, to contain damages when mistakes are made, to create a fairer environment. Secondly, some form of economic planning must be adopted to ensure that coordination mechanisms will be continuously in operation, that possibilities will be adequately assessed and the social interactions necessary to full employment will take place. Finally, an active day-to-day integrated policy must be implemented to face unpredicted events and developments, and to correct courses when necessary.

Social reforms are important to orient the future behaviour of agents, by explicitly signalling rules of behaviour and ways of solving conflicts and by making explicit social goals and values. An example of the latter was the promotion, already mentioned above, of distributive reforms, such as the adoption of social security nets for lower-income groups, through the Beveridge Plan, or the far-reaching asset-redistribution plan contained in the suggestion to transform the compulsory loan proposal, originally made to obtain non-inflationary means of financing the war, into a permanent distributive mechanism to be financed out of capital levies.[2] Reforms were needed, however, not only to change the social structure but also to improve the efficiency of the existing structure. Modern institutional rules should be instrumental in achieving more stable environments in which agents could make their decisions. Foremost among these institutional reforms were monetary reforms, another lifelong concern of Keynes, who saw them as logically taking priority over the definition of other economic rules and institutions.

Planning, for Keynes, was the assumption of the conscious direction of the economy, both to manage its everyday operation and to orient economic change towards socially accepted objectives, such as industrial reform (see *CWJMK*, XIX, part 2). It is important to note that Keynes did not see any contradiction between his brand of liberalism and the defence of planning, since his view of the latter would preserve individual freedom of choice. Planning was a coordination device to promote the goals set by society itself, not an imposing form of control over society.[3] Compliance would be ensured by a structure of differentiated rewards to some chosen activities. As Tobin (1987) has correctly identified, Keynes's approach was close to the French type of indicative planning: long-term, non-compulsory orientations that serve to signal to private agents expected (or stimulated) future developments. Favours and penalties may be associated with such a plan but no commands are issued against recalcitrant private agents that decide to resist it. As Sir Alec Cairncross has shown, it is orientation, not compulsion, that agrees with Keynes's view as to the intervention of the state in the economy (Cairncross, 1971).

A well-designed institutional environment and a well-chosen plan are not enough, in any case, to prevent unpredictable events from happening. The everyday management of the economy, that is, active economic policies, is not made useless by those other two lines of action. Rather, they give the framework within which one can be sure that economic policy will be coherently directed to achieve society's goals. It is important to note that, seen from this angle, the role of economic policy is not to delude or to surprise agents, but to orient and to inform, and to keep coherence. Nothing was farther from Keynes's mind than the peculiar notion entertained by modern-day new classical economists that the state can only operate through deception.[4]

Post Keynesian economic policy is thus essentially reformist without neglecting the need for an efficient day-to-day economic operation. There will be different instruments for each of the goals and the general objective is to allow private agents to decide in more safety and with better knowledge of actual possibilities. The state can see further because it can influence the economy. It has to use this influence to make explicit to agents how the environment is likely to evolve in the relevant future, within which private allocative decisions are to be made. In sum, the nature of the state intervention should be of global orientation as to the spheres upon which its influence is acknowledged as, for instance, the guarantee of full employment. Sectoral intervention that tends to influence resource allocation, in principle, should be avoided.[5]

The first duty of the state in a monetary economy, in sum, can be defined as providing the information the market fails to generate. The goal is to support and to extend the possibilities of conscious steering of the economy, reducing the number of decisions that are made out of ignorance and fear rather than because of a calculation of advantages; to supply data about the future that the private decision maker can assume, with confidence, to describe the path to the future. Thus the state is able to reduce uncertainties and to minimize the search for defences against them. Liquidity preference may be reduced and prices of non-liquid assets may increase towards levels compatible with full employment investments. Full employment is a benefit for all: wage-earners, capitalists, everybody. There should be no quarrel against it.[6]

As to income distribution, the question is more complicated. It deals with the need to take resources from some agents to redistribute them to others. The political unanimity that was expected in relation to full employment would not take place here. The community should be able to choose the distribution profile it considered fair. It is a political problem, influenced by all kinds of extra-economic considerations. What the theoretical model of a monetary economy showed was the existence of degrees of freedom in this question. There is no unique profile of personal income distribution adequate to any given economy. Practically infinite possibilities, ranging from complete equality to serious inequality, were possible. No position could be technically or scientifically argued to be superior to any other.

The design of policies should contemplate three general principles: (1) institutions should be created to achieve more efficient and permanent coordination of agents, allowing them to develop coherent strategies; (2) a set of instruments must be developed, paying particular attention to the timing of their operation; and (3) specific policies should be chosen not in isolation but as parts of a global plan to control and to steer the economy – there should not be fiscal policies decided independently of monetary policies or of any other; the state should intervene to coordinate, which requires that its action itself be coordinated.[7]

One important aspect of Keynes's thought as to these matters which should be stressed is that he believed that he had found, with the principle of effective demand, a truly 'scientific' principle of macroeconomic management. Full employment represented more profits and more wages. It also represented the long-term possibility of overcoming scarcity and of changing society towards a more agreeable form of organization, not one based on greed and competition. No one would object to such an arrangement. Conflict would be a characteristic of the past. But even before he got to it, Keynes strongly believed in the possibility of scientific management of the economy. In this sense, the state intervention in the economy would be peculiarly 'depoliticized' in Keynes's view. As he wrote in 1930: 'I look forward with every emotion of satisfaction to the prospect that the world may be forced in my lifetime to the substitution of a scientific control of the lever which works the balancing factor in our economic life' (*CWJMK*, XX, pp. 164–5).

Earlier, he had defended a proposal to form a body of economic counsellors to the British government by stating:

The foregoing may be open to the charge of magnifying unduly the functions and the importance of what is proposed. But a move along these lines would indeed be an act of statesmanship, the importance of which cannot easily be exaggerated. For it would mark a transition in our conceptions of the functions and purposes of the state, and a first measure towards the deliberate and purposive guidance of the evolution of our economic life. It would be a recognition of the enormous part to be played in this by scientific spirit as distinct from the sterility of the purely party attitude, which is never more out of place than in relation to complex matters of fact and interpretation involving technical difficulty. (*CWJMK*, XX, p. 27)

The faith of Keynes in the possibilities of economic science may have been exaggerated. Conflict has not disappeared from modern market economies. As another strand of Post Keynesian theory, following Kalecki's seminal (1943) paper, has pointed out, the capitalist social order may be in assent on the existence of unemployment as a means to discipline workers. Full efficiency in the employment of production factors may then be incompatible with this social order, requiring other types of social and political reform if full employment is ever to be attainable and sustainable (see, for instance, Asimakopulos, 1980/1).

Be that as it may, this discussion makes clear the need to go beyond the borders of economics to fulfil the Post Keynesian programme. This certainty cannot be pursued on this occasion. Our contribution to this debate can only be to make clear the economic side of the argument.

POLICY INSTRUMENTS

Full employment policies should be implemented by the combination of three types of instruments: fiscal policies, income policies and monetary policies. Fiscal policy should be designed to obtain global long-term employment stability; incomes policies should obtain price stability. Monetary policy would then have the role of accommodating transactional demands for money and of preventing changes in the state of liquidity preference from having an impact upon the prices of non-liquid assets. Structural reforms could also take place through industrial, (foreign) commercial and commodity policies. In what follows, we will briefly review the main influences expected from each of these instruments.

Fiscal policy has to achieve three simultaneous goals: (1) to organize the normal affairs of the state; (2) to regulate aggregate demand; and (3) to promote personal income redistribution. To regulate aggregate demand, the state should prepare and divulge long-term investment programmes that would signal the state's readiness to compensate for reductions in private investments with its own expenditures (cf. *CWJMK*, XXVII, p. 322). The goal, besides solving problems such as supplying low-price housing, is to show the disposition to sustain long-term aggregate demand if private demand flags. The complement should not be seen as permanent but as a cyclically available device. Public works could be accelerated when employment was less than full, or decelerated if aggregate demand was too high.

To organize this kind of intervention, Keynes suggested that two budgets should be prepared. The first, a current budget, containing the routine public expenditures, that would thus describe those activities that had to be sustained independently of current economic conditions. Referring to reasonably stable expenditures, the current budget should be balanced at all times, which is to say, it should be neutral with respect to aggregate demand. A second, capital budget would cover the discretionary expenditures of the state, the amount of which would vary with the cycle in order to smooth its way.[8] This budget should generate deficits or surpluses, depending on whether the economy is going through a recession or a boom.

It is important to realize that, in the long-term average, all budgets would be balanced. The role of budgetary policy was to signal precisely the long-term commitment to sustaining an adequate level of employment. Fiscal policy was not thought to be a quick lever to be pulled when an actual recession took place. Expenditure policies are much too heavy and slow to allow reactions of this nature. Ideally, given its timing, there should be reserved for fiscal policy the role of smoothing the trade cycle and, thus, for signalling to private agents the safe level of income they should include in their expectations as to the future.[9] If private agents confidently accepted the income projections divulged by the state, 'animal spirits' could be enhanced and private investments take place. In this case, the other instruments, and in particular the appeal to budget deficits, could, in practice, even be dispensed with.

Fiscal policy was also a crucial instrument for obtaining social change in Keynes's and Post Keynesian theory. Both taxation and the choice of expenditures can promote personal income redistribution in a monetary economy. Progressive income taxes and capital levies are recurrently proposed by these economists as means to organize redistribution. A careful design of expenditures, be they in social services or in public goods for low-income areas, can much improve the standard of living of poorer people while preserving the profit motive that stimulates private activity.

One non-orthodox instrument of redistribution was also developed by Keynes in the 1940s: the use of compulsory loans in times of excess demand (such as the Second World War) that would avoid having incomes dissipated by inflation if aggregate supply was insufficient to meet demands, transforming them, in contrast, into assets to be accumulated and liberated in slack periods. The proposal made by Keynes initially as part of a stabilization policy during the war quickly became a redistribution proposal, when Keynes suggested that the repayment of the loans should be made with capital levies.

New Perspectives

In sum, and to emphasize the point, despite the fiscalist mythology developed by the neoclassical synthesis and its monetarist critics, fiscal policy should not generate permanent deficits. In the long term, budgets should be neutral with respect to full employment aggregate demand. This would be achieved by the separation of the routine activities of the state, to be performed on any occasion, and the discretionary expenditures to be activated only when necessary and safe from generating inflationary pressures on aggregate demand.

If aggregate demand could be smoothed through fiscal policies, the other kind of inflationary pressures, income inflation, caused by attempts of social groups to increase their share of national income, should be dealt with by incomes policies. Incomes policy is a typical Keynesian (and not only Post Keynesian) prescription. The basic assumption made by their proponents is that money wages are the main component of money prices. Whether because of marginal costs being mainly labour costs or because of mark-up pricing, as we saw in Chapter 10, it is believed that wage bargaining is a very poor arena for redistributive initiatives but a powerful instrument for generating inflationary pressures. Wage bargains do not necessarily have any influence on the size of mark-ups or on market power of firms. As Weintraub (1978) has shown, mark-ups have been reasonably constant in the long term, despite pressures from rising wages that have only been dissipated in inflation.[10]

For Post Keynesians, redistribution is mainly a matter for fiscal policy, particularly progressive taxation and social expenditures by the state. Incomes policies are intended to regulate the formation of money wages and prices in order to suppress cost inflation. The design of feasible incomes policies has to face the difficulties brought about by the politicization of the process of factor pricing. As Appelbaum (1982) has noted, most incomes policies proposals go little beyond suggesting restraint upon union demands. For an effective incomes policy to be implemented it is necessary that a political consensus be formed around the desirability of price stability and around current mark-ups. On the other hand, incomes policy is more efficient at conserving a situation than at promoting any change. But the very introduction of such policies tends to change the political balance of power that, as is the experience of many incomes policies (such as those applied in Great Britain under

Labour governments), ends up by eroding the political deals that made them feasible to begin with (cf. Tarling and Wilkinson, 1977).

Proposals attempting to deal with precisely this difficulty try to create 'automatic' forms of incomes policy, such as Wallich and Weintraub's Tax-based Incomes Policy (TIP), that would be embodied in the tax system. These policies have been favourably received by most Post Keynesians, but have not yet had any chance to be tried in the real world.

If incomes policies are implemented to control cost inflation and aggregate demand is regulated by long-term fiscal policy, the role of monetary policy becomes two-fold: (1) to satisfy the needs for active balances created by an expanding output; and (2) to prevent autonomous changes in expectations and shifts in the liquidity preference schedule from disturbing the prices of non-liquid assets. In an adequately controlled economy, the money supply should become endogenous, since increases in demand caused by expansion of industrial circulation should be satisfied and increases because of precautionary or speculative motives should have their effects contained within the confines of the money market. A flexible monetary policy would be able to isolate movements in the demand for money due to changes in uncertainty from changes in interest rates that could have an impact upon the demand for investment goods and affect aggregate demand.[11]

This combination of the three legs of economic policy would allow the adequate macroeconomic management that would maintain full employment and price stability. Actual policies are in fact very far from being so harmonious in content and in handling. To achieve such results, some major institutional reforms would have to be made. Keynes dedicated intense efforts in the last years of his life to designing institutions that would be efficient and fair. These efforts occupy three volumes of his *Collected Writings* and much more is scattered throughout the other volumes. Themes such as monetary reform, intended to create the safe and flexible monetary system to which we referred above, were a concern Keynes had entertained since his youth.

The proposals of Keynes, the reformer, cannot be adequately examined here. Post Keynesians have not yet, in general, given to these ideas the attention they deserve.[12] The same is true of other fields of policy, such as commercial and industrial policies. In these matters, agreement is more difficult because, contrarily to the three policies discussed above, destined to promote full employment and price stability, there are no consensual targets among Post Keynesians, or anybody else for that matter, for transformation policies such as, for instance, commercial protectionist policies or industrial policies to change the productive structure of a given economy. These are, from a theoretical point of view, ad hoc policies to achieve definite goals that are not identified in any particular detail by Post Keynesian foundations.

SUMMING UP

This chapter was intended to sketch the main policy implications of Keynes's and Post Keynesian concepts of monetary economy. This kind of economy fails to achieve full employment because uncertainties about the future lead agents to adopt defensive strategies that are harmful to employment. The state can intervene then to supply information for the formation of expectations and to generate a state of confidence adequate to sustain these expectations.

The basic policies were outlined. Fiscal policy was destined to sustain long-term expectations as to the aggregate level of income the state was committed to support. Incomes policies would regulate the wage/price relation to avoid cost inflation. The role of monetary policy, under these conditions, would be to provide active balances for transaction needs and to prevent increases in liquidity preference from being translated into higher interest rates that could threaten investment. These policies should be jointly implemented. None of them can be thought of as Keynesian when taken in isolation because they would create difficulties for the economy that could end up in a crisis. To a certain extent, the crisis in Keynesian economic policy in the late 1960s was caused by an excessive concentration on fiscal matters. Monetary policy was neglected; monetarism could be revived with the motto 'money matters', something that can be used against Keynes's ideas only with a strong dose of irony.

Finally, it is argued that Keynes has also proposed many sorts of institutional reforms intended to make the system more efficient and fair. Unfortunately, these reforms have yet to receive an integrated and extensive study, which cannot be made in a work such as the present one.

NOTES

1. The belief that the price system could obtain satisfactorily the adequate allocation of resources was a principle, but not a dogma. In his last published paper Keynes warned 'revolutionaries' who wanted to go too far that not everything in the classics' teachings was wrong, in a clear reference, given his other works, to the performance of the price system. However, although never reneging on his allegiance to 'free' markets, Keynes also reproached 'conservatives' for allowing themselves to be deceived by the price system (*CWJMK*, xxvi, p. 297). The point was to complement the forces in operation in a market economy with those of the state, not to replace the market economy altogether.

2. For the discussion of the compulsory loan as an instrument for demand management see *CWJMK*, xxii, pp. 123, 138. Its potential for social reform is pointed out in *CWJMK*, ix, pp. 368, 379; *CWJMK*, xxviii, p. 138.

3. On planning, see *CWJMK*, xii, pp. 238–9 and the numerous remarks scattered throughout Keynes's works, particularly in *CWJMK*, xxi; *CWJMK*, xxv.

4. The need for the adoption of truth-revealing economic policies, including monetary policy, is presented in *CWJMK*, xx, pp. 198, 262–3.

5. Again one should not be dogmatic about this statement. In specific cases, the social interest could be to preserve or to promote some specific kinds of action. Keynes himself defended a protective intervention in coal production (*CWJMK*, xix, part 2) and the use of discriminatory commercial policy to promote infant industries (*CWJMK*, xxvi, chap. 2). Modern-day Post Keynesians are usually favourable to the definition of industrial policies to increase competitiveness of declining economies. In any case, the general principle that detailed allocative intervention should be avoided remains. The point is that most often the state has no better information or more efficient instruments of intervention than the very agents operating in these markets. Moreover, there is the important political problem of distributing privileges and allocating the costs of such policies. Macroeconomic intervention, in contrast, may lead to situations that are superior to the non-intervention case for all agents.

6. That the control of investment and income distribution may be both fair and efficient was stated by Keynes in *CWJMK*, xxi, pp. 36–7.

7. On the need for integrated policies, see *CWJMK*, v, p. 337.

8. The requirement of balanced ordinary budgets is stated in *CWJMK*, xxvii, p. 225. The 'desperate' character of deficit financing is proposed in the same work, pp. 352–3. See, for a very good discussion of these papers, Kregel (1983).

9. The limitations of expenditure policies against cyclical downswings are pointed out by Keynes in *CWJMK*, xxvii, p. 122 and *CWJMK*, xiv, p. 49.

10. The inadequacy of wage policies to redistribute income and the need for an incomes policy are discussed in *CWJMK*, xx, pp. 102–6. The fact, as Davidson and Davidson (1988) acknowledge, that 'from the early 1970s into the 1980s . . . profit margins also rose substantially' (p. 157n) significantly complicates the argument in favour of income policies that only restrain wages.

11. The role of monetary policy to stabilize the price of securities accommodating shifts in liquidity preference is identified in *CWJMK*, xxii, p. 414.

12. One important exception is Davidson's attempts to present proposals for international monetary reform based on Keynes's original Clearing Union proposals. See Davidson (1985).

13. Conclusions

Post Keynesian theory was born of the critique of neoclassical theory. In its beginnings, the label served as a portmanteau for several schools of thought that had little in common besides their rejection of neoclassical economics and their dissatisfaction with Marxism as an alternative to neoclassicism.

The alliance between critics of orthodoxy has, without a doubt, extended their reach and has contributed, through many debates, to the clearing up of the most important issues being examined. After the negative stage is over, however, criticism alone is not enough to build an alternative to orthodoxy. Different schools have to go their separate ways when the time comes to develop modes of thought alternative to the dominant views.

Post Keynesian economics has been living this second stage in recent years. It is developing and clarifying its main themes and approaches as a solid foundation for the definition of a coherent school that can sustain and extend a genuine research programme. The fundamental proposal of this book is that the core of this programme should be seen as the concept of monetary production economy.

Keynes believed himself to be starting a revolution in the way people think about economic problems when he published *The General Theory*. It certainly became a very influential book, especially in terms of policy matters people thought were implied by its model. As a theoretical revolution, however, it was much less of a success, since most of the economics profession learned to see it as one more demonstration that rigid wages could cause unemployment, something any orthodox economist has always known. For orthodox economists, the novelty of *The General Theory* was nothing more than the introduction of some new analytical concepts, that were progressively emasculated or abandoned. Many economists, certainly even among Keynes's avowed followers, would think that the Keynesian revolution was due more to the power Keynes had of generating publicity around his book than to his analytical talent.

Post Keynesians start from a radically different assessment of Keynes's intentions and realizations. The revolutionary approach to economics was rooted not in his policy proposals but in his perception that what he called classical economics was focused on kinds of economies that had little in common, even in the most abstract sense, with modern, complex, capitalistic, monetary economies. The problem with classical economics was in its foundations, not in its instruments or conclusions. It was necessary to start again from a different point at which one could recognize the essential constitutive elements of the kind of economic society in which we live.

Post Keynesians have been known for their treatment of the concepts of uncertainty, money, financial relations, unemployment and so on. What unifies these studies is the perception that it was a new conception of economy that was needed to define a new research programme. Davidson's concept of monetary economy, Minsky's Wall Street paradigm and so on were all attempts to make explicit these new beginnings. The present work is not intended as anything more than a systematization of these and other attempts, using as a guiding map Keynes's own attempts to develop an alternative concept of economy in the drafts for *The General Theory*.

To this end, in the first four chapters we developed the main features of a monetary economy, trying to establish some of the methodological particularities of the Post Keynesian approach, especially those relative to the concepts of uncertainty, gravitation processes, probability and so on. After this preparation was completed, a mode of reading *The General Theory* compatible with this approach was presented, centred upon Chapter 17 of *The General Theory* where Keynes shows that the dynamics of a monetary economy is ultimately dependent on the way the public, including capitalist firms, decides on the ways to store and accumulate wealth. It is a specificity of monetary economies that money becomes an asset, alternative to producible assets, and whose yield comes in the form of safety against uncertainty; that is, as liquidity.

Depending on the choices of the public as to the ways of storing wealth for the future, producers of capital goods will or will not be called to increase their employment to offer new items to investors.

If they are called to produce, repercussions will be generated in the consumption goods sector, summarized in the multiplier mechanism, causing income and employment to grow beyond the original stimulus.

Important but somewhat lateral aspects of these processes were examined, particularly the financial conditions that have to be satisfied for the whole sequence to start. Imbalances were also addressed, particularly those generated by inflationary processes and price instability. In the end, we suggested that the concept of monetary economy opens the way for an activist view of economic policy, since it defines problems the solution of which is beyond individual private action.

The whole effort of this book, as has already been said, was intended to introduce the monetary economy paradigm in a systematized way. It is not complete nor should it be thought to be a deep or even fair rendition of most topics discussed. It is intended as a map or a manifesto in favour of the notion of monetary economy as the core of the Post Keynesian paradigm.

Many important topics for the development of the paradigm (or important in Keynes's own debates) have not even been mentioned. They should, of course, be explored and integrated in a further study of the development of Post Keynesian theory. Studies on international aspects of the workings of a monetary economy, particularly of monetary arrangements, are badly needed, to be integrated into such a larger theoretical reconstruction. Microeconomic questions, given the importance conferred by Post Keynesians on decision making, are also largely absent from this work. Growth and development were briefly referred to in the discussions of the concepts of long run and long period but the effective implications of the Keynesian approach to gravitation process in these fields of study are still to be developed. The same applies to the discussion of perspectives on policy in Chapter 12. Proposals to reform capitalist economies, to change institutions to make them more efficient and fair, have to be studied and, when necessary, amended or extended. The study of the political foundations of Post Keynesian economics is also underdeveloped, except for important but still sporadic attempts, such as O'Donnel (1989).

All these are matters for further study. Most of the topics that were treated in this book will also deserve deeper examination. However, if this work contributes to the organization of a Post

Keynesian research programme around the notion of monetary economy, the author's ambitions will be vindicated.

References

Amadeo, Edward, 'Teoria e Metodo nos Primordios da Macroeconomia: a Revolucao Keynesiana e a Analise do Multiplicador' Catholic University of Rio de Janeiro, Discussion Paper, 1986.

Appelbaum, Eileen, 'The Incomplete Incomes Policy Vision', *Journal of Post Keynesian Economics*, Summer 1982.

Arrow, Kenneth, *Collected Papers of Kenneth Arrow, v. 2: General Equilibrium*, Cambridge: Harvard University Press, 1983.

Asimakopulos, Athanasios, 'The Determination of Investment in Keynes's Model', *Canadian Journal of Economics*, Aug. 1971.

Asimakopulos, Athanasios, 'Themes in a Post Keynesian Theory of Income Distribution', *Journal of Post Keynesian Economics*, Winter 1980/1.

Asimakopulos, Athanasios, 'Kalecki and Keynes on Finance, Investment and Saving', *Cambridge Journal of Economics*, July 1983.

Asimakopulos, Athanasios, 'Long-Period Employment in The General Theory', *Journal of Post Keynesian Economics*, Winter 1984/5.

Asimakopulos, Athanasios, 'Keynes and Sraffa: Visions and Perspectives', *Political Economy, the Surplus Approach*, 1985.

Asimakopulos, Athanasios, 'Post Keynesian Theories of Distribution', in A. Asimakopulos (ed.), *Theories of Income Distribution*, Boston: Kluwer Academic Publishers, 1988.

Barrere, Alain (ed.), *Keynes Aujourd'hui*, Paris: Economica, 1985.

Baumol, William, 'The Transactions Demand for Cash: An Inventory Theoretic Approach', *Quarterly Journal of Economics*, 1952.

Benassy, Jean-Pascal, *Macroéconomie et Théorie du Déséquilibre*, Paris: Dunod, 1983.

Bharadwaj, Khrishna, 'The Subversion of Classical Analysis: Alfred

Marshall's Early Writings on Value', *Cambridge Journal of Economics*, Jan./Mar. 1978.

Bresciani-Turroni, Constantino, *The Economics of Inflation*, London: George Allen and Unwin, 1937.

Cagan, Phillip, 'The Monetary Dynamics of Hyperinflation', in M. Friedman (ed.), *Studies in the Quantity Theory of Money*, Chicago: University of Chicago Press, 1956.

Cairncross, Alec, *Essays in Economic Management*, London: George Allen and Unwin, 1971.

Carabelli, Anna, *On Keynes's Method*, London: Macmillan, 1988.

Carvalho, Fernando Cardim de, 'On the Concept of Time in Shacklean and Sraffian Economics', *Journal of Post Keynesian Economics*, Winter 1983/4.

Carvalho, Fernando Cardim de, 'Alternative Analyses of Short- and Long-run in Post Keynesian Economics', *Journal of Post Keynesian Economics*, Winter 1984/5.

Carvalho, Fernando Cardim de, 'Inflation and Indexation in a Post Keynesian Model of Asset-Choice', unpublished PhD dissertation, Rutgers University, 1986.

Carvalho, Fernando Cardim de, 'Keynes on Probability, Uncertainty and Decision-Making', *Journal of Post Keynesian Economics*, Fall 1988.

Carvalho, Fernando Cardim de, 'Tempo e Equilibrio nos Principles of Economics de Marshall', Annals of the 18th National Meeting of Economists of Brazil, ANPEC, 1990.

Carvalho, F. C. and Oliveira, L. C., 'An Outline of a Short-Period Post Keynesian Model for the Brazilian Economy', forthcoming in W. Milberg (ed.), *The Megacorp and Macrodynamics. Essays in Memory of Alfred Eichner*, Armonk: M. E. Sharpe, 1991.

Chick, Victoria, *The Theory of Monetary Policy*, Oxford: Basil Blackwell, 1979.

Chick, Victoria, *Macroeconomics After Keynes*, Cambridge, Mass.: The MIT Press, 1983a.

Chick, Victoria, 'Monetary Increases and their Consequences: Streams, Backwaters and Floods', University College London Discussion Paper, 1983b.

Davidson, Greg and Davidson, Paul, *Economics for a Civilized Society*, London: Macmillan, 1988.

Davidson, Paul, *Money and the Real World*, London: Macmillan, 2nd edn, 1978a.

Davidson, Paul, 'Why Money Matters', *Journal of Post Keynesian Economics*, Fall 1978b.

Davidson, Paul, *International Money and the Real World*, New York: John Wiley and Sons, 1982.

Davidson, Paul, 'The Marginal Product Curve is not the Demand Curve for Labor and Lucas's Labor Supply Function is not the Supply Curve for Labor in the Real World', *Journal of Post Keynesian Economics*, Fall 1983.

Davidson, Paul, 'Reviving Keynes's Revolution', *Journal of Post Keynesian Economics*, Summer 1984.

Davidson, Paul, 'Propositions Concernant la Liquidité pour un Nouveau Bretton Woods', in Barrere, 1985.

Davidson, Paul, 'Finance, Funding, Savings and Investment', *Journal of Post Keynesian Economics*, Fall 1986.

Davidson, Paul and Davidson, Greg, 'Financial Markets and Williamson's Theory of Governance', *Quarterly Review of Economics and Business*, Winter 1984.

Davidson, Paul and Kregel, Jan (eds), *Macroeconomic Problems and Policies of Income Distribution*, Aldershot: Edward Elgar, 1989.

Debreu, Gerard, *Theory of Value*, New Haven: Yale University Press, 1959.

Deleplace, Ghislain, 'Ajustement de Marché et "Taux d'Intérêt Spécifiques" chez Keynes et Sraffa', *Cahiers d'Economie Politique*, no. 14/15, 1988.

De Pablo, J. C. and Dornbusch, R., *Deuda Externa e Inestabilidad Macroeconomica en la Argentina*, Buenos Aires: Sudamericana, 1988.

Dillard, Dudley, *The Economics of John Maynard Keynes*, New York: Prentice Hall, 1948.

Dutt, Amitava and Amadeo, Edward, *Keynes's Third Alternative*, Aldershot: Edward Elgar, 1990.

Eichner, Alfred, 'A Post Keynesian Short Period Model', *Journal of Post Keynesian Economics*, Summer 1979.

Eichner, Alfred, *The Megacorp and Oligopoly*, Armonk: M. E. Sharpe, 1980.

Feijo, Carmem A. V. C., 'Economic Growth and Inflation in Brazil in the 1970s: A Post Keynesian Interpretation', unpublished PhD dissertation, University of London, 1991.

Feijo, Carmem and Carvalho, Fernando, 'The Resilience of High

Inflation: Brazilian Recent Failures with Stabilization Policies', mimeo, 1991.

Fisher, Irving, *Le Pouvoir d'Achat de la Monnaie*, Paris: Marcel Giard, 1926.

Fitzgibbons, Athol, *Keynes's Vision*, Oxford: Oxford University Press, 1988.

Frenkel, Roberto, 'Decisiones de Precio en Alta Inflacion', Buenos Aires: Estudios CEDES nu. 6, 1979.

Friedman, Milton, 'The Quantity Theory of Money: A Restatement', in M. Friedman (ed.), *Studies in the Quantity Theory of Money*, Chicago: The University of Chicago Press, 1956.

Friedman, Milton, 'A Theoretical Framework for Monetary Analysis', *Journal of Political Economy*, 1970.

Garegnani, Pierangelo, 'Notes on Consumption, Investment and Effective Demand', *Cambridge Journal of Economics*, 1978/9.

Garegnani, Pierangelo, 'On a Change in the Notion of Equilibrium in Recent Work in Value and Distribution', in J. Eatwell and M. Milgate (eds), *Keynes's Economics and the Theory of Value and Distribution*, Oxford: Oxford University Press, 1983.

Gordon, Robert J., 'A Century of Evidence on Wages and Price Stickiness in the US, the UK and Japan', in J. Tobin (ed.), *Macroeconomics, Prices and Quantities*, Washington: The Brookings Institution, 1983.

Hahn, Frank H., *Equilibrium and Macroeconomics*, Cambridge, Mass.: The MIT Press, 1984.

Hansen, Alvin, *A Guide to Keynes*, New York: McGraw-Hill, 1953.

Harcourt, Geoffrey C., *Some Cambridge Controversies in the Theory of Capital*, Cambridge: Cambridge University Press, 1972.

Harcourt, Geoffrey C., *The Social Science Imperialists*, London: Routledge and Kegan Paul, 1982.

Harcourt, Geoffrey C., 'Keynes's College Bursar View of Investment: Comment on Kregel', in J. Kregel (ed.), *Distribution, Effective Demand and International Economic Relations*, London: MacMillan, 1983.

Harcourt, Geoffrey C., *Controversies on Political Economy*, New York: New York University Press, 1986.

Harcourt, G. C. and Kenyon, P., 'Pricing and the Investment Decision', in Harcourt (1982).

Hayek, Friedrich, *Prix et Production*, Paris: Calmann-Levy, 1975.

Heymann, D. *et al.*, 'Conflicto Distributivo y Deficit Fiscal: Algunos

Juegos Inflacionarios', *Annals of the 16th National Meeting of Economists*, ANPEC, Brazil, 1988.

Hicks, John, *Value and Capital*, Oxford: Oxford University Press, 2nd edn, 1946.

Hicks, John, *A Contribution to the Theory of the Trade Cycle*, Oxford: Oxford University Press, 1954.

Hicks, John, *Critical Essays in Monetary Theory*, Oxford: Oxford University Press, 1967.

Hicks, John, *The Crisis in Keynesian Economics*, New York: Basic Books, 1974.

Hicks, John, *Causality in Economics*, New York: Basic Books, 1979.

Jackson, D., Turner, H. and Wilkinson, F., *Do Trade Unions Cause Inflation?*, Cambridge: Cambridge University Press, 1975.

Kahn, Richard, *Selected Essays on Employment and Growth*, Cambridge: Cambridge University Press, 1972.

Kahn, Richard, *The Making of the General Theory*, Cambridge: Cambridge University Press, 1984.

Kaldor, Nicholas, *Essays on Economic Stability and Growth*, New York: Holmes and Maier, 1980.

Kaldor, Nicholas, *The Scourge of Monetarism*, Oxford: Oxford University Press, 1982.

Kalecki, Michal, 'Political Aspects of Full Employment', 1943, reprinted in Kalecki, 1971.

Kalecki, Michal, *Selected Essays in the Dynamics of Capitalist Economies*, Cambridge University Press, 1971.

Katzner, Donald, 'Potential Surprise, Potential Confirmation and Probability', *Journal of Post Keynesian Economics*, Fall 1986.

Keynes, John Maynard, *The Economic Consequences of Peace*, London: Macmillan, 1920.

Keynes, John Maynard, *Essays in Biography*, London: Rupert Hart Davis, 1951.

Keynes, John Maynard, *The General Theory of Employment, Interest and Money*, New York: Harcourt, Brace, Jovanovitch, 1964.

Keynes, John Maynard, *The Collected Writings of John Maynard Keynes*, edited by D. Moggridge, London: Macmillan and Cambridge: Cambridge University Press, 1971–89. Volumes are referred to as *CWJMK*, followed by the volume number in roman numerals.

Kindleberger, Charles, *Manias, Panics and Crashes*, New York: Basic Books, 1978.

Klein, Lawrence, *La Revolucion Keynesiana*, Madrid: Editorial Revista de Derecho Publico, 1952.

Kregel, Jan, *Rate of Profit, Distribution and Growth: Two Views*, London: Macmillan, 1971.

Kregel, Jan, *The Reconstruction of Political Economy. An Introduction to Post-Keynesian Economics*, London: Macmillan, 1975.

Kregel, Jan, 'On the Existence of Expectations in English Neoclassical Economics', *Journal of Economic Literature*, June 1977.

Kregel, Jan, 'Markets and Institutions as Features of a Capitalistic Production System', *Journal of Post Keynesian Economics*, Fall 1980.

Kregel, Jan, 'Money, expectations and relative prices in Keynes's monetary equilibrium', *Economie Appliquée*, 1982.

Kregel, Jan, 'Finanziamento in Disavanzo, Politica Economica e Preferenza per la Liquidità', in F. Vicarelli (ed.), *Attualità di Keynes*, Rome: Laterza, 1983.

Kregel, Jan, 'Expectations and Rationality within a Capitalist Framework', in E. Nell (ed.), *Free Market Conservatism*, London: George Allen and Unwin, 1984.

Kregel, Jan, 'Constraints on the Expansion of Output and Employment: Real or Monetary', *Journal of Post Keynesian Economics*, Winter 1984/5.

Kregel, Jan, 'Le Multiplicateur et la Préférence pour la Liquidité: Deux Aspects de la Théorie de la Demande Effective', in Alain Barrere (ed.), *Keynes Aujourd'hui*, Paris: Economica, 1985.

Kregel, Jan, 'Irving Fisher, 'Great-Grandparent of the General Theory: Money, Rate of Return over Cost and Efficiency of Capital', *Cahiers d'Economie Politique*, no. 14/5, 1988.

Kregel, Jan, 'Keynes, Income Distribution and Incomes Policy', in P. Davidson and J. Kregel (eds), *Macroeconomic Problems and Policies of Income Distribution*, Aldershot: Edward Elgar, 1989.

Lawson, Tony, 'The Relative/Absolute Nature of Knowledge and Economic Analysis', *The Economic Journal*, Dec. 1987.

Lawson, Tony, 'Probability and Uncertainty in Economic Analysis', *Journal of Post Keynesian Economics*, Fall 1988.

Leijonhufvud, Axel, *On Keynesian Economics and the Economics of Keynes*, New York: Oxford University Press, 1968.

Leijonhufvud, Axel, *Information and Coordination*, New York: Oxford University Press, 1981.

Lerner, Abba, 'Saving Equals Investment', in S. Harris (ed.), *The New Economics*, London: Dennis Dobson, 1947.

Lerner, Abba, 'The Scramble for Keynes's Mantle', *Journal of Post Keynesian Economics*, Fall 1978.

Lucas Jr., Robert, *Studies in Business Cycle Theory*, Cambridge, Mass.: The MIT Press, 1981.

Marshall, Alfred, *Principles of Economics*, London: Macmillan, 1924.

Marx, Karl, *Capital*, vol. 2, Harmondsworth: Penguin, 1978.

Minsky, Hyman, *John Maynard Keynes*, New York: Columbia University Press, 1975.

Minsky, Hyman, *Can 'It' Happen Again?*, Armonk: M. E. Sharpe, 1982.

Minsky, Hyman, *Stabilizing an Unstable Economy*, New Haven: Yale University Press, 1986.

Modigliani, Franco, 'Comment on Summers', in J. Tobin (ed.), *Macroeconomics, Prices and Quantities*, Washington: The Brookings Institution, 1983.

Moore, Basil, *Horizontalists and Verticalists*, Cambridge: Cambridge University Press, 1988.

Moore, Geoffrey, *Business Cycles, Inflation and Forecasting*, Cambridge (Mass.): Ballinger, 1983.

Muth, John, 'Rational Expectations and the Theory of Price Movements', *Econometrica*, 1961.

O'Donnel, Rod, *Keynes, Philosophy, Economics and Politics*, London: Macmillan, 1989.

Okun, Arthur, *Prices and Quantities*, Oxford: Basil Blackwell, 1980.

Pasinetti, Luigi, 'Rate of Profit and Income Distribution in Relation to the Rate of Economic Growth', *Review of Economic Studies*, Oct. 1962.

Penrose, Edith, *The Theory of the Growth of the Firm*, Armonk: M. E. Sharpe, 1980.

Reynolds, Peter, 'Kalecki's Degree of Monopoly', *Journal of Post Keynesian Economics*, Spring 1983.

Reynolds, Peter, 'Kaleckian and Post-Keynesian Theories of Pricing: A Comparison and Some Implications', mimeo, 1987.

Ricardo, David, *Principles of Political Economy and Taxation*, Harmondsworth: Penguin, 1971.

Robinson, Joan, *The Accumulation of Capital*, London: Macmillan, 1969.

Robinson, Joan, *The Generalization of the General Theory and Other Essays*, London: Macmillan, 1979.

Rosenberg, Nathan, *Inside the Black Box*, Cambridge: Cambridge University Press, 1982.

Sargent, Thomas, 'The Demand for Money during Hyperinflations under Rational Expectations', in R. Lucas and T. Sargent (eds), *Rational Expectations and Econometric Practice*, Minneapolis: University of Minnesota Press, 1981.

Sawyer, Malcolm, *Macroeconomics in Question: The Keynesian–Monetarist Orthodoxies and the Kaleckian Alternative*, Brighton: Wheatsheaf Books, 1982.

Schumpeter, Joseph, *Theory of Capitalist Development*, Cambridge, Mass.: Harvard University Press, 1934.

Schumpeter, Joseph, *Business Cycles*, New York: MacGraw Hill, 1939.

Shackle, George L. S., *Expectation in Economics*, Cambridge: Cambridge University Press, 1952.

Shackle, George L. S., *The Years of High Theory*, Cambridge: Cambridge University Press, 1967.

Shackle, George L. S., *Expectations, Enterprise and Profit*, London: George Allen and Unwin, 1970.

Shapiro, Nina J., 'Pricing and the Growth of the Firm', *Journal of Post Keynesian Economics*, Fall 1981.

Shapiro, Nina J., 'The Product Life Cycle and the Life of the Firm', Rutgers University, mimeo, 1984.

Skott, Peter, 'The Integration of Neo-Marxian and Post Keynesian Distribution Theory. Some Problems and Suggestions', mimeo, 1988.

Smith, Adam, *The Wealth of Nations*, Harmondsworth: Penguin, 1974.

Soskice, David and Carlin, Wendy, 'Medium-Run Keynesianism: Hysteresis and Capital Scrapping', in P. Davidson and J. Kregel (eds), *Macroeconomic Problems and Policies of Income Distribution*, Aldershot: Edward Elgar, 1989.

Sraffa, Piero, 'Dr. Hayek on Money and Prices', *The Economic Journal*, 1932.

Steindl, Joseph, *Maturity and Stagnation in American Capitalism*, New York: Monthly Review Press, 1976.

Sylos-Labini, Paolo, *Oligopolio y Progreso Tecnico*, Madrid: Oikos Tau, 1966.

Sylos-Labini, Paolo, *Ensaios sobre Desenvolvimento e Precos*, Rio de Janeiro: Forense, 1984.

Tarling, Roger and Wilkinson, Frank, 'The Social Contract: Post-War Incomes Policies and their Inflationary Impact', *Cambridge Journal of Economics*, (1), 1977.

Terzi, Andrea, 'The Independence of Finance from Saving: A Flow-of-Funds Interpretation', *Journal of Post Keynesian Economics*, Winter 1986/7.

Tobin, James, 'The Interest Elasticity of Transactions Demand for Cash', *Review of Economics and Statistics*, 1956.

Tobin, James, 'Liquidity Preference as Behaviour Toward Risk', in *Essays in Economics, vol. 1: Macroeconomics*, Cambridge (Mass.): MIT Press, 1987. Originally published in 1958.

Tobin, James, 'Friedman's Theoretical Framework', *Journal of Political Economy*, Sept./Oct. 1972.

Tobin, James, 'Stabilization Policy Ten Years After', *Brookings Papers on Economic Activity*, no. 1, 1980.

Tobin, James, *Policies for Prosperity*, Cambridge, Mass.: The MIT Press, 1987.

Townshend, Hugh, 'Liquidity Premium and the Theory of Value', *The Economic Journal*, Mar. 1937.

Vicarelli, Fausto, *Keynes: The Instability of Capitalism*, Philadelphia: The University of Pennsylvania Press, 1984.

von Neumann, J. and Morgenstern, O., *Theory of Games and Economic Behavior*, Princeton: Princeton University Press, 1953.

Walras, Leon, *Elements of Pure Economics*, London: George Allen and Unwin, 1954.

Weber, Max, *Historia Geral da Economia*, São Paulo: Mestre Jou, 1968.

Weintraub, Sidney, *Capitalism's Inflation and Unemployment Crisis*, Reading: Addison-Wesley, 1978.

Wells, Paul, 'A Post Keynesian View of Liquidity Preference and the Demand for Money', *Journal of Post Keynesian Economics*, Summer 1983.

Name Index

231

Subject Index